GENDER INCLUSION AT WORK:

A Guide to Supporting Transgender and Nonbinary Employees, Clients & Colleagues

By AMELIA J. MICHAEL

PYP Publish
Your Purpose

PRAISE FOR *GENDER INCLUSION AT WORK*

Amelia Michael's Gender Inclusion at Work is an insightful and essential guide for businesses and professionals looking to foster a truly inclusive workplace. The book takes a practical and empathetic approach to educating readers on how to support transgender and nonbinary employees, customers, and colleagues, offering real-world strategies that go beyond surface-level diversity efforts. One stand-out feature of this book is its balance between research-based insights and actionable recommendations. Michael breaks down complex topics such as gender identity, pronoun usage, and workplace policies in a way that is accessible to all, regardless of prior knowledge. The book also includes case studies, personal anecdotes, and legal considerations, making it a valuable resource for HR professionals, managers, and organizational leaders. What makes Gender Inclusion at Work particularly impactful is its emphasis on the why behind inclusion, highlighting not only the ethical and human aspects but also the business case for fostering a diverse and supportive work environment. Michael does an excellent job of addressing potential challenges and providing constructive solutions for companies striving to create lasting, meaningful change. Whether you're an executive, a team leader, or an ally looking to deepen your understanding, this book is what I consider to be a "must-read." It's a timely, well-researched, and necessary resource for anyone committed to building a more inclusive and equitable workplace.

Keshia Butler-Thomas, M.M. (she/her/hers)
Founder & Creative Director, LCK Consulting Services | Director of Media & Technology, Business Administration, Esperanza College of Eastern University | Adjunct Professor, Temple University | Democratic Committee Member, Collingswood, NJ

In a world where gender inclusion has been turned into a taboo subject by design, it's heartening that Amelia Michael takes such a thoughtful and brave approach to demystify what these practices actually are, how to employ them, and why they remain an important business strategy. Their efforts to demonstrate how gender inclusive practices sit at the intersection of the right thing to do for people and the best thing to do for the bottom line are needed more than ever.

Zach Wilcha, Chief Executive Officer,
Independence Business Alliance,
Greater Philadelphia's LGBTQ+ Chamber of Commerce

At the Food Bank of South Jersey, diversity, equity, inclusion, and belonging are more than just words—they are the foundation of our mission and the heartbeat of our work. We are deeply committed to creating a space where everyone feels seen, valued, and empowered, ensuring that our impact extends beyond food to true community transformation. It was an absolute pleasure to work with Amelia, whose expertise and passion for equity shine through in their book, Gender Inclusion at Work. This powerful and practical resource is a must-read for any organization striving to create genuine, lasting inclusion. Amelia's presentation to our team was engaging, insightful, and deeply affirming, reinforcing our commitment to championing equity and uplifting every voice in our community. Together, with leaders like Amelia guiding the way, we are not just feeding communities—we are fueling change for all.

Fred C. Wasiak, President and CEO,
Food Bank of South Jersey

Gender Inclusion at Work is a long overdue answer to the gender inclusivity questions we all struggle with. By addressing the needs of each workplace department, Amelia Michael ensures that we can all speak the same language, use technology to our best advantage, and demonstrate understanding and respect for our clients.

Kyle Kurzet, MD (they/them),
Transition Health

This book is looong overdue! We are evolving, and nothing is evolving faster than the ways that we communicate with and about each other in the workplace. IMHO, every leader, manager, and team member needs to have a copy of "Gender Inclusion at Work" on their desks for the profound education that this book provides on the importance of ensuring gender inclusion in the workplace. Amelia clearly explains, in a concise, honest, fun, and open way, the implications and applications of this important workplace topic. I found myself humbled by the constant insights shared in this brilliant book. Amelia also does the hard work of answering questions I didn't even know I had about gender inclusion in ways that are practical and easy to apply daily in my professional and personal life.

Erica Woods (she/her/ella),
Co-Founder, HumanTech Consulting

Gender Inclusion at Work is a bold and timely call to reject the radicalisation of sameness and harness the transformative power of difference. Amelia provides a blueprint for building workplaces that celebrate individuality, empower authenticity, and unlock the full potential of every person. As someone who knows how inclusivity drives innovation and builds stronger teams, I know this book is more than a resource—it's a revolution. It reminds us that embracing difference is both a moral imperative and a strategic advantage. Different is the new normal, and this book shows us how to make it our greatest strength.

Isobel Elton (she/her),
Co-Founder, Future of the Office

As a clinician working with diverse populations, this book has transformed my approach to gender-affirming care. It expertly blends clinical insights with research on the mental health challenges of gender-diverse individuals—like depression (54%) and anxiety (30%) in trans communities. Its guidance on transgender youth—who are 8 times more likely to attempt suicide—reshaped how I assess and treat clients. Strategies like affirming language and addressing unconscious bias have made my space safer and more welcoming. More than a guide, this is a call to action—an essential tool packed with ethical considerations, case studies, and real-world applications to reduce disparities and improve outcomes.

Amy M. Shaitelman (she/her), LPC, CAGS, NCC, Licensed Clinician & Certified Psychedelic Therapist

Gender Inclusion at Work is such an important resource for business owners and leaders who want to create a truly inclusive workplace. As both a business leader and a member of the LGBTQ+ community, I know how powerful it is to build environments where everyone feels respected and valued. This book gives practical, easy-to-follow advice for supporting transgender and nonbinary employees, clients, and colleagues—perfect for anyone who's unsure where to begin. It helps break down the basics and offers real steps to make your organization a place where everyone can show up as their authentic selves. In today's world, that kind of inclusivity isn't just important—it's essential for long-term success.

Matt Tinney,
Windows Management Experts

This guide provides creative ways to incorporate gender inclusivity in any organization, with common sense tips for all those who work in a team environment. Anyone who is passionate about contributing to a more inclusive and empathetic world can gain invaluable insight from this book and will be able to immediately impart positive change at any organization.

Chloe Mullen-Wilson (she/her),
Esquire, Orphans' Court Litigator, Probate Practitioner, and Probate Section Diversity Committee Chair

Here is the guide that employers and managers need to read more than ever. In this book, written with professionalism, courage, and sensitivity, we can learn actionable ways to make our workplaces more inclusive. Many of these steps are so simple and easily

implemented! If you work in Human Resources and care about your workplace culture, pick up this book.

Scott Agostini (he/him/his),
Senior Director of Human Resources at Rowan University |
Executive Council, DisruptHR South Jersey

Gender Inclusion at Work is an essential guide for anyone committed to fostering an inclusive and supportive workplace. The book offers clear, actionable insights into the unique challenges transgender and nonbinary individuals face and provides practical strategies to create environments where everyone can thrive. From leadership to frontline employees, this guide empowers organizations to embrace diversity, strengthen collaboration, and build inclusive cultures. It's a must-read for businesses looking to stay ahead in today's evolving workforce landscape. I am passionate about this topic, being the father of a transgender son and experiencing the joys and challenges of our family's journey through this process. I have also been very fortunate to have worked the past 25 years for a company that has always been at the forefront of diversity and inclusion and a strong supporter of the LGBTQ community.

Ken Bode,
Senior Business Development Manager at
Integrity Staffing Solutions

Amelia throws their heart and soul into this book. They share from their personal experience navigating their own journey in gender identity to writing an incredible resource guide on how companies can navigate gender inclusion for their employees. From the basics on why gender inclusion matters to more complex issues such as strategy, HR and legal, Amelia covers it all in this thorough guide for companies. Plus, they give real life examples at major corporations of how this can work in your own organization. This is a MUST READ book for any business leader looking to create more inclusive environments in their company culture.

Chantelle Fitzgerald (she/her),
Founder/CEO, Mindset Strategies, LLC

For permission requests, write to the publisher, addressed "Attention: Permissions Coordinator," at the address below.

Publish Your Purpose
141 Weston Street, #155
Hartford, CT, 06141

PYP **Publish**
Your Purpose

The opinions expressed by the Author are not necessarily those held by Publish Your Purpose.

Ordering Information: Quantity sales and special discounts are available on bulk purchases by corporations, associations, universities, and other educational institutions. For details, contact sales@ameliajmichael.com. For general inquiries, contact info@ameliajmichael.com.

Edited by: Brandi Lai, Jill Kramek, and Kelsey Spence
Cover design by: Rebecca Pollock
Typeset and e-book design by: Amit Dey

ISBN: 979-8-88797-161-2 (hardcover)
ISBN: 979-8-88797-162-9 (paperback)
ISBN: 979-8-88797-163-6 (ebook)

Library of Congress Control Number: 2025901890

First edition, May 2025

The information contained within this book is strictly for informational purposes. The material may include information, products, or services by third parties. As such, the Author and Publisher do not assume responsibility or liability for any third-party material or opinions. The publisher is not responsible for websites (or their content) that are not owned by the publisher. Neither the Author nor the Publisher assumes any liability for actions taken based on the information provided in this book. Readers are advised to do their own due diligence when it comes to making decisions.

Publish Your Purpose is a hybrid publisher of non-fiction books. Our mission is to elevate the voices often excluded from traditional publishing. We intentionally seek out authors and storytellers with diverse backgrounds, life experiences, and unique perspectives to publish books that will make an impact in the world. Do you have a book idea you would like us to consider publishing? Please visit PublishYourPurpose.com for more information.

DEDICATION

To Sagan Janet Michael.

So much of who I am, I owe to you.
Thank you for making me face my fears. I love you forever.

ACKNOWLEDGMENTS

It takes a village to make big things happen. This book would not be in your hands without the support, encouragement, and love from my village. I owe special thanks:

To Spencer Broad, for your calming presence that brings peace to every moment. Your quiet strength has been my anchor on this journey. Thank you for listening as I think out loud, for lifting me up when I was tearing myself down, and for taking charge of your three things so I could focus on writing. The road to paradise is paradise, and I'm so grateful that you are walking this road with me.

To Anna Carhart, for demonstrating again and again that any obstacle can be overcome if we are willing to do the work. Your commitment to doing the next right thing continues to inspire me, both in life and in everything we create together at polycute. com. You are the embodiment of a safe space for trans folk, and for that, both my child and I thank you deeply.

To Daniel Lipton, my most special, who has been involved in and supported every big idea I've ever had since age seventeen. You are my chosen family, and our friendship has empowered me for forty years (and counting).

To Ann Wolf, a very special thanks to you for getting me through the tough times during this undertaking, and in life, with your dark sense of humor that so perfectly matches mine. You remind me that anything can be funny, which makes everything easier.

To Edie Nugent, for sending me current events and facts to help with my research. Much of what you shared made it into this book. Thank you for being the perfect example of allyship: cheerleading and supporting me during my own coming out and beyond.

To Stephanie Smith, my most valuable beta reader, for the depth and breadth of your professional knowledge, and the gentle hand you used to guide me.

To my publishing team, Jenn T. Grace, Dawn and Chris Agnos, Alexander Loutsenko, and especially my editor, Brandi Lai. Thank you for bringing this book to life. Brandi, your knowledge and expertise took my book from an accomplishment to a true source of pride for me.

To my mom, Irene Brown, for making me take typing in seventh grade instead of AP Biology. You were right, Ima. I love you.

I also owe a debt of gratitude to the following individuals whose presence and support have enriched this journey in ways both big and small: Jamie Fearson Bost, Marla Becker, Finnegan King, Castin Carhart, Kate Nachman, and Susan Medoff.

TABLE OF CONTENTS

FOREWORD BY HRH PRINCE MANVENDRA SINGH GOHIL PRINCE OF RAJPIPLA | GLOBAL LGBTQ + ADVOCATE

There is something profoundly sacred about being seen, not just for who we are, but for all that we carry. In every culture, there are rituals for recognizing the soul in another. And in every generation, there are those called to insist that no one be denied that recognition.

As the first openly gay royal in India, my life has stood at the intersection of tradition and truth. My coming out was not merely a personal milestone; it was a public reckoning with silence, stigma, and the inherited weight of cultural expectations. I know, intimately, the cost of visibility. But I also know its liberating power. To be seen is to be set free.

This book is a testament to that power.

Gender Inclusion at Work is more than a manual. It is a mirror, a roadmap, and a rallying cry. It meets this moment with clarity and compassion, offering us tools for transformation, not just in policy, but in practice; not only in corporations, but in the quiet courage of daily decisions. It invites us to expand our understanding of gender, identity, and dignity, so we may expand the horizons of inclusion for everyone.

The author, Amelia Michael, writes with the authenticity of someone who has walked this path, not as a theorist, but as a parent, a teacher, and a nonbinary leader navigating a world too often designed to exclude. Their voice, steady, wise, and deeply human, guides us through complex terrain with empathy and expertise. In sharing their own truth, Amelia affirms countless others.

Inclusion is not a Western ideal; it is a global imperative. In India, we speak of Vasudhaiva Kutumbakam— the world is one family. In that family, each person, including our transgender and nonbinary siblings, holds equal worth. From Delhi to Detroit, from boardrooms to back offices, we must recognize that culture does not shift solely through compliance. It evolves when we choose compassion. It grows when we make space for authenticity.

This is not work for tomorrow. It is for now.

To those reading this book: whether you are a business leader, a colleague, a parent, or simply someone learning anew, know that your courage matters. Every small act of inclusion changes lives. Every choice to affirm another's humanity brings us closer to the world we are meant to build.

May this book illuminate your way, challenge your assumptions, and inspire your commitment. And may it remind us all that in embracing the full spectrum of identity, we are not breaking with tradition; we are returning to a deeper truth: that love, dignity, and visibility belong to everyone.

HRH Prince Manvendra Singh Gohil
Prince of Rajpipla | Global LGBTQ+ Advocate

AUTHOR'S NOTE

This book was completed in 2024, with the publishing process beginning before the US presidential election. My goal was always to create a guide that would be useful no matter who held power, because workplace inclusion should not be dependent on politics. Now, as the book reaches publication, the reality has shifted. The administration in power is systematically dismantling every mechanism that protected marginalized communities under federal law. This is an all-out war on trans people, racial justice, and equity—executed through bureaucratic and legal erasure. It is not just an attack on policy; it is an attack on existence itself.

In times of political upheaval and rising fascism, simply existing as yourself becomes an act of defiance. What started as a guide has also become a refusal to let trans and nonbinary people be erased—a reminder that justice must be fought for, especially when those in power are working to drag us backward.

History tells us exactly what happens when authoritarian movements take hold. It starts with controlling language, restricting rights, and dehumanizing entire groups of people. The goal isn't just to make life harder—it's to make us disappear. And right now, we are watching that play out in real time.

From the moment Trump returned to office, his administration wasted no time dismantling protections, stripping gender identity from federal policies, and gutting DEI initiatives. This isn't a random attack. It's part of a much larger strategy—one laid out in *Project 2025*, a blueprint for a far-right takeover that explicitly lays the groundwork for eliminating trans rights, women's rights, and any form of diversity that doesn't fit their narrow, regressive vision. This is not a drill.

And make no mistake: silence is compliance. There is no neutral ground when one side is actively working toward erasure. This is about survival and resistance in a political climate intent on erasing trans and nonbinary people from public life.

This book isn't just a guide; it's a record of what they want to erase. Some policies and case studies in this book may already be erased by the time you read this. That doesn't mean they were never valid. It means they were powerful enough that those in control felt the need to destroy them. Erasure is not the same as illegality, and removing protections from government websites does not mean businesses and individuals must comply with discrimination. Compliance is a choice, and they are relying on people believing they have none.

This book isn't just about defending trans rights. It's about celebrating the beauty, resilience, and undeniable humanity of trans and nonbinary people. It's about refusing to let our identities be rewritten by bigots with an agenda. To read these words—to understand, to speak up, to act—is to stake your claim in this fight.

For allies, this book is a call to sharpen your tools and step up. For those just waking up to the reality of what's happening, it's time to move beyond awareness and into action. And for every trans and nonbinary person navigating this world right now:

You are real. You are worthy. You are not alone. And no amount of hate, no law, no government edict will ever change that.

We will not be erased.
Amelia

WHO I AM AND HOW I TEACH

Over the last thirty years, my consulting work has evolved to encompass a range of interconnected roles, including process consultant, change management specialist, and productivity consultant. But if there was one thing that I would say I "am," it's a teacher. I teach. If someone wants to learn, I can teach them anything. Interest is the only requirement, regardless of the rationale. So, whether your motivation is that you think gender inclusion is the right thing to do or you're looking to attract younger generations, this book is for you.

My teaching philosophy focuses on helping people become comfortable with things that make them uncomfortable: whether it is gender inclusion, technology, meditation, or communication. My superpower is breaking down intricate ideas and making complex concepts accessible to those who fear change. Over decades, I have guided executives and organizations through significant changes, honing my ability to engage and educate even the most hesitant audiences. As a crisis counselor, I've developed skills in emotional support and conflict resolution, making me particularly adept at helping individuals and teams navigate their fears and anxieties related to change, essentially "talking people off ledges," especially when addressing sensitive issues (for them) such as gender identity and inclusion in the workplace.

What began as offering gender-inclusive information to technology projects turned into offering technology help with gender inclusion projects. I've managed website redesign jobs to make them gender inclusive and I've coded templates for law firm document management systems with logic that will insert "he," "she," or "they" and the appropriate honorifics based on a gender field in the system. When someone says, "We can't do that because our software only offers two options for gender," I helped them overcome the issue by editing database tables or by communicating with a vendor to identify and manage what needed to be done. My role evolved to providing gender inclusion workshops to my IT and legal clients.

To understand where my passion for gender inclusion comes from, it's important to look at the personal and professional journey that led me here. The seeds for this book were planted long ago, though I didn't fully grasp how both my personal and professional experiences were driving me to create this book until, frankly, writing this introduction.

My early commitment to gender equity started while traveling abroad at age eighteen. I participated in an underground feminist movement focused on protecting women from gender-based violence. This experience laid the foundation for my dedication to intersectional feminism and my work in advocacy, eventually leading me to become a certified crisis and domestic abuse counselor.

While working at my IT firm and later in my current consultancy, I repeatedly encountered the challenge of departmental silos, where departments operate in isolation, often purchasing redundant software or failing to communicate effectively. My role as a process consultant frequently involved untangling these situations, aligning business processes and communication across an organization to optimize efficiency.

For years, I've been delivering keynote speeches and gender inclusion workshops, and while these were impactful, I often left with a sense of wanting to do more. Over time, I developed custom talks to leadership and various departments that addressed their specific needs. Through this work, I realized that silos persisted in the context of gender inclusion as well. This recognition led me to research and compile data with a "What if I could train the entire organization?" approach, sparking the idea of creating a book that addresses every department and the interdepartmental collaboration that must happen to achieve success.

Identifying as bisexual, I have always been dedicated to supporting the LGBTQ+ community. Later, as the parent of a transgender child, I embarked on a path of learning and advocacy to support my family. This personal journey informed my professional work. I cofounded a second business dedicated to creating products that celebrate diverse identities.

I was inspired by my child's generation, or as I lovingly call them, the "gender bendy generation." Generation Z cares less about what other people think about their identity labels than any other generation before them, and I wanted businesses to keep up with them.

As I was writing this book, I came out as nonbinary at age fifty-four. I realized this book wasn't just for the younger generations; it was also for those of us who live every day in the workplace hiding who we truly are.

So, why did I write this book? Because I needed to. Because it was in me and like my own identity, I had to let it out. Gender inclusion isn't just about being kind, it's about being educated. I have educated businesses for decades to become more efficient; now it's time to help them become a kinder and more inclusive space for all of us.

The same strategies I've used to facilitate technological changes are applied in this book to implement gender-inclusive changes using the ADKAR model. Part One raises *Awareness* about why gender inclusion matters and begins fostering *Desire* by emphasizing its importance. Part Two builds *Knowledge* with effective communication strategies. Part Three ensures *Ability* through practical departmental guidelines, and the last chapter *Reinforces* these changes with real-life examples.

HOW TO USE THIS BOOK

As a teacher at heart, I've designed this book to guide you through your journey at your own pace, in a way that feels comfortable and manageable. Much like in my workshops, I break down intricate concepts into accessible pieces, allowing you to choose the areas most relevant to your role while encouraging exploration beyond your comfort zone.

This book is designed as a choose-your-own-adventure business book. Just like the classic adventure stories where you decide the next step, this book allows you to chart your own course based on your job role and current needs, with the option to circle back and explore other areas as your journey evolves. Whether you're looking to gain a general understanding, dive deep into a specific department, or see the full picture of what your business needs to do, you have the freedom to explore the chapters that make the most sense for you.

There are four essential chapters that you should read (Chapters 1–4), regardless of your position. Chapter 1, "Why Gender Inclusion at Work Matters," lays the groundwork by explaining the importance of gender inclusion. While you might already recognize its significance, this section will provide you with the necessary insights and arguments to communicate its value to others in your organization.

Chapter 2, "Terminology," covers the essential terms and concepts related to gender identity and experiences. This shared vocabulary forms the building blocks of future communication, getting everyone on the same page.

Chapter 3, "Principles of Gender-Neutral Communication," and Chapter 4, "Strategies for Gender-Inclusive Communication," offer guidelines and strategies that will be beneficial for everyone. Here, you'll learn about gender-neutral language techniques and common dos and don'ts that apply to all workplace interactions across all departments.

The following ten chapters are broken down by department: leadership, HR, legal, IT, marketing, sales, customer service, procurement, facilities, and security. This is where the adventure begins. If you are a business owner, C-suite executive, HR professional, compliance officer, or in any leadership role, I encourage you to read the book in its entirety. Otherwise, choose the chapters that fit your goals and needs. For example, if you are a department director or manager, or an employee on a leadership track, I recommend reading "Leadership: Setting the Tone for Inclusion," followed by the chapter about your department.

In some cases, you may read something in the chapter about your department that leads you to want a better understanding of another department. For example, "Marketing and Branding: Crafting Inclusive Narratives," may lead you to read about IT if you work directly with them to develop your online presence. Similarly, reading "Security and Safety Services: Protecting with Inclusive Awareness" may cause you to want a better understanding of what HR will be doing.

The final chapter, Chapter 15, "Real-Life Examples of Inclusion at Work," presents case studies of companies across various industries implementing gender inclusion.

As you go through this book, you might find some concepts repeated in different sections. This is intentional. I designed the book so you can jump into the chapters that best fit your role or current needs. If you read it cover to cover, some points may seem redundant, but that's because they are essential principles that apply across different areas. Repetition can help reinforce these ideas, especially since they may challenge deeply ingrained habits or information that we might not even realize we hold.

Often, when people learn new technology, they just want to know the steps: "Just tell me what to do." They jot down a numbered list, certain that's all they'll need. But when unexpected issues arise (and with technology, it's a "when," not an "if"), people get flustered and sometimes even angry, confused by the situation. That's why, when I teach an executive–perhaps one who used to rely on support staff and a "big red appointment book"–I start by turning off the computer. We have a conversation about technology. The more someone understands the background and concepts, the better equipped they are to handle any situation with ease, knowing exactly what to do next. I call it Technotherapy™. The same applies to gender inclusion.

This is why I have structured this book to lay out core concepts first, building a foundation of understanding before progressing to more nuanced or detailed information. By taking this approach, you'll be able to handle unexpected situations and navigate gender inclusion in your organization with greater confidence and clarity.

If some of this feels confusing or you don't grasp it right away, that's completely okay. Change takes time, especially when it involves unlearning ideas that have long been presented as "normal." If you're curious, I invite you to explore the entire book at your own pace. The journey of learning and inclusion is ongoing, and every step you take contributes to making your organization a more welcoming space for everyone.

We do this work not just for ourselves, but for the benefit of others. It's about creating a workplace where everyone feels seen, valued, and respected. Consider this your guide on that path, one chapter at a time.

This resource is designed to provide practical strategies for driving gender inclusion in any organization, regardless of size or structure. Whether you're working within a small business with limited resources or a larger corporation with more complex structures, it will help you implement gender inclusion effectively and efficiently. For organizations looking to scale up their efforts, it offers a roadmap to identify gaps, develop comprehensive strategies, and foster sustainable inclusion across all levels of the business.

Gender Inclusion at Work is for people who want to make a difference in their workplace. Whether you're driven by a desire to do the right thing, attract younger generations, comply with or navigate legal or potential client requirements, improve employee engagement and morale, enhance your company's performance, or address a recent issue, this guide will provide the guidance you need.

PART ONE:

Getting on the Same Page

CHAPTER 01

WHY GENDER INCLUSION AT WORK MATTERS

This is the most academic, number-filled chapter in this book (consider this your heads-up if you're like me and numbers aren't your thing!). It's designed to equip you with the knowledge and tools to communicate the importance of gender inclusion effectively. Whether you're advocating for gender-inclusive policies at work, educating peers, or striving to create a more inclusive world, this chapter lays a solid foundation for the journey ahead.

We'll explore the shifting demographics of the workforce, the importance of authenticity, the business benefits of gender inclusion, the cost of exclusion, and the legal landscape in detail. With this deeper understanding, you'll be better equipped to promote and build an inclusive environment within your organization.

If you're already well-versed in the importance of gender inclusion, you might be thinking, "I get it, but how do I convey the significance to others?" Maybe you're an HR professional, an educator, a manager, or just someone who values diversity and inclusion. You know that fostering an inclusive environment is a necessity in today's world. However, you may find yourself in situations where those around you need a bit more enlighten-ment on the subject. To that end, I offer you this information.

Embracing the Change: Shifting Demographics

As our society evolves, so do the demographics of our workforce. Recent Gallup polls have shown a remarkable increase in the number of people in the United States who identify as LGBTQ+ over the past decade. Approximately 9.3% of the population identifies as LGBTQ+, a figure that has nearly tripled since the study began in 2012, when it was just 3.5%. Among Generation Z, almost one in four identify as LGBTQ+.[1]

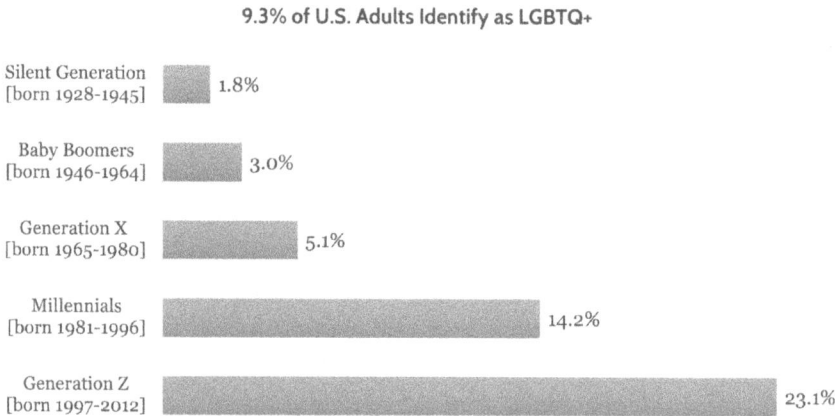

9.3% of U.S. Adults Identify as LGBTQ+

Silent Generation [born 1928-1945] — 1.8%

Baby Boomers [born 1946-1964] — 3.0%

Generation X [born 1965-1980] — 5.1%

Millennials [born 1981-1996] — 14.2%

Generation Z [born 1997-2012] — 23.1%

Notice how the percentage increases with each younger generation. This doesn't mean that more people are becoming LGBTQ+. It instead suggests that each new generation feels more comfortable being open about their identity. In other words, these numbers likely reflect that younger generations are less concerned with societal judgment and more willing to express their true selves than older generations.

I'm often asked, "Why are there so many more transgen-der people now?" The answer isn't that people are suddenly becoming trans. Think of it like what happened with left-handedness. For years, being left-handed was stigmatized as "evil" or "unnatural" due to cultural and religious beliefs. People were forced to write with their right hand–literally forced to be something they weren't, causing emotional and psychological harm. Once society let that nonsense go, people felt comfortable writing with their natural hand. It's the same with gender identity; as society becomes more accepting, more people feel empowered to be their authentic selves without fear of being forced into a box where they don't belong. So, it's not that there are more transgender people now. It's that more people are willing to share their true selves with the world. This does not change when any new administration attempts to dismantle the growing acceptance of any group. Historically, as with the 1969 Stonewall Riots[2] or the 1955 Montgomery Bus Boycott,[3] visibility creates allies and galvanizes opposition to regressive policies.

Similarly, I'm also asked whether someone can be "made" transgender. It is worth noting that, just as you cannot make someone gay, you cannot make someone trans. Case in point: my child came out as transgender, and through that learning process, I came to understand my own identity and came out as nonbinary (meaning my gender identity does not align with my sex assigned at birth). While supportive environments can encourage people to explore who they truly are, identities emerge naturally–not through coercion or pressure. This challenges the misconception that having an LGBTQ+ child, or more than one, somehow makes someone a "groomer." According to Tara Tull, former chair in the Department of Human Services and Counseling at the Metropolitan State University of Denver, we have over the past decade created "space for people to explore their identities in ways that there didn't used to be that social room to maneuver in."[4]

Determining how many transgender people there actually are is a bit tricky. Until recently, the US Census didn't even ask about sexual orientation or gender identity, so we've been lacking big-picture data. Instead, we rely on surveys and estimates. And, depending on the source, the numbers might vary. Globally, under 3% of people identify as transgender or nonbinary, while in the US, that figure is closer to 2%.[5]

A Pew Research Center study shows that about 1.6% of US adults identify as transgender or nonbinary.[6] While this might seem like a small percentage, it's equivalent to the entire population of Montana. Imagine meeting every single person in Montana, each with their own unique story. Not so small now, right?

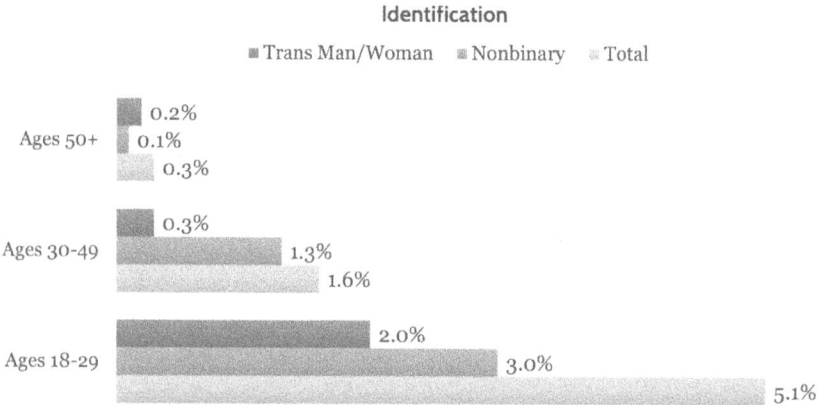

Identification

■ Trans Man/Woman　■ Nonbinary　▨ Total

Ages 50+
- 0.2%
- 0.1%
- 0.3%

Ages 30-49
- 0.3%
- 1.3%
- 1.6%

Ages 18-29
- 2.0%
- 3.0%
- 5.1%

Plus, more people are getting to know transgender individuals. On average, 44% of adults know someone who is transgender, and 20% know someone who is nonbinary.[7] This growing familiarity means that if you don't already know a transgender or nonbinary person, chances are, you will soon! Of course, it's also possible you already do; they just might not have shared it publicly yet.

We can expect these numbers to continue to rise. Cultural shifts make it difficult to undo acceptance once it's reached. As more people personally know someone who is transgender or LGBTQ+, this familiarity fosters understanding and support, making it harder to justify actions that seek to reverse progress toward inclusion. In other words, the 2025 rollbacks of DEI might make headlines, but they won't erase decades of progress—or the connections you've made with your friend, sibling, or coworker.

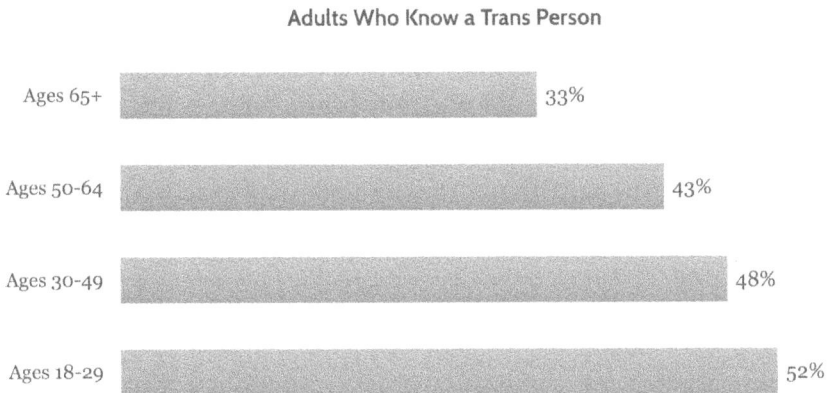

Adults Who Know a Trans Person

Age Group	Percentage
Ages 65+	33%
Ages 50-64	43%
Ages 30-49	48%
Ages 18-29	52%

The growing visibility of this demographic is largely due to cultural representation. Public figures like Miss Nevada USA Kataluna Enriquez, *Sports Illustrated* cover models Valentina Sampaio and Kim Petras, and actors such as Asia Kate Dillon and Elliot Page are challenging traditional gender norms and gaining prominence in mainstream media. In 2022, Laverne Cox became the first transgender woman to have a Barbie fashioned after her. A Barbie doll! There is little that represents popular culture more than Barbie. The presence of these humans paves the way for broader acceptance across all sectors of society. Take the NFL, for example. Many people never considered the presence of trans people in this space, yet 2024 marked the third season for Justine Lindsay, the first openly transgender cheerleader for the Carolina Panthers.

The political arena, traditionally slow to change, is also undergoing a transformation. The number of transgender or nonbinary LGBTQ+ elected officials has skyrocketed, with a staggering 1,183% increase from 2017 to 2022.[8] Politicians like Mauree Turner, the first out nonbinary person elected to the Oklahoma state legislature, and Sarah McBride, the first out transgender state senator, are further normalizing diverse gender identities in spaces that were once rigidly binary (strictly identified as male or female). This significant rise shows that change is happening at all levels of society.

Born between the late 1990s and early 2010s, Generation Z is poised to usher in significant societal change. In 2023, twenty-five-year-old Maxwell Frost became the first member of Generation Z elected to public office.[9] The World Economic Forum predicts that by 2025, Generation Z will account for almost 30% of the global workforce.[10] Their unique characteristics and perspectives are already shaping the future of gender inclusion and acceptance.

I am often brought into law firms to discuss Generation Z and what makes them different, particularly what they want and need in the workplace. There are many factors that make Gen Z unique. For example, they are the most diverse generation in history.[11] To me, one of the most fascinating aspects of Generation Z, though not directly related to gender, is how their collective experiences have shaped their priorities. This generation has grown up in the shadow of multiple major global events: the 2008 financial recession and, more importantly, the COVID-19 pandemic. If you think about it, not since the Great Depression have we seen such a powerful shaping of a generation's mindset due to economic upheaval. Much like the children of the Great Depression, Gen Z has witnessed financial instability, watching their parents lose jobs, businesses shutter, and entire industries pivot overnight. This generation, however, has the added influence of social media and a hyper-connected world. As a result, while they still value passion and purpose, their focus on financial stability is stronger than their Millennial counterparts.[12]

Gen Z is embracing and openly identifying with diverse gender identities and sexual orientations. While the previously mentioned Gallop poll reported that 23.1% of Generation Z adults identified as LGBTQ+, a CDC survey across 152 high schools nationwide found that 28% of teens identify as LGBTQ+.[13] That number could be so high because it includes people who are questioning. "People feel more comfortable saying that they're not heterosexual and don't feel forced into that category," reports Gregory Phillips II, PhD, author of the study.[14]

A significant aspect of Gen Z's perspective is their comfort with gender-neutral pronouns. Many know people who use nonbinary pronouns, and a large number expect options beyond the traditional "man/woman" on forms and documents.[15] Roughly half of both Gen Z-ers and Millennials believe that society isn't accepting enough of transgender, nonbinary, and gender nonconforming individuals.[16]

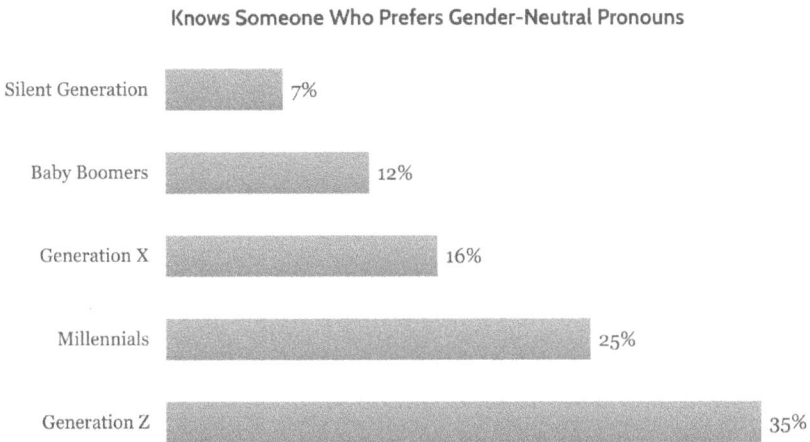

Knows Someone Who Prefers Gender-Neutral Pronouns

Generation	Percentage
Silent Generation	7%
Baby Boomers	12%
Generation X	16%
Millennials	25%
Generation Z	35%

For Gen Z, Diversity, Equity, and Inclusion (DEI) are non-negotiable. They expect to see diversity, especially in leadership roles. They want a workplace culture that truly fosters inclusion. In fact, 63% say it's important to work alongside people from diverse educational backgrounds, and 20% emphasize the need for culturally diverse teams.[17] Their view of diversity and inclusion pertains to gender as well. According to a Tallo Gen Z Benchmarking study of over 5,000 high school and college students, 88% of Gen Z-ers agree that recruiters or potential employers should ask for their pronouns; with 65% strongly agreeing.[18]

Gen Zers Believe Recruiters Should Ask for Their Pronouns

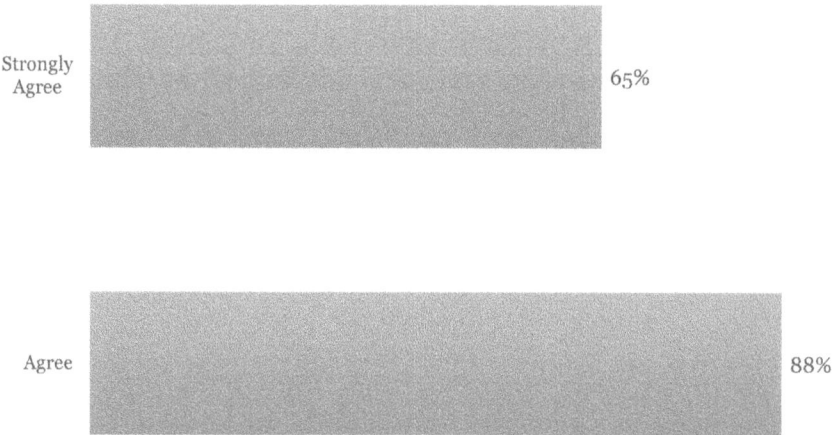

Strongly Agree	65%
Agree	88%

But it's not just about their own experiences. For Generation Z, it's equally important for others to feel safe expressing their true selves. A 2023 EY Gen Z Segmentation Study of more than 1,500 participants across the United States shows that 91% of Generation Z place authenticity among their highest values. This thinking carries over not only to how they expect businesses to operate internally but also to how they engage in the consumer marketplace.[19] They're not just seeking inclusivity for themselves; they're looking for companies that support everyone in being their authentic selves.

The Power of Being Real: Authenticity in the Workplace

In the professional world, the importance of authenticity, especially around gender identity, has been gaining momentum beyond just Generation Z. A 2017 study found that transitioning at work isn't just a preference for many transgender individuals, it's a necessity. This holds true regardless of the level of support from coworkers, supervisors, or the organization. One participant shared,

> "I'm just tired of not being authentic. I dealt with that with every faculty member who walked in my door. Thinking, 'I'm a liar. I'm a fraud.' I'm not a fraud. And that means I have to make some more changes [by transitioning]."[20]

However, as authenticity gains momentum in workplaces, it faces new challenges. Recent political shifts, including the 2025 dismantling of DEI protections and the rollback of key workplace policies like Lyndon Johnson's 1964 executive order prohibiting discrimination, threaten this progress.[21] Yet, history shows that the need for authenticity is resilient—once individuals have tasted the freedom of being their true selves, it becomes nearly impossible to return to the shadows.

While the need for genuine self-expression has always existed, the need was accelerated as a result of the pandemic. Picture this: you've spent a year working from home, free from rigid dress codes, small talk, and the subtle pressures to fit in. You've been living each day as your true self. Then, suddenly, you're expected to go back to an environment where you once felt the need to conform, and you just can't do it anymore. A LinkedIn survey from early 2021 supports this.

Job Seekers on Gender and Authenticity Post COVID-19

More Willing to be Open About Their Gender Identity	46%
See Gender as Central to Their Identity	55%
Recruiters Should Recognize and Respect Their Pronouns	70%

Almost half of job seekers were more willing to be open about their authentic gender identities at work than before COVID-19. About 55% saw gender as central to their identity, both in their career and personal life, and a significant 70% emphasized the importance of recruiters and hiring managers recognizing and respecting their gender pronouns.[22] This shift highlights the growing importance of authenticity in professional settings.

Allowing employees to acknowledge and share their gender identity in the workplace contributes to a profound sense of belonging, which boosts mental health, job satisfaction, engagement, and creativity. On the flip side, hiding or suppressing gender identity can cause significant stress, which takes a toll on their focus and productivity. Inclusive environments where gender identity is recognized and celebrated lead to higher job satisfaction and better overall performance.[23]

Psychological safety is all about creating a space where people feel they can express their thoughts, ideas, and identities without fear of backlash. In terms of gender inclusion, it means employees can openly discuss their gender identity and share their experiences without worrying about being judged or side-lined. This kind of environment isn't just good for the soul, it's good for business. When employees don't have to waste energy hiding or conforming, they can put that energy into being inno-vative and collaborative.

A 2017 study of transgender employees' work-related attitudes and experiences reveals valuable insight into the importance of psychological safety and the successes of living authentically at work:

> "I feel more included. I feel like I'm living as an authentic person. When I wasn't me, I was miserable. It created work-related conflicts. Pretransition conflicts are not an issue now . . . I feel like I fit better with the faculty I work with, with everyone."[24]

> "Before, she [a coworker] said I was unapproachable, untalkative, seemingly upset, and now I'm smiling, enjoying myself, enjoying others' company and doing work better and reacting to others in a more positive way."[25]

Case Study: Caroline Farberger: Leading with Authenticity

Caroline Farberger, the former CEO of Swedish insurance com-pany ICA, shared her journey from hiding her true feminine identity for decades to embracing her authentic self. As the first CEO in the Nordics to publicly transition while in office, Caro-line's journey represents a profound shift in what it means to lead with authenticity.

For nearly five decades, Caroline lived as a man, rising through the corporate ranks with what she referred to as "the full package:" a prestigious role, a wife and three children, and socioeconomic success. However, as Caroline later shared, she spent those years feeling as though she were playing a character on stage. She hid her true identity for years, only fully embracing her authentic self at age forty-nine with the support of her wife.[26] Having come out at fifty-four myself, I resonate with her journey and the weight of revealing one's true identity after so many years.

Caroline's transition marked a pivotal moment, not just in her personal life but also in her leadership approach. Prior to transitioning, she admitted that she viewed diversity as a "statistic," something to be checked off in the corporate world. She felt obligated to recruit a certain number of women to meet perceived expectations, but her own lived experience hadn't allowed her to grasp the depth of systemic barriers. After her transition, she gained a new understanding of the privileges she once held as a white heterosexual male. "I genuinely thought the playing field was even when I lived as a man," she reflected, "but I only had to live as a woman for a few months to realize how wrong I had been."[27]

This shift fundamentally changed Caroline's leadership style. She recognized the unspoken challenges faced by women and other marginalized groups in the workplace, challenges she hadn't seen before, such as not being heard, facing subtle discrimination, and being sidelined in male-dominated environments. "It is a privilege in business to be a white heterosexual male," she acknowledged.[28] "It's very hard to understand your privileges if you yourself belong to the privileged category."[29]

Caroline's leadership transformation emphasized the importance of authenticity and inclusivity at the highest levels of business. She understood that inclusion had to start at the top, not just in policy but also in the behavior of leadership. "As a leader who's responsible for the corporate culture, the way I behave sets the tone for the entire organization," she said. If leaders aren't authentically inclusive, it's unlikely their managers or teams will be. Caroline also shared that her transition gave her the courage to promise herself and others that she would never "play theater" again. Her commitment was to create a corporate environment where everyone, regardless of gender identity or background, could be their authentic selves.[30] By being true to herself and embracing her transition openly, she set a powerful example for others in the workplace. She also learned valuable lessons about privilege, lessons she could not learn until after transitioning from her life as a man.[31]

This new understanding led Caroline to implement more inclusive practices. By listening to diverse voices, particularly women, and ensuring gender balance in decision-making spaces, her company began making better decisions. This inclusive leadership approach fostered more innovative solutions, reduced implementation mistakes, and improved employee retention. Diverse team members, especially women in compliance and risk management, chose to stay despite higher offers elsewhere, feeling valued and included. As a result, the company saw tangible business benefits, including stronger engagement, better decisions, and measurable P&L improvements.[32]

Beyond Good Intentions: The Business Benefits of Gender Inclusion

Embracing gender inclusion offers a range of business benefits, from unlocking new economic opportunities and enhancing innovation to boosting brand reputation and attracting top talent. These advantages not only improve profitability but also position companies as leaders in an increasingly diverse and values-driven marketplace.

Statistics show that transgender adults are twice as likely to be unemployed compared to cisgender adults. Even when they have similar or higher levels of education, transgender employees still earn 32% less on average annually compared to their cisgender colleagues.[33]

These disparities go beyond income. Many transgender employees face challenges in the workplace environment itself. More than half of transgender employees feel uncomfortable being open about their gender identity at work, and two-thirds stay in the closet even during professional interactions outside their organizations.[34]

The challenges don't stop there. Transgender individuals often feel less supported at work. They find it harder to navigate workplace culture, access benefits, secure promotions, and gain their managers' support.[35]

Economic Advantages of Gender Inclusion

Pursuing gender inclusion at work is a potential source of significant economic growth. Research shows that improving employment and wage equity for transgender people could lead to an annual increase in consumer spending of $12 billion, as transgender individuals gain greater financial stability and spending power.[36]

One powerful example of how gender inclusion impacts business is the economic force known as "pink money," which refers to the purchasing power of the LGBTQ+ community. World LGBTQ+ annual spending power currently stands at $3.9 trillion and continues to grow. Even with the financial disparities for transgender individuals, the LGBTQ+ community represents the fastest-growing minority segment in America with regard to purchasing power.[37]

Even when DEI initiatives face increased scrutiny, the economic benefits of inclusion remain undeniable. Companies that continue to champion gender equity can tap into the growing purchasing power of the LGBTQ+ community, ensuring they stay ahead in a rapidly evolving marketplace.

The Growing Influence of Gen Z

The future is indeed Gen Z, and while their current purchasing power is modest, their earnings are poised to reach $33 trillion by 2030, accounting for a quarter of all global income. By 2031, they will surpass millennials in spending power.[38] With one in nearly four Gen Z individuals identifying as LGBTQ+, this generational shift will further fuel the growth of pink money, ensuring that the economic influence of the LGBTQ+ community will only continue to expand as this generation enters its prime earning years.

Gen Z places a strong emphasis on transparency, with more than half of them prioritizing purchases from businesses that align with their values. This generation is highly informed, using social media and personal networks to investigate whether companies genuinely uphold the inclusive principles they claim to support.[39]

However, many businesses still struggle to meaningfully engage LGBTQ+ consumers. While most advertising professionals recognize the importance of representing gender and sexual orientation diversity, the challenge of doing so authentically remains a hurdle. Many fear that misrepresentation or tokenistic gestures (commonly referred to as "pinkwashing") could backfire, leading to backlash for inauthentic efforts. For businesses to truly succeed, they must go beyond performative actions and develop strategies that genuinely reflect the diversity of their audience. In a time when diversity initiatives face increasing opposition, these efforts not only resonate with values-driven consumers like Gen Z but also future-proof a company's reputation and success. One company that has successfully embraced inclusion in a way that resonates with consumers is Mastercard.

In today's information age, a company's success heavily relies on its image and branding. Companies seen as inclusive and progressive attract top talent among those who prioritize diversity and equity and enjoy a better public image. According to a global study by TechTarget's Enterprise Strategy Group (ESG), sponsored by Amazon Web Services, 86% of respondents said their organization's diversity and inclusion strategies positively impact the company's reputation.[40] Mastercard's True Name Program is a noteworthy example of this. Their initiative not only won the Cannes Brand Experience and Activation Grand Prix in 2020 and the Grand Clio for Integrated Campaign in 2021, but it also bolstered Mastercard's reputation as a leader in diversity and inclusion.

In light of the early 2025 rollbacks of DEI, some businesses have pulled back from publicly advertising their diversity efforts due to political pressure or fear of backlash. While these concerns are understandable, companies that maintain their commitment to inclusion—even in the face of opposition—not only stand by their values but also retain the loyalty of employees and consumers who prioritize diversity.

Case Study: Mastercard's True Name Program

Mastercard's commitment to inclusivity goes beyond recognition in the business world; it directly impacts the lives of its customers. The True Name Program, launched in 2019, allows customers to use their chosen name on their cards, addressing a critical need for the transgender and nonbinary community.

Asher DiGiuseppe, a Toronto resident, often faced uncomfortable situations when using his credit card, which still showed the name he used before his transition. "When trying to do something as simple as making a purchase," Asher shared, "the last thing anyone wants is to explain their entire gender journey to strangers." He often found ways to avoid these awkward encounters but stressed that trans individuals shouldn't have to be so creative just to use a credit card. Having a card with a name that matches their identity can make a big difference.

Mastercard recognized this challenge and made a groundbreaking move in the financial world. In 2019, they launched the True Name feature in the US, which allowed customers to use their chosen name instead of their legal name. The impact was immediate. By January, T-Mobile MONEY's debit card had integrated the True Name feature. Amsterdam's challenger bank, Bunq, soon followed, becoming the first in Europe to offer this feature across thirty countries. Recently, BMO Financial Group became the first major financial institution in Canada to embrace this initiative, extending its availability to thirty-two countries across North America and Europe.

BMO customers can now have their chosen name on both their consumer and business debit and credit cards, as well as on their monthly statements. Reflecting the importance of non-gender-specific titles, customers can also choose the prefix "Mx.", the nonbinary alternative to "Mr." or "Ms."

This commitment to inclusivity isn't just about goodwill. Research by Mastercard across sixteen countries in North America and Europe revealed that 59% of nonbinary individuals have felt unsafe while shopping. Additionally, 57% said it's important for companies to address them in ways that respect their identity.

Improving Corporate Image

Mastercard's True Name program teaches a vital business lesson: understanding and responding to the diverse needs of customers not only boosts brand reputation but also builds stronger, more trusting relationships with clients.[41]

Conversely, companies that fail to approach inclusion authentically risk damaging their reputation and alienating both supporters and detractors. A notable example is Bud Light's collaboration with trans influencer Dylan Mulvaney. While the partnership initially sparked backlash from anti-trans groups, Bud Light's subsequent decision to apologize and distance itself from the campaign backfired. Instead of diffusing the situation, these actions prolonged media coverage, keeping the controversy in the spotlight and leading to deeper, more long-lasting effects on the brand's reputation.[42]

The core issue wasn't the inclusive marketing itself, but rather a conflict in values. Consumers, whether conservative or supportive of the transgender community, responded because they felt that Bud Light's actions (or lack thereof) didn't align with their values. This misalignment cost the company the loyalty of both sides, showing that inclusion needs to be backed by genuine commitment rather than wavering support.[43]

A similar miscalculation played out at Target in early 2025. Long recognized as a leader in corporate DEI initiatives, Target cultivated a reputation for supporting LGBTQ+ rights, racial equity, and diverse hiring. In January 2025, however, the company abruptly reversed course, eliminating DEI hiring goals, disbanding its racial equity committee, and distancing itself from external diversity evaluations. Target framed these moves as a shift toward a broader inclusion strategy, but customers weren't convinced. Progressive consumers, who had long supported the brand because of its commitment to DEI, saw it as a betrayal—an arbitrary decision based on political pressures rather than business strategy.[44]

This shift wasn't just a change in policy; it was a fundamental break in the trust Target had built with its customers. The backlash was immediate: protests erupted outside Target's headquarters, prominent civil rights figures condemned the decision, and even the daughters of one of Target's co-founders publicly denounced the rollback.[45] Just as Bud Light's attempt to placate both sides led to a loss of consumer trust, Target now faces a growing boycott movement from the very communities that once championed its brand.

While some companies may recover from boycotts, regaining the trust of consumers once it's lost—especially due to a perceived inconsistency in values—can be far more difficult. Bud Light's initial misstep alienated both sides, illustrating how important it is for brands to maintain authenticity and stand firmly by their commitments. Target risks learning that same lesson the hard way.

Driving Innovation and Profitability

In today's global economy, businesses interact with a diverse and varied clientele. By building a diverse workforce, organizations can better understand the unique needs and preferences of different customer segments. These insights, drawn from a range of perspectives, can drive the creation of innovative products, services, and solutions that appeal to a broader audience. Supporting this idea, a study by the Boston Consulting Group found that companies with above-average diversity in their leadership teams had innovation-related revenue that was nineteen percentage points higher than companies with less diverse leadership: 45% versus 26% of their total revenue.[46]

Impact of Leadership Diversity on Innovation-Related Revenue

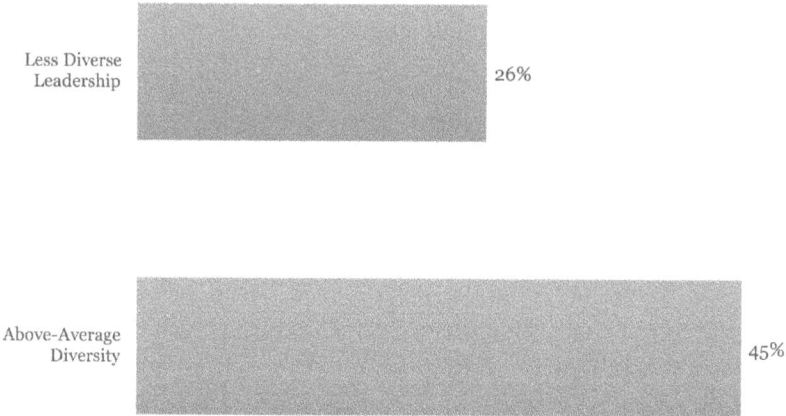

Less Diverse Leadership	26%

Above-Average Diversity	45%

Essentially, diversity can spark innovation that aligns with customer needs. A report by McKinsey & Company found that companies in the top quartile for gender diversity are 21% more likely to outperform those in the bottom quartile in terms of profitability.[47] These businesses benefit from a mix of experiences, worldviews, and skills, allowing them to tackle challenges more holistically and find solutions that might be missed in a more uniform setting.

Gender diversity encompasses all women, including transgender women, and studies show a strong link between inclusivity and organizational performance.

Including women in corporate leadership can significantly boost a firm's performance in several ways. For one, having a diverse skill set within corporate boards enhances their oversight of management, which can improve profitability and stock market valuation.[48] Companies that discriminate against a large portion of the talent pool, like women, are at a competitive disadvantage. US research indicates that twenty to forty percent of productivity growth over the past five decades can be attributed to better talent-job matching, including the inclusion of women and Black Americans in highly skilled positions.[49] This is an efficiency gain that shouldn't be overlooked.

Having women in top management roles can also provide both informational and social diversity benefits, potentially improving the performance of other managers and motivating mid-level female managers. This impact is especially strong in sectors like technology, in firms with many female employees, and in companies with weak governance structures. For instance, firms that transitioned to a female CEO from a male predecessor and had a workforce that was 25% female saw an average sales boost of over 3%. Additionally, increasing female representation in corporate leadership from 0 to 30% was associated with a 1 percent rise in net profit margins, translating to a significant 15% profitability surge.[50]

Inclusive leadership unlocks the full potential of a diverse workforce. A study highlighted by the *Harvard Business Review* in 2013 underscores the significant impact that diversity in leadership, specifically two-dimensional diversity, which combines inherent and acquired traits, has on innovation and market growth. This research defines inherent diversity as involving traits you're born with, like gender, ethnicity, or sexual orientation, while acquired diversity comes from life experiences, such as working in different cultures or advocating for gender equality in the workplace. A company is said to have two-dimensional diversity when its leaders possess at least three inherent and three acquired diversity traits.[51]

Organizations led by individuals with two-dimensional diversity are not only better at innovation but also enjoy a substantial market advantage. These companies are 45% more likely to see market share growth and 70% more likely to enter new markets.[52] This success comes from creating an environment where a variety of perspectives are welcomed and encouraged, leading to a richer pool of ideas and strong deci-sion-making processes.

Hiring new talent comes at a cost. Recruitment expenses, training, the learning curve for new hires, potential severance costs, and the loss of productivity when an experienced employee leaves all add up. Retaining employees is a cost-effective strat-egy. Young professionals look for diversity in leadership roles, but genuine inclusion only happens once they're on board. Firms need to not only project diversity but also practice deep-rooted inclusion. Otherwise, they risk cycling through hires without truly cultivating talent.

When employees feel genuinely valued and respected for who they are, without being constrained by outdated gender norms, they perform better and are more likely to stay loyal to their organization. A survey by Glassdoor found that 76% of job seek-ers consider workplace diversity an essential factor when looking for jobs. Financially, more inclusive companies have seen a 2.3 times higher cash flow per employee over a three-year period.[53]

Talking about diversity is one thing but showcasing it in hir-ing statistics is another.

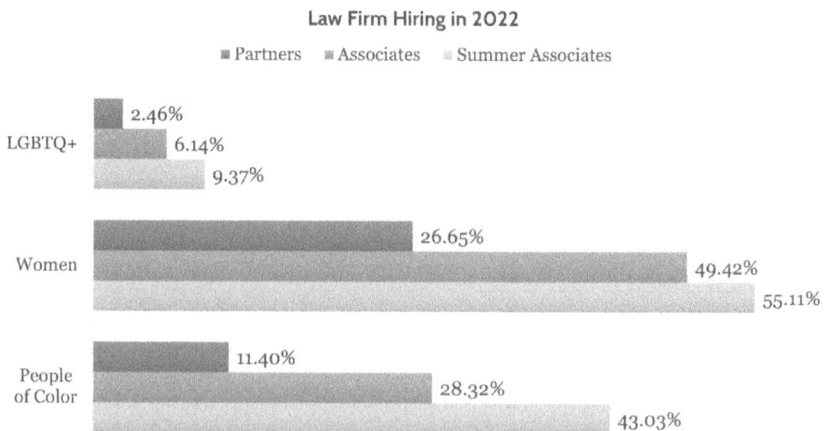

Law Firm Hiring in 2022

■ Partners ■ Associates ▪ Summer Associates

LGBTQ+
- 2.46%
- 6.14%
- 9.37%

Women
- 26.65%
- 49.42%
- 55.11%

People of Color
- 11.40%
- 28.32%
- 43.03%

According to the National Association-Law Placement, 2022 saw law firms recording their highest diversity figures for summer associates: 43% were people of color, over 55% were women, and more than 9% identified as LGBTQ+. However, these numbers drop significantly when looking at full-time associates and partners. For example, while people of color make up 43% of summer associates, only about half of that number are represented among associates, and the proportion shrinks even further, with nearly four times fewer people of color reaching partner level.[54]

Ignorance Isn't Bliss: The Costs of Exclusion

When we talk about why gender inclusion matters in the workplace, we need to look at the significant costs of not being inclusive. This includes not just overt discrimination or hostility but also rolling back existing DEI initiatives in favor of so-called "merit-based" systems that fail to account for systemic inequities. Ignoring gender diversity and failing to create an inclusive environment can hit an organization hard in terms of financial health, talent acquisition, employee retention, innovation, and public perception.

Non-inclusive workplaces create environments where discrimination and hostility lead to increased absenteeism, lower motivation, and reduced productivity. A study by the Human Rights Campaign found that employee engagement in non-inclusive workspaces can drop by up to 30%.[55] While this research mainly looked at the broader LGBTQ+ community, I can tell you firsthand that transgender individuals face these same challenges.

In fact, a comprehensive 2015 survey of 27,715 transgender individuals in the US revealed alarming statistics: 77% had taken steps in the previous year to avoid workplace mistreatment related to their gender identity. This included not revealing their true identity, postponing their gender transition, or quitting their job due to a hostile environment. Sadly, 67% reported direct negative job outcomes tied to their gender identity, from being unfairly fired to being denied promotions. Nearly a quarter faced further indignities, such as being denied access to the correct restroom or having private information disclosed without consent.[56]

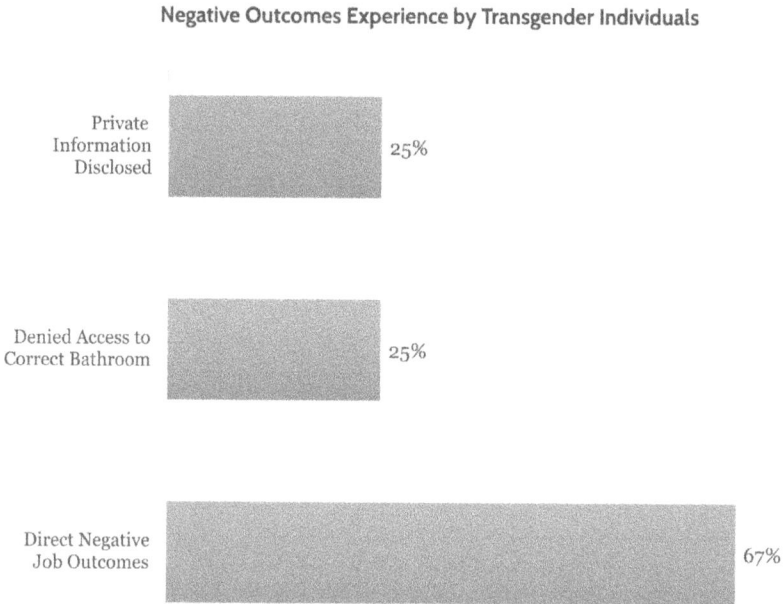

Negative Outcomes Experience by Transgender Individuals

Private Information Disclosed — 25%

Denied Access to Correct Bathroom — 25%

Direct Negative Job Outcomes — 67%

A 2020 study using daily survey data from 105 transgender employees in the US showed that almost half experienced daily discriminatory behaviors, such as transphobic remarks or pressure to conform to traditional gender norms. These incidents led to heightened hypervigilance and rumination at work, resulting in diminished focus and productivity the following workday.[57]

Neglecting to cultivate an inclusive culture makes your workplace genuinely unwelcoming. This unwelcoming environment, and the reputation it creates, harms your employees and damages efforts to recruit and retain top-tier talent. According to the Level Playing Field Institute, one in four people who experience unfairness at work are highly unlikely to recommend their organization to others.[58]

This reluctance to endorse the company can seriously hinder recruitment efforts. A 2022 study by the Boston Consulting Group showed that more than half of transgender and nonbinary employees in the US have dropped out of the recruiting process, declined job offers, or left a company due to a lack of gender-inclusive culture and policies.[59] Establishing a gender-inclusive environment supports employees and provides substantial financial benefits by reducing turnover and associated hiring costs. Replacing an employee can cost a company between six to nine months of that employee's salary, according to SHRM (Society for Human Resource Management).[60] Additionally, the total expense of hiring a new employee can reach three to four times the position's salary.[61] On the flip side, employees who feel safe to be their authentic selves are happier, more motivated to give their best, feel like their perspectives matter, and are nearly 2.4 times less likely to quit.[62]

Beyond the personal and emotional toll on employees, businesses also face operational and legal risks. While prepping for a custom workshop on the cost of exclusion for a law firm, an example unfolded in real time that illustrated the significant consequences of ignoring inclusivity, and how easily some of these risks can be mitigated.

Case Study: The New Jersey Municipalities Incident

In 2022, twenty-eight municipalities in New Jersey received violation notices from the state attorney general for failing to comply with anti-discrimination laws regarding marriage licenses. Many of these municipalities were not using the state-provided forms, which had included a third gender option since 2019. Instead, they continued to use their own outdated forms with gender-restrictive language, such as "Bride" and "Groom," or stated that marriage licenses were only available to opposite-sex couples. In some cases, this exclusionary language appeared on both the forms and the websites.[63]

This issue came to light after a resident noticed that her borough's website incorrectly stated that marriage licenses were only available to opposite-sex couples. She reported the issue, which sparked further investigation by advocacy groups, leading to a review of all 565 municipal websites across the state. Their findings revealed that twenty-eight municipalities were non-compliant with the state's anti-discrimination laws, leading to the attorney general's intervention.[64]

These municipalities faced the risk of fines for failing to comply with the state's anti-discrimination policies, with potential penalties reaching up to $10,000. But the necessary fixes were relatively simple. Most municipalities didn't even have to create new forms. Instead, they could simply update their websites to link directly to the Department of Health's standardized marriage license form, which already included a third gender option. For many towns, the issue arose because data on their websites had become outdated, and they simply hadn't noticed.[65]

In some cases, like in Linden, towns went beyond minimal compliance by quickly updating their websites to explicitly welcome "all gender compositions, including same-gender, same-sex, and nonbinary applicants."[66] Others, like Vineland, realized the issue was as small as a single outdated link that had been missed during routine website updates. The required changes, updating links, modifying website language, and providing brief employee training, were relatively minor but had a significant impact on both legal compliance and inclusivity.[67]

This case shows that ignoring inclusion doesn't just carry financial and reputational costs; it's often avoidable. Proactively tackling these issues before they snowball into bigger problems can avoid fines, protect reputations, and foster an environment of equality. And it doesn't have to be a massive overhaul. Sometimes, it's as simple as updating a form, training your staff, or fixing a link—little changes, big difference.

While the laws in this case were clear and enforceable, the legal landscape around inclusivity continues to evolve—or devolve under targeted efforts to dismantle protections. Regardless of shifts in federal or state policies, organizations that prioritize proactive inclusion will be better positioned to navigate changes and uphold equitable practices.

Legal and Financial Consequences

But while some issues can be addressed with minor adjustments, others involve significant financial and operational consequences.

In 2020, a landmark US Supreme Court case, Bostock v. Clayton County, tackled whether Title VII of the Civil Rights Act of 1964, which prohibits employment discrimination based on sex, also protects employees from discrimination based on their sexual orientation or gender identity. The Court ruled that firing someone for being gay or transgender is discrimination based on sex, which Title VII prohibits. This decision marked a significant victory for LGBTQ+ rights and workplace equality.

Since the Bostock v. Clayton decision, several federal and district court cases have made it clear: the law now unequivocally protects against discrimination based on gender identity. However, under the current administration, the federal agency responsible for enforcing these protections—the Equal Employment Opportunity Commission (EEOC)—has actively abandoned its role in protecting transgender workers.

In 2025, the EEOC announced it would no longer investigate cases of anti-trans workplace discrimination, removed pronouns from federal complaint forms, and even endorsed corporate bathroom bans.[68] This does not mean discrimination is now legal. It simply means that federal enforcement is being obstructed.

Even as federal protections are actively rolled back, the legal precedent set by Bostock and subsequent cases remains in place. Organizations that fail to uphold inclusive policies still face significant liability through state-level discrimination laws, private litigation, and lawsuits from advocacy groups such as Lambda Legal and the ACLU.

Proactively aligning with best practices is still the smartest legal and business decision, even as federal enforcement wavers. While the EEOC is no longer acting as a reliable enforcer, companies that abandon inclusive policies risk lawsuits, reputational damage, and workforce instability. Compliance with Bostock and state laws remains essential, even if federal agencies fail to act.

EEOC v. R.G. & G.R. Harris Funeral Homes, Inc. (884, F.3d 560, 6th Cir. 2018)[69]

Aimee Stephens, a transgender woman, worked as a funeral director at R.G. & G.R. Harris Funeral Homes, Inc. She was fired after telling her employer she planned to transition from male to female and would present herself as a woman at work. In 2014, Stephens filed a complaint with the Equal Employment Opportunity Commission (EEOC), claiming unlawful sex discrimination.

The EEOC investigated and found that Stephens had been fired because of her transgender status and her refusal to conform to sex-based stereotypes, which violated Title VII of the Civil Rights Act of 1964. They also discovered the funeral home gave clothing allowances to male employees but not to female employees.

The funeral home argued that enforcing Title VII's anti-discrimination provisions would significantly burden the owner's religious beliefs, citing the Religious Freedom Restoration Act (RFRA).

This case made its way to the US Supreme Court and became a crucial part of the landmark Bostock v. Clayton County decision in 2020. The court ruled that the funeral home had indeed engaged in unlawful sex discrimination and that enforcing Title VII didn't substantially burden the owner's religious exercise. In short, this case confirmed that firing employees for not conforming to sex stereotypes or for being transgender is illegal under Title VII. The funeral home's religious objections didn't exempt it from following the law. Sadly, Aimee Stephens passed away before the case was resolved in her favor.

The financial consequences for the funeral home were significant.[70]

- $130,000 in back pay and compensatory damages to Stephens's estate
- $120,000 in attorney fees
- $3,705 in clothing benefits for approximately seventeen female front-facing employees

In addition to the financial penalties, the funeral home was required to:

- Provide anti-discrimination training
- Revise its anti-discrimination policy
- Implement new procedures for handling discrimination complaints

EEOC v. A&E Tire (1:17-cv-02362, D. Colo. Sept. 5, 2018)[71]
In this case, A&E Tire, a Colorado tire company, offered a job to Egan Woodward that was contingent on a background check.

When A&E Tire saw that Woodward had identified as female on his background paperwork and realized he was transgender, they decided not to hire him and chose another candidate instead.

The EEOC filed a lawsuit, and after months of investigation and a court order denying A&E Tire's motion to dismiss, the court allowed the lawsuit to proceed. The court found the EEOC's claims plausible, asserting that A&E Tire didn't hire Woodward because he didn't conform to sex stereotypes. The court recognized that discrimination against transgender individuals is a form of sex stereotyping, as they identify as a gender different from the one assigned at birth.

The resolution of the lawsuit included A&E Tire paying Woodward $60,000 and sending him a letter of apology. The company also had to update its employment policies to explicitly prohibit sex discrimination, including discrimination based on sex stereotyping and transgender status. Additionally, A&E Tire was required to provide training to managers and employees on these anti-discrimination laws.

EEOC v. Deluxe Financial Services, Inc. (0:15-cv-02646. D. Minn. Jan. 20, 2016)[72]

Britney Austin, a transgender woman, had been a long-time employee of Deluxe Financial Services. She was hired in 2007 when she presented as a man. She began to present as a woman in 2010 and informed her supervisors of her transition. She requested permission to use the women's restroom and to update her records to reflect her gender identity. Instead of honoring these requests, the company refused to let her use the appropriate restroom, only partially updated her personnel records, and allowed supervisors and coworkers to make derogatory statements and intentionally use the wrong pronouns for her.

The case was settled in 2016, with Deluxe required to pay $115,000 in back pay and compensatory damages, along with

$39,962.11 in attorney's fees. In addition to these financial penalties, Deluxe had to:[73]

- Revise its employment policies to explicitly protect against sex discrimination, including gender identity and sex stereotyping
- Ensure its health benefits cover medically necessary care for transgender employees
- Provide annual anti-discrimination training to employees, ensuring everyone understands that discrimination against transgender employees is illegal under Title VII

These changes were overseen by the court for three years, during which Deluxe was under scrutiny to ensure compliance. Additionally, the company was required to issue Britney Austin a letter of apology and a reference for future employment opportunities.

While past EEOC cases highlight the financial risks of discrimination, the agency itself has now turned against trans workers.[74] But legal liability has not disappeared. Discriminatory policies still violate state laws, company policies, and the ethical foundations of an inclusive workplace. Even as federal agencies refuse to act, private lawsuits, advocacy groups, and state-level enforcement will continue to hold companies accountable.

Under the Microscope

Beyond legal penalties, businesses are increasingly being evaluated on how they handle inclusion, not just by courts but also by employees, customers, and advocacy groups. This growing scrutiny is fueled by tools like the Human Rights Campaign's Corporate Equality Index (CEI), which evaluates businesses on their treatment of LGBTQ+ employees. Established in 1980, the HRC is the nation's largest LGBTQ+ civil rights organization, boasting over three million members and supporters. The Corporate Equality Index serves as a national benchmark for assessing how businesses treat LGBTQ+ employees. For companies, participation is a conscious choice; any private sector, for-profit employer with five hundred or more full-time US employees can request to be evaluated.[75] Businesses that earn a top score of one hundred are celebrated as Best Places to Work for LGBTQ+ Equality. However, once a company opts in, its score is made public, so there's no escaping the spotlight of a low score. The HRC CEI evaluates companies on LGBTQ+ inclusive workforce protections, benefits, and culture, with dedicated criteria for transgender inclusion best practices.[76]

While the HRC CEI is perhaps the most well-known, it's not the only tool companies should be paying attention to. In 2024, *Newsweek* and Plant-A Insights released their America's Greatest Workplaces for LGBTQ+ ranking for the second year. Unlike the HRC CEI, companies are not asked to participate. Instead, they are evaluated based on feedback from more than 29,000 LGBTQ+ employees, who contributed over 205,000 reviews. The 2024 list features over four hundred companies across sixty-five industries.[77]

Beyond corporate settings, the Campus Pride Index has provided a National Listing of LGBTQ+-Friendly Colleges and Universities since 2007. The index includes a gender identity/ expression ranking, and tracks inclusive policies, academic life, student life, housing, and campus safety. While it primarily serves as a guide for students, it is also a valuable resource for faculty and staff considering where to work.[78] States are similarly ranked on their LGBTQ+ policies by the think tank Movement Advancement Project (MAP), which monitors over fifty LGBTQ+-related laws, including those specific to gender identity. Journalist and activist Erin Reed maintains a regularly updated Anti-Trans Legislative Risk Map, which evaluates current policies and projected future risks over the next two years, guiding decisions about where people live and work.[79]

It's not just advocacy groups and think tanks keeping score; companies that prioritize Gen Z hires and inclusive workplaces are increasingly eager to advertise their DEI policies and achievements. Many businesses proudly announce when they hit 100% on the HRC CEI, showcasing it as a badge of honor. Alaska Airlines, for instance, actively promoted its perfect score, highlighting its gender inclusion initiatives, such as offering expanded gender options for bookings, using gender-neutral greetings in inflight announcements, and curating a Pride Month collection for inflight entertainment.[80]

Even when a company chooses not to promote its inclusion efforts, platforms like Glassdoor and Indeed give employees the opportunity to share their experiences anonymously. On Glassdoor, for instance, employees can rate companies on metrics like Culture & Values and Diversity & Inclusion. Reviews can even be filtered to show feedback from transgender and nonbinary employees. With 86% of job seekers researching company reviews before applying, a company's practices around inclusion rarely remain hidden.[81]

Following the 2025 presidential executive orders dismantling workplace protections, an analysis of Google Trends revealed an 822% increase in searches for "companies with DEI."[82] While it's difficult to determine whether these searches were driven by support or opposition, the spike highlights a growing public awareness of corporate inclusion policies. Consumers—particularly younger generations—are paying close attention to which companies remain committed to DEI and which quietly walk back their efforts.

When inclusion initiatives face growing political scrutiny, tools like the HRC CEI, even with a potentially smaller pool of participating companies, will continue to hold significant value. These benchmarks, along with non-participation-based rankings from MAP, Erin Reed, and employee review platforms, ensure accountability and transparency, helping companies demonstrate their commitment to inclusive environments regardless of shifting federal or state policies.

We've covered a lot of immediate costs, both for employees and employers, including personal, legal, and financial consequences. But the impact of exclusion doesn't stop there. A significant and often overlooked cost is how innovation and creativity are stifled. When diversity is left out of design and development stages, products and systems are designed without fully considering the needs of all users.

Take car crash test dummies, for example. For decades, they were designed based on the average male body, which meant that safety technologies protected men far better than women. As a result, women are a staggering 47% more likely to suffer serious injuries in car accidents. Even when female dummies were finally introduced in 2011, they still didn't accurately represent the average woman, continuing to widen the safety gap.[83]

The medical field has a long history of exclusion as well. It wasn't until the NIH Revitalization Act of 1993 that women and people from racial and ethnic minority groups were included in clinical research. Prior to that time, most medical trials were conducted on men under the belief that all results would pertain to women as well. As a result, women are often overmedicated, suffering adverse drug reactions nearly twice as often as men.[84] Exclusion in medical research means real-world consequences for health and safety.

Failing to include diverse perspectives in product development limits creativity, compromises safety, leads to costly oversights, and disproportionately endangers underrepresented groups. No policy change, corporate trend, or government action can erase the real-world consequences of exclusion.

CHAPTER 02

TERMINOLOGY

anguage is a powerful tool capable of conveying nuanced meanings. The English language gives us countless words to describe different aspects of the human experience. Consider, for example, the many words we have for "love"—affection, adoration, infatuation, devotion, and so on—each capturing a different shade of emotion. In much the same way, labels and terminology allow individuals to express their identities with clarity and precision. But when it comes to gender, society often reduces this complexity to just two basic categories: man and woman. Before we even begin defining new terms, let's identify an old concept with a potentially new term for it: "binary."

In technical spaces, "binary" denotes two options: 0 or 1, on or off, yes or no. For a long time, many people believed gender worked the same way—only two options: man or woman. No gray area, no space between, no room to move.

However, just like there are many ways to describe love, there are many ways to describe gender, and as we'll explore in the coming pages, each term carries its own unique meaning. This chapter will introduce terminology related to various aspects of gender identity, expression, orientation, and experiences. We need to share a common vocabulary in order to discuss transgender and nonbinary inclusion. This is especially critical in a time when misinformation is often passed around as fact—even by those in positions of power. Having accurate, clear definitions allows us to cut through noise and ensure discussions are grounded in truth rather than rhetoric.

In a 2020 survey, 40,000 LGBTQ+ youth aged thirteen to twenty-four identified with more than one hundred different combinations of terms to describe their gender identity.[85] Due to this diversity of language, it would be impossible to write a simple chapter that covers all the words and the nuances associated with them. The terminology presented in this chapter has been thoughtfully selected to address the specific needs of gender inclusion in the business world. For those looking for a more extensive list, Michigan State University's Gender and Sexuality Campus Center offers an online glossary covering a wide range of gender, sexuality, and romantic identity terms, as well as legal and legislation terms, terms for kinds of oppression and racial identity, and racial justice terms. The list is updated regularly and includes contact information should you notice a term that needs to be added.[86]

While the acceptance of gender diversity may vary across administrations, regions, and cultures, the reality of gender's complexity remains unchanged. Science, lived experiences, and language continue to evolve together, providing the tools we need to better understand and describe the human experience. Regardless of external attempts to simplify or regulate these concepts, the terminology in this chapter reflects the diversity and richness of gender as it exists today.

As we begin this journey, let me remind you that you do not have to be a gender expert or know every term perfectly to be respectful. You are already on the right track for having the interest and willingness to learn.

Gender 101: Foundations of Gender and Expression

Before diving into specifics, it's important to understand the core concepts of gender identity, gender expression, and sexual orientation. To help illustrate these ideas clearly, we'll start with the Gender Unicorn, a graphic created by Trans Student Educational Resources.[87]

The Gender Unicorn

Graphic by:
TSER
Trans Student Educational Resources

⌒ Gender Identity
Female/Woman/Girl
Male/Man/Boy
Other Gender(s)

Gender Expression
Feminine
Masculine
Other

Sex Assigned at Birth
Female   Male   Other/Intersex

♡ Physically Attracted to
Women
Men
Other Gender(s)

♥ Emotionally Attracted to
Women
Men
Other Gender(s)

To learn more, go to:
www.transstudent.org/gender

Design by Landyn Pan and Anna Moore

I will break down what each of these sections means, but first, I'll present a quick primer on how to use the Gender Unicorn. The Gender Unicorn is a tool designed to help you explore, understand, and communicate the various aspects of identity beyond the rigid boxes that society often tries to put us in. This exercise isn't just for LGBTQ+ people; it's for anyone who wants to better understand the nuanced ways we all experience gender and attraction. You can fill out your own gender unicorn by marking a circle or an "X" on each of the arrows to signify where you identify in each category. Let's dive into the terms and then revisit how to fill out your own Gender Unicorn.

Sex Assigned at Birth

If you've ever seen a movie or TV show where a baby is born, or if you've ever witnessed or participated in the experience yourself, you may recall that almost immediately after the baby is delivered, someone calls out, "It's a boy" or, "It's a girl." This announcement is based solely on a visual inspection of the baby's external genitalia. Typically, this assignment is not influenced by any other factors unless specific medical studies are performed.

This label, "sex assigned at birth," becomes the letter "M" or "F" written on official documents, like a birth certificate or medical records, based on that initial visual assessment. Whether it's announced verbally, recorded in documentation, or listed in official records, the assignment is just that: the label given at birth. While the initial categorization is based on this visual assessment, the biological understanding of someone as male or female involves more complex factors such as chromosomes, hormonal profiles, and both external and internal anatomical features.[88]

Intersex

Not all bodies are obviously male or female. Whether at birth or later in life, if a person does not fit the typical definitions of male or female, they may be labeled "intersex." Intersex individuals possess physical characteristics that encompass a range of variations in chromosomes, hormones, and anatomical features. These variations mean that an intersex person may have biological traits of both males and females or traits that do not fit traditional binary notions of male and female bodies. For example, an intersex individual might be born appearing female on the outside but have internal testes, or a person might have a combination of male-typical and female-typical genital characteristics.

In many cases, doctors assign either male or female at birth based on visible characteristics, and sometimes this assignment may not reflect the person's full biological complexity. Many intersex individuals do not discover they are intersex until later in life, during medical examinations such as fertility treatments or diagnosis of unrelated health conditions. It's also important to note that being intersex does not mean a person will necessarily identify as something other than their sex assigned at birth, regardless of when they learn this fact.

Gender Identity

If sex assigned at birth is how you are labeled, then gender identity is who you are. It's your internal sense of your gender, which might match that birth label, or it might not.

Gender pertains to the roles, behaviors, and expectations society assigns to us based on being "male" or "female." These roles shape how we act, relate to others, and even view ourselves. While biological sex has certain universal features (like chromosomes and anatomy), gender varies a lot; it's flexible and largely influenced by cultural norms. Gender roles, behaviors, and norms vary significantly between cultures and time periods. For instance, some Indigenous cultures have long recognized more than two genders, such as the Two-Spirit identity in certain Native American tribes. This highlights the importance of understanding that gender is not universally binary and is often a social construct shaped by the environment in which one lives.[89] We will discuss various gender identities in the coming sections of this chapter.

A January 20, 2025, executive order in the US asserts that gender is limited to binary categories of 'man' and 'woman,' defined at conception.[90] This perspective contradicts established scientific understanding and the lived experiences of countless individuals worldwide. Gender identity, as we know it, encompasses a wide spectrum that has been recognized across cultures and history. Science, anthropology, and sociology all show us that gender is not fixed at birth but shaped by complex biological, social, and cultural factors. While policies may attempt to enforce rigid definitions, these efforts cannot erase the reality of gender diversity.

The term "gender ideology," while defined in the executive order and used in some circles, is not defined in this book. Gender is not an ideology; it is an identity.

One final note on the science behind defining gender as sex at conception—because how could we let this one slide? If that were true, then congratulations: we live in a world with no men. Why? The SRY gene, located on the Y chromosome, doesn't activate until weeks after conception to begin male development. Until that point, everyone follows the default developmental pathway, which is female.[91] By the logic of this rule, everyone is a woman!

Gender Expression

This is how you present yourself to the world. Gender expression refers to how you outwardly express yourself through your appearance, behavior, clothing, and more.

One of the most important lessons to learn when becoming a more gender-inclusive person is that gender expression does not necessarily equal gender identity. For generations, more senior generations have shown confusion, and often disapproval, about the fashion choices and appearances of younger generations.

These critiques often miss that fashion choices are more about individuality and creativity than about gender; a way for people to push back against rigid norms and explore self-expression.

In retrospect, many iconic fashion moments are now celebrated for expanding our understanding of gender expression. They remind us that appreciating the choices of younger generations requires a willingness to embrace change and the diversity of human expression.

Here are some examples of American subcultures that did not adhere to traditional gender norms of the time:

- **Flappers in the Roaring Twenties:** During the 1920s, some women known as "flappers" rebelled against traditional gender norms by adopting a more androgynous style. They wore shorter dresses, bobbed their hair, and openly challenged societal expectations for women's behavior.

- **Hippies of the 1960s:** The counterculture movement of the 1960s included individuals who embraced a free-spirited and nonconformist lifestyle. This often included wearing unconventional clothing, growing out their hair, and exploring alternative forms of gender expression. "Get a haircut, you look like a girl," was commonly said by parents to their hippie sons.

- **Punk Rockers:** In the punk rock scene of the 1970s and 80s, people engaged in a rebellious and gender-nonconforming style. Many punk rockers adopted hairstyles, clothing, and accessories that challenged traditional gender expectations.

- **Glam Rock Artists:** Some cisgender male musicians in the glam rock era, such as David Bowie and every member of the band Roxy Music, incorporated elements of androgyny and theatricality into their stage personas. They challenged conventional masculinity through their gender-bending performances.

- **Goth Subculture:** Within the goth subculture, both men and women may adopt a gender expression that challenges conventional gender norms. They may wear dark makeup, clothing, and accessories that do not conform to typical gender expectations.

Each person is unique in the way they choose to present themselves to others. Some people enjoy expressing themselves in multiple ways, so their gender expression can change daily. When you see someone, remember that how they look does not tell you everything about who they are.

Sexual Orientation

In the Gender Unicorn, "physically attracted to" and "emotionally attracted to" together make up what we commonly refer to as "sexual orientation," even though the term "sexual orientation" itself isn't labeled on the graphic.

Sexual orientation encompasses both who you love and who you're attracted to. It's important to understand that physical (or sexual) attraction and emotional (or romantic) attraction, while related, are not the same thing. Physical attraction refers to who you find yourself physically drawn to, which may or may not include a sexual component, depending on the individual. Emotional attraction refers to the deeper, romantic connection you seek with others. Some people experience both, while others may experience one or neither.

It's not uncommon to hear statements like, "I don't know if he's gay or trans." These aspects are separate and distinct. Someone can be both gay and trans, as sexual orientation and gender identity are completely different facets of a person's identity. Sexual orientation is outward: who you love. Gender identity is inward: who you are. Some examples of sexual orientation labels include lesbian, gay, bisexual, and straight (heterosexual). These labels can also be used to describe romantic attraction.

Now that we've covered the basics of gender identity, expression, and sexual orientation, it may become clearer that the arrows in each section of the Gender Unicorn represent the range of possibilities for how people identify and express themselves. These arrows highlight the fluidity within each category, showing that gender, expression, and attraction are not confined to rigid boxes.

For example, on a given day, someone might not feel connected to either masculine or feminine expression at all, choosing to wear an oversized sweatshirt and sweatpants.

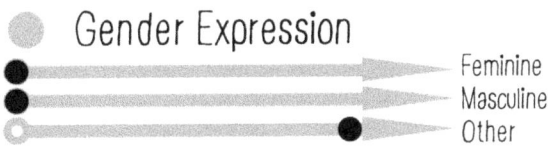

Gender Expression

Feminine
Masculine
Other

That same person might feel equally connected to both feminine and masculine ways of expressing themself the following day, blending traits from both categories while also feeling some connection to expressions that don't fit into either box. A button-down men's shirt with dangling earrings and makeup, paired with loose, neutral-toned trousers and sneakers, allows them to mix traditionally masculine and feminine elements while still adding a unique touch that doesn't fit neatly into either category.

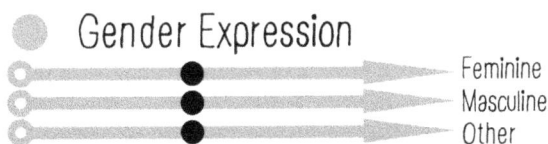

Gender Expression

Feminine
Masculine
Other

By seeing these examples, it's clear that gender identity and expression exist on a spectrum of possibilities. There is no one "right" way to experience or express gender and no one "right" way to fill out the Gender Unicorn. Each person's experience is unique, and each day could be different.

Understanding the Spectrum

You may have heard the statement, "Gender is a spectrum"; the gender spectrum is the most popular model of gender. Simply stated for the purpose of our conversation, the entirety of gender identity falls within a spectrum between man and woman, allowing people to identify anywhere along this continuum.

Spectrum

Sex Assigned at Birth *(how you are labeled)*

Male	Intersex	Female

Gender Identity *(who you are)*

Man	Nonbinary Identities	Woman

Gender Expression *(how you present yourself)*

Masculine	Androgynous	Feminine

Sexual Orientation *(who you love)*

Heterosexual	Bisexual/Pansexual/Asexual/Aromantic	Homosexual

The term "spectrum" is used to explain many things within an LGBTQ+ context. Throughout this book, we will refer to the spectrum of gender identity, as this is the most popular concept and can be a helpful starting point if you are new to it or explaining gender identity to someone who is not familiar.

When I teach technology and can't separate users by skill set, I often must explain both basic and advanced concepts at once. In those cases, I'll say, "For those of you who already know this part and want more, here's something extra, and if you just learned this and aren't ready for more, feel free to tune me out."

So, for those of you who already understand the spectrum model and are ready for more, I offer you this (and feel free to tune me out!): if the point is to reject gender as a binary concept of man and woman, then putting nonbinary identities on a line *between* man and woman fails to do that.

Instead, I invite you to consider gender as a constellation.

Constellation

In a gender constellation, gender identity can exist in "multiple dimensions and permits fluidity and change in both the individual elements and their interrelationships."[92] This is a growing concept as it is a more complete departure from the concept of binary identity.

Please note that the point here is not to get "lost among the stars" but instead to be open to the concept of gender as a much more expansive concept than we may have previously understood. It's very okay not to fully grasp any of this just yet.

Beyond the Binary: Exploring Gender Identities

Cisgender: Navigating Familiar Territory

Cis is a prefix that comes from Latin, meaning "on this side of." Cisgender individuals are those whose gender identity aligns with the sex they were assigned at birth. The word draws inspiration from the field of chemistry; "cis-" refers to molecules with atoms grouped on the same side. The adoption of "cisgender" in everyday language took time, eventually gaining recognition in dictionaries, legal works, and medical documents.

While it gained more prominence in the early twenty-first century, its roots can be traced back to discussions within the transgender community. Dana Defosse, PhD, MPH, a graduate student at the time, coined the term "cisgender" in 1994 to facilitate discussions on gender identity without inadvertently framing cisgender individuals as the norm and making transgender identities appear as the "other."[93] This was in response to the previously prevalent norm of referring to such individuals simply as "normal," "non-transgender," or even just by their gender identity without any modifier, which inadvertently positioned transgender identities as deviations from the norm. The goal of introducing "cisgender" was to create a more equitable linguistic framework, acknowledging that both transgender and cisgender experiences are valid and encompass a diverse range of identities. This linguistic shift aimed to promote understanding and foster conversations that transcend the binary gender construct.

The term has since been embraced by various communities, including academia, advocacy groups, and the broader public. It has played a significant role in challenging traditional norms and fostering discussions around gender diversity and inclusion. The use of "cisgender" reflects a growing recognition of the importance of respectful and accurate language when discussing gender identities.

Cisgender Privilege and Intersectionality

Cisgender individuals experience a set of privileges because their gender identity aligns with the sex they were assigned at birth. While many may not realize these privileges, they can make daily life easier in ways that transgender and nonbinary individuals often cannot take for granted. Some of these privileges include:

- **Ease with Identification Documents:** Cisgender people may not love the photo on their driver's license, but they don't have to fear that their ID might reveal a gender or name that doesn't align with their identity. For transgender individuals, their license may show a name, gender marker, or photo that's drastically different from how everyone knows them. This mismatch can lead to uncomfortable or even unsafe situations in everyday interactions, from something as simple as being carded to more serious encounters with law enforcement or travel security agents.

- **Restroom Access Without Fear:** The ease with which cisgender people use public restrooms is a privilege that many never even have to think about. Public restrooms are often gender-segregated, and transgender individuals must navigate which one to use, balancing their gender identity with the fear of confrontation, harassment, or even violence. This fear is not a minor inconvenience; it's an ongoing, daily struggle. Many transgender people avoid public restrooms entirely, planning their day around places where they feel safe or simply not drinking enough water to avoid needing to use one.

- **Not Being Misgendered in Everyday Interactions:** Cisgender people are typically referred to by the correct pronouns or gendered language based on how they present. In fact, they may never consider what it feels like to go through the day being misgendered with every interaction. For example, when a cisgender person walks into a store, they're often greeted as "sir" or "ma'am" without question. Transgender individuals, however, concern themselves about every interaction with strangers. Constant misgendering can be emotionally exhausting for transgender people, leading to feelings of invalidation, frustration, and even anxiety or distress.

Recognizing privilege is not about placing blame or guilt. It's about using the awareness of the advantages that cisgender people hold to stand up against discrimination, advocate for equal rights, and contribute to creating a more inclusive society.

Cisgender individuals, while experiencing privilege in terms of their gender identity aligning with their assigned sex at birth, may also belong to marginalized groups based on other aspects of their identity, such as race, sexual orientation, or socioeconomic status. Privilege is not a one-size-fits-all concept and can intersect with various dimensions of identity. For example, a cisgender Black woman may benefit from cisgender privilege, but she still faces systemic racism and sexism in her daily life. These overlapping forms of marginalization influence how she experiences the world.

Myth: Cis Is a Slur

The term "cisgender" is a valuable term when discussing gender identity. However, some misconceptions surround it, with individuals mistakenly viewing "cisgender" as a slur or an unnecessary label.[94]

Despite its legitimate origins and utility, some people perceive "cisgender" negatively. They argue that it is a slur or that it forces an unwanted label upon them. This misconception, however, misses the point of the term. Cisgender is not intended to be derogatory but rather serves as a linguistic tool to distinguish individuals whose gender identity aligns with the sex assigned to them at birth from those whose gender identity does not. It provides a framework for more precise discussions surrounding gender and identity, ultimately contributing to a more inclusive and equitable society.

The negative perceptions of "cisgender" are not a result of the word itself but stem from broader societal discomfort with discussions of gender identity and the questioning of traditional gender roles. Cisgender privilege is sometimes misunderstood as a personal attack rather than an acknowledgment of the advantages that come with aligning with societal norms. However, the term "cisgender" is not the cause of these issues; rather, it brings attention to existing disparities in our understanding of gender.

In today's climate of exclusion and violence against transgender and gender-nonconforming individuals, the term "cisgender" is not the enemy. It is a tool that fosters understanding and promotes equitable dialogue about gender identity. Rather than attacking the word itself, we should address the root causes of discomfort surrounding discussions of gender identity and work toward a more inclusive society where all individuals can express their identities freely and authentically. We will address some of the root causes of this discomfort in later chapters.

Transgender: Crossing the Boundaries of Identity

The conceptual opposite of "cisgender," the term "transgender" comes from the Latin prefix "trans-" meaning "across, beyond, or on the other side of." A transgender individual has a gender identity that differs from the sex they were assigned at birth.

Like the prefix "cis," "trans" draws inspiration from the field of chemistry, referring to molecules with atoms on opposite sides.

This term emerged in the twentieth century and initially gained traction within academic and medical communities. However, it has since evolved into a self-identifying and empowering term for a broad spectrum of people who do not conform to traditional gender norms. While "cisgender" refers to alignment with assigned sex, "transgender" encompasses a range of gender experiences, some of which include challenges to the traditional understanding of gender as a binary concept.

Intersectionality and Transgender Identity

Intersectionality acknowledges that our identities are not isolated but rather intricate webs encompassing multiple facets of our lives, including race, ethnicity, socioeconomic status, disability, and more. For instance, consider a Black nonbinary person, a Christian trans man, or a Spanish and Chinese disabled trans woman. Each of these individuals holds multiple identities that interact to shape their unique experiences. Intersectionality helps us understand that we are more than just one label; each identity plays a role in how we navigate the world. By understanding and addressing these intersections, we can work toward a more holistic and inclusive approach to supporting transgender and nonbinary individuals, recognizing that their experiences are shaped by a complex interplay of factors.

This section applies to both the transgender and nonbinary communities; we will delve deeper into the unique experiences and identities within the nonbinary community in the subsequent section.

Race, Ethnicity, and Transgender Identity

The intersection of race and transgender identity illuminates the diverse struggles faced by transgender and nonbinary individuals from different racial and ethnic backgrounds. People of color within the transgender community often experience compounded discrimination due to both their racial identity and gender identity. Conversations about transgender rights and representation must acknowledge the distinct challenges faced by trans individuals of color.

Transgender women of color, especially Black transgender women, experience alarmingly high rates of violence and discrimination. One in six people who identify as transgender report having been incarcerated at some point in their lives; this figure jumps to nearly three in six for Black transgender women.[95] Layleen Polanco, a transgender Afro-Latina woman, died due to neglect at Rikers Island, having been left alone in solitary confinement for three times as long as the procedural limit.[96]

Socioeconomic Status and Transgender Identity

Socioeconomic factors intersect with transgender identity, leading to varying access to resources and opportunities. Transgender individuals from marginalized socioeconomic backgrounds may encounter barriers to education, stable employment, and healthcare, contributing to economic disparities. Addressing these challenges requires a comprehensive approach that includes economic empowerment as a key component of gender inclusion.

Many transgender individuals experience significant economic hardship, including lower employment rates, lower household incomes, and higher poverty rates. According to a 2020 study, the first to document the socioeconomic struggles of transgender populations, transgender individuals in the United States are approximately 14% less likely to have obtained a college degree and 14% more likely to experience poverty compared to the general population. Interestingly, even after adjusting for factors such as educational attainment and other visible distinctions, transgender Americans still face an 11% lower likelihood of employment when compared to similarly situated cisgender men.[97]

Disability and Transgender Identity

The intersection of disability and transgender identity emphasizes the importance of creating inclusive spaces that accommodate diverse needs. Transgender individuals with disabilities often face unique challenges related to accessibility, healthcare, and social inclusion. Advocacy efforts must recognize the specific experiences of individuals at the intersection of gender identity and disability, working to remove barriers to full participation in society.

A survey conducted in 2022 revealed that individuals who identify as both transgender and disabled were nearly three times more prone to indicate having unmet healthcare needs when compared to disabled cisgender individuals. A more in-depth examination also disclosed that LGBTQ+ individuals with disabilities not only confront discrimination but also encounter challenges related to accessing services, social support systems, and community connections.[98]

Furthermore, transgender individuals with disabilities had a higher likelihood of experiencing economic difficulties, mental health issues, and mistreatment by healthcare providers compared to transgender individuals without disabilities. The survey also highlighted an increased incidence of denials for gender-affirming healthcare among disabled transgender individuals.[99]

Age and Transgender Identity

The intersection of age and transgender identity reveals evolving challenges across different life stages. Transgender youth may face bullying and discrimination in school, which can impact their mental health and academic performance. In contrast, older transgender individuals may struggle with accessing age-appropriate healthcare services related to gender-affirming care or gender-related surgeries. Older transgender adults are also at an elevated risk of experiencing poor physical health, disability, and symptoms of depression compared to their cisgender peers. These health challenges often stem from their exposure to victimization and stigma.[100]

Cultural and Religious Diversity Within Transgender Identity

Cultural and religious backgrounds intersect with transgender identity, shaping perceptions of gender diversity. Various cultures and religions may have distinct terminology and understandings of gender, influencing how individuals express themselves and come out. Acknowledging and respecting these intersections ensures that transgender individuals can navigate their gender journeys while honoring their cultural or religious beliefs.

For example, certain cultures recognize traditional gender identities that diverge from the Western binary concept. In Indigenous cultures in North America, Two-Spirit individuals embody both masculine and feminine qualities. Understanding and respecting these cultural nuances is vital for supporting transgender individuals across diverse cultural and religious contexts.

Common Misconceptions

As we delve into the terminology and concepts that shape our understanding, it becomes clear that certain myths and biases persist, perpetuating stereotypes and hindering genuine empathy. By shedding light on these myths, we hope to foster a deeper appreciation for the unique and diverse journeys of transgender individuals, ultimately promoting an environment of greater acceptance and understanding.

Myth: Transgender Identity Is About "Passing"

Assuming that transgender individuals are primarily concerned with "passing" as a specific gender oversimplifies the complexity of their experiences. As we will learn later in this chapter, passing refers to whether a transgender individual is perceived as the gender with which they identify. Just as cisgender women are often criticized for not meeting societal beauty standards, transgender individuals may encounter similar pressures to conform to a particular image.

However, not all transgender individuals prioritize "passing" in the same way. Many choose to prioritize self-expression, authenticity, and the acceptance of their diverse identities over conforming to conventional standards. They may reject the notion that their worth is determined by how well they "pass" as cisgender and instead embrace their unique journey and appearance.

This concept might be more familiar in the traditional cisgender community, where women may or may not choose to conform to the standard of beauty that has been established by the patriarchy. In other words, women don't always conform to the Barbie ideal, and men don't always look like Ken. Just as some cisgender women prefer not to wear high heels or makeup and some men might skip the suit and tie, transgender individuals express their gender in ways that feel true to them, not according to rigid stereotypes. "Passing" is not always the goal for anyone, whether they are transgender or cisgender.

Myth: Gender Identity Is Just a Phase

A common misconception is the notion that transgender identity is temporary or merely a phase. Gender identity is a core aspect of an individual's sense of self and is not determined by passing trends. An individual's gender identity is intrinsic and enduring, akin to other fundamental aspects of their identity, such as their ethnicity or sexual orientation.

Just as cisgender individuals have a stable and lasting gender identity, so do transgender individuals. The idea that transgender identity is fleeting or influenced by passing trends is not only incorrect but also invalidates the authentic experiences of transgender people. Recognizing the permanence and validity of transgender identities fosters inclusive and supportive environments where individuals can express their true selves without fear of judgment or dismissal.

Myth: The Transgender Experience Is Defined Solely by Challenges and Struggles

Assuming that the lives of transgender individuals are solely defined by challenges and adversity overlooks their successes, achievements, and resilience. While the transgender experience does involve overcoming obstacles, it is also marked by personal growth, self-discovery, and moments of triumph. Celebrating these positive aspects contributes to a more balanced and compassionate understanding.

Myth: Transgender Identity Is a Western Concept

Transgender identities are sometimes inaccurately viewed as a concept specific to Western cultures. In truth, transgender experiences and identities exist across diverse cultures and histories. Many societies around the world have long recognized and integrated nonbinary or third-gender roles into their cultural frameworks. For example, Hijras in South Asia are recognized as a third gender, with legal acknowledgment in countries like India and Pakistan. In Indonesia, Bissu individuals hold a sacred role in Bugis society as a fifth gender, encompassing the entire gender spectrum. Khawaja Sira in Pakistan also represents a traditional third-gender community with recognized cultural roles.

These examples illustrate that diverse gender identities have existed globally for centuries, challenging the notion that transgender identities are solely a Western concept. We will explore these identities and others in greater depth later in this chapter.

Nonbinary: Expanding the Spectrum

The term "nonbinary" refers to a gender identity that doesn't fit within the traditional binary framework of male and female. The word "binary" itself comes from the Latin root "bini," which means "two together." The prefix "non-" negates this, indicating that nonbinary people do not strictly adhere to a dualistic view of gender. The word nonbinary is both an identity and an umbrella term, encompassing a variety of gender experiences and identities that don't align with the conventional male/female dichotomy.

Nonbinary individuals may identify with aspects of both male and female genders, neither gender, or they may define their gender in completely different terms altogether. The term challenges the cultural and social expectations associated with one's assigned sex at birth, offering a more fluid understanding of gender that allows for a broader range of identity and expression.

A common slang for "nonbinary" is "enby." When pronounced, it sounds like you are saying the *n* and the *b* in "nonbinary."

Being nonbinary is not a new concept. Nonbinary identities have been recognized in various cultures and communities around the world and throughout history, often holding special roles or statuses within those societies. For example, Muxes in Zapotec culture in Mexico represent a recognized third gender. Stepping beyond the binary of male and female has long been part of cultural understandings around the globe.

Nonbinary individuals often seek recognition and respect for their identity, expressing themselves in ways that feel authentic to them. Each person's experience is unique and deeply personal.

We will review several nonbinary identities within this umbrella term, but first, let's dig a little deeper into the concept of stepping beyond the binary of man and woman.

Diverse Expressions of Nonbinary Identities

Genderqueer

Genderqueer typically refers to individuals who reject or challenge the binary concept of gender altogether. They may not identify strictly as male or female and may view their gender identity as existing outside of these categories (a great example of where constellation is better than spectrum). Genderqueer individuals may have a more expansive understanding of their gender, and their identity might incorporate elements from various gender expressions.

Genderfluid, Genderflux, and Fluidflux

Genderfluid describes individuals whose gender identity changes over time. A person who identifies as genderfluid may feel more connected to different gender identities at different moments. This change can include anything along the gender spectrum.

Genderflux individuals experience a changing intensity of their gender identity rather than changing their actual identity. This means that their connection to their gender might feel stronger or weaker at different times. For example, someone who identifies as feminine might feel a very strong connection to that identity on some days, and on others, it might feel less pronounced or distant.

Fluidflux is a combination of genderfluid and genderflux; both one's gender identity and the intensity of that identity can change. This means that both the identity itself and the strength of connection to that identity can shift over time.

Other Nonbinary Identities

This is in no way a comprehensive list of nonbinary identities. In fact, there are many more than I could possibly list here. The goal is to give you a snapshot of the wonderfully varied identities that fall under the nonbinary umbrella and to remind you that it's okay to not know them all. Some other examples of nonbinary identities include:

- **Agender:** A person who identifies as having no gender or an absence of gender altogether, experiencing a sense of being outside the traditional categories of male or female.
- **Neutrois:** Similar to agender, some neutrois individuals identify as genderless or have a neutral internal sense of gender.
- **Bigender:** The experience of two distinct gender identities, either simultaneously or at different times.
- **Demigender:** A partial connection to a specific gender, such as demiboy or demigirl.
- **Pangender:** A broad connection to many gender identities, sometimes feeling too diverse to fit into one category.

Third Gender

Throughout history, thriving societies worldwide have recognized, revered, and integrated more than just two genders, challenging the Western notion of a strict male-female binary. This recognition has often granted individuals distinct roles and statuses within their communities. However, the recognition of a third gender can also subject these individuals to different forms of discrimination or marginalization.

Two-Spirit

Two-Spirit is a term used within Indigenous or Native American cultures to describe individuals embodying both masculine and feminine qualities. Historically, Two-Spirit people held revered positions within their tribes as healers, mediators, and spiritual leaders due to their unique ability to understand and encompass both male and female perspectives.

The impact of colonialism disrupted these traditional roles, forcing heteronormative roles onto Indigenous children. This led to a loss of cultural identity and erosion of the respect once accorded to Two-Spirit individuals within society. Homophobic attitudes further marginalized them.

Despite these challenges, many Two-Spirit individuals have worked to reclaim their cultural heritage and regain their place in the community. Education and healing processes have been instrumental in this restoration of identity, leading to a renewed recognition of Two-Spirit people as sacred members of Indigenous communities.

The concept of Two-Spirit individuals is culturally specific and varies among Indigenous peoples and cultures. It cannot be generalized to all Indigenous worldviews, and it is not an identity that non-Indigenous individuals can adopt or claim. Respect for cultural diversity and sensitivity to these traditions are of utmost importance when discussing Two-Spirit identities.[101]

Hijras

In South Asia, Hijras serve as a prominent example of a culturally recognized third gender, a status legally acknowledged in countries like India, Nepal, and Bangladesh. Hijras encompass individuals who may identify as intersex, transgender, eunuchs, or who don't conform strictly to binary male or female genders. This recognition, although not without challenges, grants them a unique societal role distinct from both men and women.

Hijras have a longstanding tradition in India, where they are often invited to bestow blessings upon newborns and newlyweds. These blessings are highly valued and believed to bring good fortune and fertility to the recipients. This cultural niche has become somewhat institutionalized over time, solidifying Hijras' place in society. Nevertheless, beyond their ceremonial role, Hijras frequently encounter discrimination in various aspects of life, such as employment and healthcare.[102] While their legal recognition as a third gender marks a significant step toward social acceptance and inclusion, it does not eliminate the challenges and biases they continue to face.

Diverse Third Genders Worldwide

Across the globe, diverse cultures have long recognized and integrated third-gender identities, offering unique perspectives on gender that transcend conventional binaries.

Americas

- **Muxe:** Among the Indigenous Zapotec people in Mexico, muxes represent a recognized third gender. Muxe individuals often present themselves in a traditionally feminine manner, and their roles span from caretakers to merchants and artisans, showcasing the diversity of experiences within this identity.

- **Nádleehí:** In Diné culture, nádleehí is a gender category specific to their traditions. Historically, those embodying this gender have assumed roles as negotiators, caretakers, and healers, but the cultural roles and expressions of nádleehí vary.

Pacific Islands

- **Akava'ine:** In the Cook Islands within Māori culture, akava'ine is a community of people who may live, present themselves, and identify as women, representing a distinct third gender within their culture.

- **Fa'afafine:** In Samoan culture, fa'afafine are individuals who may adopt specific cultural roles, including caring for elders and providing education about various topics, including sex. Fa'afafine often embody feminine traits, but their gender expressions vary.

- **Fa'afatama:** Also within Samoan culture, fa'afatama is a community of people who may adopt cultural roles like caring for the elderly. They often embody more masculine traits and may live and identify as men.

- **Fakafifine:** In Niuean culture, fakafifine represents a community of individuals who may take on traditionally feminine roles and expressions, distinguishing themselves as a recognized third gender.

- **Fakaleitī:** Tongan culture acknowledges fakaleitīs or leitīs as individuals who often assume a feminine gender role and expression, though this can vary. Many consider leitīs to be a distinct third gender in their society.

- **Māhū:** Indigenous Hawaiian and Tahitian cultures recognize māhūs as individuals who embody both male and female spirits. Historically, māhūs have played essential roles in their communities as caretakers, healers, and keepers of sacred knowledge.

- **Palopa:** In Papua New Guinea, the term "palopa" may encompass those who identify as gay, transgender, and/or belonging to a cultural third gender.

- **Vaka Sa Lewa Lewa:** Fijian culture recognizes vaka sa lewa lewa as a community of individuals who may present themselves and identify as women, establishing their unique place as a third gender.

South Asia

- **Khawaja Sira:** Khawaja Sira, a traditional Pakistani third-gender community, is understood as having a "feminine soul" and has historically played specific cultural roles within society.

Southeast Asia

- **Bissu:** Within Indonesia, bissus are the fifth gender of Bugis society. They are believed to encompass the entire gender spectrum and hold significant spiritual roles in their communities.

These diverse examples illustrate the rich tapestry of third-gender identities found across different cultures and regions, challenging conventional binary perceptions of gender.[103]

Gender Questioning

"Gender Questioning" refers to the period of introspection and active exploration that some individuals undergo when they're uncertain about their gender identity. During this phase, people may assess and re-assess how they relate to traditional categories of male and female, as well as other nonbinary identities. Questioning is not a transient or trivial state; it is a valid and recognized part of the LGBTQ+ community. Some people may remain in this questioning phase for a short time, while for others, it may take years of exploration. Questioning is a personal journey that can involve varying degrees of emotional, psychological, and sometimes even physical changes.

Common Misconceptions

Myth: Nonbinary Identity Is Just About Rejecting the Binary

A common misconception is that nonbinary individuals merely reject the binary classification of male and female. However, nonbinary identity isn't solely defined by what it isn't; it's a positive assertion of diverse gender experiences. Nonbinary individuals define their identity in their own terms, often embracing unique gender expressions that reflect their authentic selves.

Myth: Nonbinary Is a New Trend

The idea that nonbinary identity is a recent trend disregards the historical and cultural roots of nonbinary experiences. Throughout history, various cultures have recognized and celebrated genders beyond the binary, as exemplified by the diverse third-gender identities we've just explored. Acknowledging the longevity of nonbinary identities counters the misconception that they are a passing fad, highlighting their enduring presence across different societies and time periods.

It's also important to note that nonbinary identity isn't exclusive to Gen Z or Millennials. Many nonbinary people belong to older generations, like Gen X (that's me!). While Gen Z might be more open about coming out, nonbinary folks have been living authentically across all ages, even before there was a Generation Z.

Myth: Transgender Identity Is Limited to Binary Transitions

A common misconception limits transgender identities to a binary framework, implying that individuals transition from one binary gender to another; from "he" to "she" or "she" to "he." However, the transgender experience encompasses a wide spectrum of identities, including nonbinary, genderqueer, and more. Recognizing this diversity challenges the binary paradigm and fosters greater inclusivity.

Myth: Nonbinary Is Merely a Subset of Transgender

A nonbinary person might not exclusively identify with the gender assigned to them at birth, which leads many to assume that all nonbinary people are inherently transgender. Some nonbinary individuals identify as transgender, while others do not. Nonbinary is a distinct identity that exists on its own. Remember that labels are identifiers, and all people have the right to use their own labels.

Myth: Nonbinary Identity Is Equally Split Between Genders

Assuming that nonbinary identity is an equal blend of male and female oversimplifies the diversity within the nonbinary spectrum. Nonbinary individuals express their identity in a multitude of ways that may not align with a perfectly even split between genders. Nonbinary identities exist everywhere along the gender spectrum.

Myth: Nonbinary Individuals Are Always Androgynous

An inaccurate stereotype is the assumption that all nonbinary individuals have androgynous appearances. Nonbinary identity encompasses a range of presentations, from androgynous to feminine, masculine, and beyond. There is no specific way to "look nonbinary."

Affirmed Gender

Affirmed gender (or "true gender") refers to an individual's self-identified gender that may be different from the gender they were assigned at birth. Using the term "affirmed gender" acknowledges that an individual's gender identity is valid and should be respected. This term is preferable to terms like "chosen gender" or "new gender," which imply a choice rather than a true gender identity. Affirmed gender emphasizes the importance of self-identification and personal experience in understanding one's own gender.

Referring to someone's true or affirmed gender is only relevant when discussing something specific about being transgender or nonbinary. In an everyday setting, everyone simply has a gender.

Connecting the Dots: Bridging Identity and Expression

Language and terminology around gender are complex and can be understood differently by individuals and communities. For example, there are certain terms that blur the lines between gender identity and gender expression, serving as either or both, depending on the individual. This section explores terms like androgynous and gender nonconforming, which can describe how someone expresses their gender but may also reflect their sense of identity.

Androgynous

"Androgynous" is often associated with a gender expression that combines elements of both masculinity and femininity. However, it can also include elements that are neither traditionally masculine nor feminine, resulting in a more neutral or non-gendered presentation. In some contexts, "androgynous" can also be used as a gender identity to describe a person who feels their gender identity is a mix of male and female or neither exclusively male nor exclusively female.

In terms of gender expression, many people wear androgynous clothing in their everyday lives without even realizing it. The term can be used to explain someone's presentation on any given day. Items like jeans, t-shirts, or blazers, which are considered neutral, can blur traditional gender lines. However, this often goes unnoticed or unquestioned for cisgender individuals, who enjoy the privilege of not having their gender expression scrutinized. For a binary transgender person, such as a transgender woman, choosing to dress androgynously on a given day may lead to misgendering or confusion from others, as their gender presentation may not align with societal expectations of how she "should" dress.

Gender Nonconforming

"Gender nonconforming" is a term that often refers to gender expression rather than identity, describing individuals whose gender expression doesn't align with societal expectations related to their assigned sex at birth. However, it can also be used more broadly to describe anyone who doesn't adhere to societal gender norms, which could include people who identify as nonbinary. It's a more overarching term, and some people do use it to describe their gender identity, especially if they don't feel that any of the more specific terms quite fit. You may see "transgender, nonbinary, and gender nonconforming people" as a way of acknowledging everyone whose gender identities or expressions fall outside the traditional cisgender framework.

Doctor's Orders: Medical and Healthcare Terms You Should Know

Gender-Affirming Healthcare

Gender-affirming healthcare encompasses a wide range of medical procedures, treatments, and interventions designed to help individuals align their physical selves with their affirmed gender identity. These may include hormonal therapies, surgeries, and even voice training, among other options.

Surgery

While the term "surgery" in the context of gender-affirming healthcare often leads people to think of "bottom surgeries," the range of available surgical interventions is much broader. Surgeries may include adjustments to primary sexual characteristics (like genital reconstruction), secondary sexual characteristics (such as facial feminization or masculinization and chest surgeries), and even tertiary characteristics like voice pitch (through procedures like laryngoplasty). This broad array of surgical options allows individuals to choose the path that most aligns with their gender identity and comfort.

Hormone Replacement Therapy (HRT)

Hormone Replacement Therapy, commonly referred to as HRT, involves the administration of hormones to align one's physical characteristics more closely with their gender identity. This can affect a multitude of characteristics, including body hair, fat distribution, and even emotional well-being.

Voice Training

Voice training, sometimes also referred to as voice therapy or voice modification, involves specialized coaching to help individuals align their vocal presentation with their gender identity. While not a medical procedure, it's a component of gender-affirming care for many people.

Gender Euphoria

Gender euphoria is the joy, affirmation, and satisfaction individuals feel when their gender identity, presentation, or the way others perceive them aligns with how they understand themselves. In the workplace, a transgender person can experience gender euphoria by having their name and pronouns used consistently.

Gender euphoria isn't exclusive to transgender and nonbinary people; cisgender people also experience it, although they may not always recognize it as such (which reflects an aspect of privilege). For example, a cisgender man might feel a sense of joy and pride when growing a beard, taking care of it with oils and products, and receiving compliments on it. The feeling a woman has when she puts on a dress that fits her perfectly, that moment of twirling around in the mirror—that's euphoria, and both trans and cisgender women can experience it.

Gender Dysphoria

Gender dysphoria is the discomfort or distress someone experiences when their gender identity does not align with the sex they were assigned at birth. For transgender and nonbinary people, this dissonance can manifest in various ways, ranging from a general sense of unease to clinically significant depression and/or anxiety. Some describe it as feeling trapped in a body that doesn't match their true self. A transgender woman described her experience of gender dysphoria in a letter she wrote to her employer, "I have felt imprisoned in a body that does not match my mind, and this has caused me great despair and loneliness."[104]

It's important to note that not all transgender or nonbinary people experience gender dysphoria. A common myth is that dysphoria is a requirement for being transgender, but this is not the case. For example, many nonbinary individuals don't feel intense discomfort with their body or assigned gender but still identify outside the traditional male-female binary.

Gender dysphoria can sometimes manifest as other mental health challenges, such as depression, anxiety, social withdrawal, or a sense of being unproductive. This makes it difficult to identify, particularly when it's masked as another condition. The level of dysphoria can vary significantly from person to person. The critical point to remember is the transformation that occurs when a person is able to live authentically. When someone is affirmed in their gender identity, whether through hormone therapy, surgery, social transition, or simply being recognized for who they are, their dysphoria can often give way to gender euphoria, allowing them to thrive emotionally, mentally, and socially.

Cisgender individuals can sometimes experience gender dysphoria in specific contexts. For instance, cisgender men undergoing hormone treatments for prostate cancer may develop gynecomastia (the growth of breast tissue), which can cause significant discomfort and distress as their physical appearance no longer aligns with their gender identity. While this can be challenging, the dysphoria experienced by transgender individuals is often far more pervasive and deeply tied to their overall sense of identity.

The Transition Journey: Navigating Change and Authenticity

Transition

Transition refers to the process through which a transgender individual makes changes to align their physical appearance, social identity, and/or legal documentation with their affirmed gender identity. This process can include medical, legal, and social steps, such as hormone therapy, pronouns and/or name change, and coming out to other people.

Transitions happen in both one's personal and professional life. While every transition is unique, one common thread is the need for understanding and support from those around them. For a transgender person, this process can involve emotional growth, self-discovery, and overcoming societal challenges. Support from friends, family, and colleagues is vital in helping someone feel validated and secure in their transition. Transition is not a one-time event but a continuous journey of living authentically.

Common Misconceptions

Myth: Transitioning Involves Surgery

One prevalent myth in understanding transgender identities is the assumption that transitioning necessitates surgery.

Too many transgender individuals and their families have faced the invasive question, "Did [he/she/they] have the surgery?" This question assumes that surgery is a defining aspect of being transgender, which is a profound misunderstanding. Transgender individuals do not need to undergo surgery to validate their gender identity. Their identity is a matter of self-realization and affirmation, not a physical transformation.

The decision to have surgery is a deeply personal one and looks different for every individual. Some transgender people choose to undergo surgery as part of their journey, while others don't. That choice is influenced by many factors, such as personal preference, financial circumstances, or access to healthcare. For many, surgery simply isn't an option, especially when faced with the reality of being turned away by family after coming out, leaving them to fend for themselves financially much earlier than most cisgender people.

Moreover, asking about a transgender person's surgical status is as inappropriate and intrusive as asking any other deeply personal medical question. It's akin to asking a cisgender person about their body in ways we all understand to be off-limits. For instance, imagine the discomfort of asking about someone's circumcision status in a casual conversation. It's not only inappropriate but also irrelevant to the person's identity and role in a professional or social setting.

Curiosity, no matter how well-intentioned, doesn't justify intrusiveness. Inquiring about someone's surgical status under the guise of curiosity can be invasive and disrespectful. Kindness and interest in someone's life should be expressed with respect for their privacy and boundaries.

As we cultivate more inclusive environments, we must move beyond the oversimplified and invasive notions about what transitioning entails. We need to focus on understanding, respect, and support for each person's individual journey toward living authentically.

Myth: Uniform Transition Narratives

One common misconception about transgender experiences is the assumption of uniformity in the journey of transitioning. Transgender individuals undergo diverse processes of self-discovery, social and medical transition, and the negotiation of personal identity.

Some people have known from an early age that they are transgender. For example, a three-year-old child assigned male at birth may consistently insist that she is a girl. This child might transition by wearing girls' clothing, changing her name and pronouns early in life, and beginning hormone therapy during her teens. She might later pursue surgery or other medical steps in her twenties, living her entire life as a woman.

In contrast, another person might not fully understand or accept their feelings until much later in life (a bit like my own journey). They may spend years in self-reflection and exploration before realizing they are transgender and may wait additional years before telling anyone. Their transition might involve changing pronouns and socially transitioning with or without medical intervention.

Myth: Transition as the Sole Focus

Another misunderstanding is the belief that being transgender revolves solely around the process of transition, such as changing one's name, pronouns, or undergoing medical procedures. For many transgender individuals, the journey is not just about altering their appearance or social roles. It also involves profound emotional growth as they learn to understand and accept their true selves. Identity exploration is a fundamental aspect of being transgender, where individuals delve into questions of who they are, their gender identity, and what it means to live authentically.

Transgender individuals often navigate complex societal expectations and norms that can differ from those placed on cisgender individuals. This includes addressing issues of discrimination, stigma, and the challenges of advocating for their rights.

What's in a Name: Understanding Names and Pronouns

Chosen Name

A chosen name (or preferred name) is the name an individual chooses to be known by, which may differ from their legal or birth name. Acknowledging this preference ensures that all individuals feel seen and acknowledged for who they are. Attempts to restrict pronoun policies are not about language; they are about denying the reality that trans women are women, trans men are men, and nonbinary people exist. But denying a fact does not change the fact, and respecting names and identities remains the right thing to do.

The concept of a preferred name is not exclusive to transgender or nonbinary individuals. In fact, it's a universal aspect of identity. Just as someone named Robert might prefer to be called Bob, a transgender person might prefer to be called something that aligns more closely with their gender identity. In both cases, these names are chosen names; they reflect the identity and preference of the individual.

Deadname

A deadname, also known as a birth name or former name, is the name assigned to a transgender person at birth but is no longer used after they transition to their affirmed gender identity. Using a person's deadname can be deeply distressing and invalidating, as it often reminds them of a time when they were not living as their true selves. Supporting transgender individuals means being sensitive to and respecting their preferred or chosen names.

This term was coined within the transgender community to express the transformative journey that accompanies transitioning. It signifies a rebirth, emphasizing the empowerment and self-discovery that comes with embracing one's true identity.

Hearing this word can evoke complex emotions, especially among parents and grandparents who might feel a sense of personal loss upon learning that the name they chose is no longer in use.

If you are struggling with the term, remember that a name is a gift a child receives, and like any gift, they are free to enjoy it and use it until it no longer serves them. Changing a name does not negate the value of the original gift.

Pronoun

Pronouns are the words used to refer to someone in the third person. For transgender individuals, using correct pronouns is paramount to respecting their identity. Binary pronouns include "he" and "she." The most common gender-neutral pronoun is "they," though there are others that we will soon review.

It's worth noting that while a name can be preferred, the same principle doesn't apply to pronouns. The term "preferred pronoun," although once intended to be affirming, is now outdated and invalidating. Every person has their own set of pronouns, which reflects their genuine identity. Referring to pronouns as "preferred" implies the existence of a "true" pronoun distinct from the one someone chooses to use, which undermines the essence of recognizing and honoring an individual's gender identity. We will cover this in more detail in Chapter 4.

Remember, "preferred name" is okay; "preferred pronoun" is not.

Understanding Pronouns

I'm often asked why people share more than one pronoun when introducing themself, like "she/her" or "he/him." It's a great question! Pronouns typically include the subject and the object. Some people also choose to include a third form, the possessive pronoun, as in "she/her/hers."

Understanding the different grammatical forms pronouns take—such as subject, object, and possessive pronoun—clarifies which forms people are referring to when they list their pronouns. This will also come in handy as we explore pronouns beyond "he" and "she." Here is a breakdown of pronoun forms:

- **Subject:** The pronoun leads the sentence, indicating who is performing an action. For instance, in the sentence, "[She] left me a voicemail," *she* is the subject.

- **Object:** The pronoun receives the action of the verb. In the phrase, "I called [her]," *her* serves as the object.

- **Possessive Adjective:** The pronoun describes a noun by indicating ownership. In the example, "[Her] office is upstairs," *her* denotes possession of the office.

- **Possessive Pronoun:** The pronoun indicates ownership without directly modifying a noun. For example, in the statement, "That is [hers]," *hers* signifies possession of something previously mentioned or understood.

- **Reflexive Pronoun:** The pronoun refers back to the subject of the sentence or clause. In the sentence, "She did it all by [herself]," *herself* emphasizes that the action was performed without any assistance.

Nonbinary Pronouns

The most common nonbinary pronoun currently in use is "they." The chief complaint I hear is that "they" is a plural pronoun, so using it for someone would be grammatically incorrect. Imagine being told that someone refuses to honor your pronouns for any reason, especially when that reason is inaccurate. Not only is "they" a grammatically correct singular pronoun, but the people who say they can't use it, in fact, use it all the time.

"They" As a Singular Pronoun

The use of "they" as a singular pronoun dates back to the fourteenth century, with literary giants like Shakespeare and Jane

Austen using it in their writing. Reputable dictionaries and linguistic references also recognize and endorse its legitimacy.

Interestingly, the singular "they" is even older than the singular "you." Historically, "thou" was used to address one person, while "ye" was used for multiple people. "Thee" was the objective case of "thou," as in the phrase "I love thee." These distinctions were common in Early Modern English from the late fifteenth century to the mid-to-late seventeenth century.

By the seventeenth century, "you" took over from "thou" and "thee" to address both singular and plural subjects. This shift shows that the singular "they" has been around for centuries, even before "you" became standard for both singular and plural. This confirms that using "they" as a singular pronoun is grammatically correct and older than the use of the singular pronoun "you."

"They" in Everyday Use

I often share a story during my workshops, one that revolves around the time I stumbled upon a wallet on the floor of a store. In this story, I brought the wallet to the cashier, who, after identifying the wallet owner's name and contact information, reached out to them. The owner of the wallet asked to speak with me directly. They expressed their gratitude and even offered a reward as a token of appreciation for my efforts. I declined the kind offer because I thought it was unfair for them to be penalized for the simple act of misplacing something.

That story is one example of using they/them in a sentence. There are other examples, such as:

In a conversation about an accident: "Oh my, were they hurt?"

Or when instructing someone about phone calls: "If anyone calls, tell them I'll call them right back."

We've established that "they" can function as both a singular and plural pronoun, depending on context. While it's commonly used as a singular pronoun, this isn't always a conscious choice, as "they" is more traditionally associated with the plural form. For example, in the wallet story, "they" works because it allows us to imagine anyone, regardless of gender.

However, when we meet the person from the story, our perceptions may influence whether we see them as "he" or "she," based on our individual experiences. Once we make this association, it can be challenging to continue using "they" as a singular pronoun.

Now, consider a world where we could reprogram our minds not to associate appearances with gender. In such a world, we'd approach each person with a fresh perspective, learning about their gender as we get to know them, much like how we learn other aspects about people.

To navigate this, remember that gender expression does not equate to gender identity. We must acknowledge that we can never accurately determine someone's gender simply by looking at them at a single point in their life. Every person's gender identity is unique and may not align with their outward appearance due to our biases, cultural influences, and preconceived notions.

Neopronouns: Beyond "They/Them"

Neopronouns are less commonly known across generations. In a 2020 survey of 40,000 LGBTQ+ young people ages thirteen to twenty-four (Gen Z), 10,000 said they use nonbinary pronouns. Only 4% of those who use nonbinary pronouns say they use neopronouns.[105]

The term "neo" suggests they are new, but some of these alternatives to "they" have been in use for hundreds of years. One early example is "thon," which was proposed by attorney and composer Charles C. Converse in 1858 as a blend of "that one" to serve as a gender-neutral pronoun. Thon was listed in the Merriam-Webster dictionary from 1935 to 1961 and then removed due to a lack of widespread acceptance.[106] I confess to putting it in this book on the chance that it catches on. I like it.

Spivak pronouns, which include "e" as the subject form and "em" as the object form (e.g., "E is going to the store. I will meet up with em later."), were coined by mathematician and writer Michael Spivak in his 1990 software guide "The Joy of TeX." Spivak pronouns were also used by LambdaMOO, an early online program where users could choose pronouns to match their avatars.[107]

To provide grammatical context before reviewing, the following list contains some of the common neopronouns. To provide grammatical context, the binary "he" and "she" as well as the nonbinary "they" are included:

Subject	Object	Possessive Adjective	Possessive Pronoun	Reflexive Pronoun
she	her	her	hers	herself
he	him	his	his	himself
they*	them	their	theirs	themself**
ze	zem	zer	zers	zemself
xe	xem	xyr	xyrs	xemself
ey	em	eir	eirs	emself
hu	hu	hume	humes	humeself
fae	faer	faer	faers	faerself
per	per	per	pers	perself
[name]***	[name]	[name]'s	[name]'s	[name]'s self

*The conjugation of "they" remains unchanged when used as the subject, such as "they are," even in singular usage.

**Some grammar checkers may not recognize "themself" and may suggest changing it to "themselves." This distinction is a grammar difference when "themself" is used as a singular pronoun.

***In cases where individuals do not use pronouns, their name is used instead of a pronoun. This practice is an alternative to traditional pronouns.

As a reminder, below is an example of each pronoun form, using she:

- **Subject:** [She] left me a voicemail.
- **Object:** I called [her].
- **Possessive Adjective:** [Her] office is upstairs.
- **Possessive Pronoun:** That is [hers].
- **Reflexive:** She did it all by [herself].

Combination Pronouns

Some people use more than one pronoun. Instead of listing the subject and object of a single pronoun, they list the subject of multiple pronouns, such as she/they or they/ze. Combination pronouns indicate that a person is comfortable being referred to by more than one set of pronouns.

The Personal Choice Behind Combination Pronouns

There is no universal reason someone chooses to use more than one pronoun. Some might be experimenting with a pronoun to see how they feel about it, some might be using two pronouns during their transition, some might be fluid, while some might simply identify with multiple pronouns. Every individual's choice of combination pronouns is deeply personal.

For instance, in my personal life, I use they/them pronouns exclusively and have since the day I came out. In professional settings, I sometimes used she/they or they/she, depending on the situation or people involved. Transitioning at work was challenging for me; I feared that a potential client would be less likely to talk to someone with "they/them" pronouns, and I didn't want to alienate my existing clients. As a consultant, eliminating the comfort of "she" for my clients was a scary risk. I made a point of revealing my combination pronoun rationale during workshops. I used to say that the combination for me wasn't about compromise but about connection and understanding. Once I realized that it wasn't about connection or understanding, that it was about fear, I changed my pronouns at work.

Tips on Using Combination Pronouns

When addressing someone who uses combination pronouns, I suggest to clients that they begin with the pronoun that they feel they can "get right." If someone says their pronouns are she/they (or they/she) and you are more comfortable using "she" than "they," you should use "she."

It is acceptable to use one pronoun exclusively, though if you want to show someone you are paying attention (or that you really care), consider incorporating the other pronoun occasionally. Using both pronouns honors their identity and acknowledges the spectrum of their gender expression. This is a great way to help a colleague feel seen.

Misgender

Misgendering occurs when someone is referred to or addressed using language that does not align with their affirmed gender identity, such as using "sir" for a nonbinary person or "she" for a man. This can be unintentional or deliberate, and it can have significant emotional and psychological impacts on transgender individuals.

If you've ever wondered what to do when you accidentally misgender someone, don't worry, we'll cover that in detail in "Strategies for Gender-Inclusive Communication" (Chapter 4). For now, know that the key is to acknowledge the mistake, correct it, and move on. Lingering on it can make things more uncomfortable for everyone involved.

Let's Talk: Social Terms and Concepts

Ally

An ally is someone who supports and advocates for the rights and well-being of transgender individuals, even if they are not part of the transgender community. Allies actively contribute to creating an inclusive and supportive work environment.

Cisgender individuals, leveraging their inherent privilege, have the capacity and responsibility to actively stand up for and support transgender and nonbinary folks, bridging gaps of understanding and fostering an environment where everyone is acknowledged, respected, and celebrated.

Myth: Allies Are Part of the LGBTQ+ Community

There is a common misconception that the "A" in "LGBTQIA+" stands for Ally. While not members of the LGBTQ+ community themselves, allies actively advocate for and support LGBTQ+ individuals, using their privilege to amplify voices and drive positive change. The community thrives with the support of allies, and we need more of them!

Outing

Outing is the act of revealing another person's sexual orientation or gender identity without their consent.

If someone trusts you enough to share this part of their identity, it's important to respect that trust. We'll explore this more, along with other dos and don'ts, in "Strategies for Gender-Inclusive Communication" (Chapter 4).

Microaggressions

Microaggressions are subtle, often unintentional words, actions, or gestures that can convey bias or exclusion. While a single microaggression may seem inconsequential, the cumulative effect can have a significant impact on the sense of belonging and emotional well-being of those on the receiving end of microaggressions.

Because microaggressions can be unintentional, it can be difficult to understand when they are being committed. For example, a meeting facilitator may say, "This meeting has been organized specifically for the women in the company," and then make eye contact with the transgender person in the room and say, "or anyone who identifies as a woman." The intention was to be inclusive, but the message subtly implies, "You're not a full member of this club."

Research has shown that these subtle yet harmful behaviors can lead to increased rates of depression, prolonged stress, and physical health issues such as headaches, high blood pressure, and sleep disturbances. Over the course of an employee's career, repeated microaggressions can also result in burnout, reduced job satisfaction, and diminished mental well-being, ultimately compromising both personal and professional growth.[108]

Microaggressions can be so commonplace that a transgender or nonbinary person may experience them daily. These comments and gestures accumulate, and while they might be excused at first, over time, they inevitably lead to questioning whether they are intentional.

For example, I went to a restaurant with my girlfriend. The host said, "This way, ladies," as she led us to our table. Our server greeted us with, "Hello, ladies," and a few moments later, checked in, asking, "Are you ladies ready to order?" I didn't love this, but I let it go, understanding that they all meant well. But by the time I heard "ladies" for the fifth time, when our server asked if we wanted more drinks and if we needed anything else, I was left wondering if it was deliberate. It felt like a constant reminder that I was being categorized in a way that doesn't reflect who I am.

Unconscious Bias

Unconscious bias is a natural human tendency to make judgments about others based on incomplete or limited information. It often occurs when we fill in gaps in our knowledge without realizing it, leading to automatic assumptions about people. These judgments happen outside of our conscious awareness, meaning that we may not recognize the biases we hold or the knowledge gaps that influence our conclusions.[109]

I often offer workshops focused entirely on unconscious bias because it's a topic that stands alone. In this book, we are focusing specifically on how unconscious bias affects gender and how awareness can help create more inclusive workplaces.

Many people think "gender bias" refers solely to the unconscious stereotyping of men and women. However, the assumption that there are only two genders, man and woman, is a bias in itself. Gender bias also includes a lack of understanding about transgender and nonbinary individuals. An example of gender bias is when a hiring manager unconsciously assumes a candidate is less qualified for a job simply because the applicant lists pronouns on their resume. Another example is assuming that this candidate would "not fit with our corporate culture," which is often code for perceiving the candidate as different and therefore difficult.

Overcoming unconscious bias requires acknowledging the gaps in our knowledge or experience and being open to learning from others rather than projecting our discomfort onto them. Reading this book and implementing new processes across the organization is a meaningful step toward addressing gender bias and closing those knowledge gaps.

Unconscious bias can be one of the greatest challenges to achieving gender inclusion. Throughout this book, we will examine different strategies for overcoming gender biases, particularly when they show up as resistance to inclusion from colleagues, customers, or external stakeholders such as vendors, business partners, and investors.

Queer

While traditionally a derogatory term, "queer" is now often used as an umbrella term to describe a sexual orientation, gender identity, or gender expression that does not conform to dominant societal norms. Some people use queer to mean that they are questioning their label and/or identity, while others use it to convey that they do not want to share anything about their identity beyond the fact that they are a member of the LGBTQ+ community. Given that some people still find it offensive, the term's usage can be complex and should be handled carefully. My rule of thumb when advising people: if you're not a member of the community, avoid using the word unless someone uses it with you first.

Cisnormativity

Cisnormativity is the assumption that all individuals are cisgender, leading to the marginalization of non-cisgender identities. For example, only having "male" and "female" on official forms and documents without providing an option for other gender identities assumes that there are no other identities.

Heteronormativity

Heteronormativity is the assumption that all individuals are heterosexual, leading to the marginalization of non-heterosexual identities. For example, only having "husband" and "wife" on forms invalidates same-sex couples.

The Big Picture: Public Perception and Identity

Intersectionality

Intersectionality refers to the interconnected nature of social identities such as race, class, gender, and much more, and how these identities overlap to shape a person's unique experiences of privilege and oppression. We've touched on this concept earlier in this chapter while discussing cisgender privilege and transgender identity.

Laverne Cox is a prominent example of someone who embodies intersectionality in both her life and activism, particularly as a Black transgender woman navigating the entertainment industry. She has achieved significant milestones, from being the first openly transgender person nominated for a Primetime Emmy to being the first transgender woman to have a Barbie doll fashioned after her. Yet, despite her success, she continues to face structural racism, transphobia, and sexism. Cox has spoken openly about how these intersecting identities amplify the discrimination she encounters, including being misgendered, experiencing harassment, and the media often sensationalizing her story by focusing on her struggles rather than her full humanity and achievements. In her own words:

> "Just because you are LGBTQIA+, I am still Black. I still experience structural racism. Trans folks still experience that on top of transphobia, on top of sexism . . . on top of classism."[110]

Passing

This term refers to the ability of a transgender individual to be perceived, at a glance, as the gender with which they identify. When a transgender woman is perceived as a cisgender woman or a transgender man is perceived as a cisgender man, they are said to be "passing." The concept of passing is often complex and can be subjective, depending not just on physical appearance but also on mannerisms, voice, and other gender cues. Passing doesn't necessarily imply that the individual is keeping their transgender identity a secret.

Stealth

This is the condition of a transgender person passing as their affirmed gender without other people realizing that they are transgender. Being "stealth" means that a transgender individual is not openly disclosing their transgender status in their day-to-day life. A person might be stealth in some contexts (like at work or in school) and not in others (such as within close friendships or family). Stealth implies a level of passing, as the individual is not readily identified as transgender by those around them, but it adds the layer of active non-disclosure. In other words, all individuals who are stealth are effectively passing, but not all individuals who are passing are stealth.

It's important to remember that every transgender person navigates this differently. For some, being stealth is necessary for their safety or comfort, while others may feel no need or desire to be stealth. This choice is deeply personal and varies from person to person.

Clocking

The term "clocking" refers to the act of recognizing or identifying someone as transgender even when they are attempting to present as cisgender or are in stealth mode. This can occur unintentionally or deliberately and may involve noticing various cues such as physical features, voice, or mannerisms that might not align with societal expectations for a particular gender. Being clocked can be a deeply personal and sometimes unsettling experience for a transgender individual, particularly if they are trying to maintain a stealth status or simply wish to go about their day without their transgender identity becoming a focus. Clocking can sometimes result in misgendering, outing, or even harassment, so it's a term often discussed in the context of privacy and safety within transgender communities.

PART TWO:

Effective Communication Strategies

CHAPTER 03

PRINCIPLES OF GENDER-NEUTRAL COMMUNICATION

Language and equality have been evolving together for a long time. Ever since the first wave of feminism, we've been challenging language that only focuses on men, pushing for more inclusive terms. This journey for gender-neutral language has always been about breaking boundaries and challenging societal norms.

Today, our quest for gender-neutral communication is broader. It's not just about equality for women anymore; it's also about recognizing and respecting the identities and experiences of nonbinary individuals. Just as our understanding of gender has evolved, so too must our language. It's time to bring these changes into the workplace, making it a key area for this evolution.

As you read through this chapter, I encourage you to think about the gendered language you use in your daily life. Many of these expressions are so ingrained in our culture that we don't even realize the impact they have. But with awareness, we can start to shift these patterns of speech to create more inclusive and respectful environments.

Speaking with Care: Gender-Inclusive Language

The words we choose carry weight. They reflect our respect for others' identities and experiences and can either create an inclusive environment or reinforce harmful stereotypes. For workplaces committed to gender inclusion, adopting gender-inclusive language isn't just a nice-to-have; it's a must-have.

Language isn't just a way to communicate; it shapes how we see the world. The terms we use to describe people and situations can subtly but powerfully influence our thoughts. When we default to gender-specific terms, like "chairman" instead of "chairperson," or use phrases like "you guys" for a mixed-gender group, we unintentionally reinforce a male-centric view. Even if these phrases are culturally ingrained and not meant to exclude, they can feel isolating for someone who doesn't fit traditional gender norms.

The way we speak and write shapes our workplace culture, influencing daily interactions and career paths. For example, terms like "manpower" instead of "workforce" or "guys" to refer to a mixed group can subtly undermine inclusivity. These seemingly small choices can impact everything from performance reviews to opportunities for advancement or even workplace morale.

Using gender-inclusive language fosters a culture of respect and dignity, making employees of all gender identities feel seen and valued. For example, replacing terms like "salesman" with "salesperson" or avoiding phrases like "ladies and gentlemen" in favor of "everyone" sends a clear message of inclusivity. These shifts help attract a diverse workforce and align with ethical imperatives. We will cover more on specific language shifts later in this chapter.

When we interact with strangers, especially regarding gender, it's essential to be mindful. The challenge here isn't about language; it's about shifting how we think about gender.

I'm often asked, "What's the most gender-neutral way of referring to someone when we don't yet know their pronouns?" I wish we had an entirely different pronoun that represented "as yet unknown," one that acknowledged the uncertainty without putting anyone in a box. But at least for now, English lacks this kind of universally accepted option. Among the pronouns available to us, "they" stands out as the most neutral choice. While it's not perfect and can still lead to unintentional misgendering, it's better than making assumptions based on appearance or societal norms.

Right now, most of us decide to use "he" or "she" (or even "they") based on how a colleague looks. We don't know, but we assume. And that's where so much misgendering happens. But what if we stopped making these assumptions? While "they" isn't a perfect fit for everyone, it's more understandable for someone to know you use "they" for everyone rather than feeling like they've been misgendered because of how they look. For example, many trans women don't want to be called "they" because it can feel like people don't see them as women. But using "they" universally, when you don't know someone's pronouns, is different; it signals that you're not making assumptions about anyone, no matter their gender expression.

This connects to one of the most important lessons in becoming more gender inclusive: gender expression doesn't have to equal gender identity. Imagine if, in the workplace, we refrained from making assumptions about our colleagues' gender identity simply because of how they present. This paradigm shift doesn't change how someone expresses themselves, but it changes how we interpret and respect that expression. By not assuming, we create a more open and respectful space, where employees are seen for who they are as opposed to who we assume them to be.

Words for Everyone: Universal Terminology

Using a gender-neutral approach to terminology goes beyond just tweaking language. It's not about whether a term seems acceptable or "not really gendered" to you. Common usage might make some words feel neutral, but for many transgender people, they aren't. For example, words like "dude" or "guys" can feel misgendering or exclusionary to a trans woman (especially if she is the only woman in the room). While these words are often used casually, they can inadvertently reinforce gender norms and make people feel unseen. We'll explore more examples of these everyday gendered phrases and their impact later in the chapter.

Rethinking Job Titles: A Step Toward Inclusivity

One area ripe for inclusive transformation is job titles. In a 2015 presentation on sexist job titles, Brigham Young University English professor Delys Snyder noted:

> "The foreman reassured himself he had made the right decision," and

> "The foreman reassured herself she had made the right decision."

Upon reading the second sentence, participants would hit the female reflexive pronoun, stop, go back, and read the sentence again, whereas with the first sentence, participants would read straight through without any hesitation.

"The change in how people saw the word itself shows that when people see m-a-n they probably don't expect woman," said Snyder, referring to the reactions participants exhibited upon seeing a female pronoun associated with a seemingly male job title. "That shows that job titles affect how we see jobs."[111]

Historically, many job titles have been unnecessarily gendered, creating a subtle yet pervasive form of exclusion. Here are some examples of words that describe roles and responsibilities that include everyone:

- General Occupational Terms
  - Chairman → Chairperson or Chair. Let's drop "Chairman." We're not in a 1950s boardroom movie.
  - Businessman → Businessperson. Because business isn't a man's world.
  - Spokesman, Spokeswoman → Spokesperson. Because anyone can speak up and represent.
  - Salesman → Salesperson. Selling skills have nothing to do with gender.
  - Steward, Stewardess → Flight Attendant. We're all stewards of our own spaces; this person attends to you in the skies.
  - Mailman → Mail Carrier or Postal Worker. They deliver mail, not just "man" the mail.
  - Repairman → Repair Technician. Because they fix things, not just "man" them.
  - Handyman → Handyworker. They're handy, period.
- Emergency Services
  - Fireman → Firefighter. Fighting fires is about courage, not gender.
  - Policeman → Police Officer. Anyone can wear the badge.
- Hospitality and Service Industry
  - Waiter, Waitress → Server or Waitstaff. Serving food isn't a gender role.

- o Host, Hostess → Greeter or Host. Welcoming people is universal.
- o Maître d' → Head of Service. A modern twist to "Maître d'."
- Entertainment and Media
  - o Actress → Actor. This one's a debate, but let's lean toward inclusivity.
  - o Cameraman, Camerawoman → Camera Operator. Operating a camera isn't gendered.
  - o Anchorman, Anchorwoman → News Anchor. Anchoring news is about credibility, not gender.
- Education and Administration
  - o Headmaster, Headmistress → Head of School. More inclusive than "Headmaster" or "Headmistress."
  - o Schoolmaster, Schoolmistress → Principal or School Leader. Leading a school goes beyond gendered titles.
- Government and Representation
  - o Councilman → Council Member. It's about representing people, not just men.
  - o Congressman, Congresswoman → Congressional Representative. Represents a broader spectrum of people.
  - o Assemblyman, Assemblywoman → Assembly Member. Assembling more than just men or women.
- Management and Leadership
  - o Foreman → Supervisor or Crew Leader. Supervising goes beyond the "foreman."
  - o Linesman → Line Technician or Line Worker. It's about maintaining lines, not gender lines.
  - o Manpower → Workforce or Personnel. Let's leave "manpower" in the past.

- Religious Titles
  - Clergyman → Clergy Person or Member of the Clergy. Faith transcends gender.

Gender-Neutral Adjectives

While striving for gender-inclusive language, we must extend our focus beyond nouns and pronouns to include adjectives. These words can subtly shape perceptions and inadvertently reinforce gender stereotypes. In many workplaces, language can exclude or marginalize based on gender. For instance, a male colleague showing firmness might be called "assertive," while a female colleague with the same behavior might be unfairly labeled "bossy." These language disparities perpetuate unfair stereotypes and create an unwelcoming culture.

Choosing gender-neutral adjectives contributes to fostering an inclusive workplace. By doing so, we avoid reinforcing outdated gender stereotypes and move toward a more equitable environment for everyone.

Here's a breakdown of some gender-neutral adjectives, categorized for ease of understanding:

- **Personal Qualities**
  - **Confident:** Suitable for any individual, regardless of gender.
  - **Adaptable:** Valued in any person, in any role.
  - **Resilient:** Suggests strength and perseverance, for anyone.
- **Professional Traits**
  - **Dependable:** A characteristic sought in every employee.
  - **Detail-Oriented:** Describes a valuable work trait.
  - **Innovative:** Appropriate for anyone with creative ideas.

- **Ambitious:** Anyone who aspires to achieve goals and reach new heights.
- **Emotional States**
  - **Content:** A state of satisfaction without gender connotations.
  - **Calm:** Describes composure without reference to gender.
  - **Energetic:** Reflects vitality and is applicable universally.
- **Interpersonal Skills**
  - **Friendly:** Universally appreciated in any workplace.
  - **Helpful:** Positive and supportive, crucial for teamwork.
  - **Collaborative:** Indicates a team-oriented approach.
  - **Supportive:** Essential for building a cooperative work environment.

As we move beyond individual qualities, it's also important to rethink the way we describe humanity as a whole. Let's talk about "mankind"—a term that's been around for ages, suggesting that humanity is predominantly male. It's time we embrace terms like "humanity," "humankind," or "peoplekind." These words reflect the diversity and richness of our species without favoring one gender over another.

So, the next time you're tempted to say "mankind," pause and opt for a gender-neutral form of the word. It's a small change with a big impact.

Gendered Expressions

A friend and I were laughing recently about a realization her daughter shared. "Mom, did you know that when I was a kid I thought 'grow a pair' meant a pair of shoes? You know, because you need to stand your ground."

If only. Gendered expressions are so commonplace, most of us don't even notice we use them. A 2011 study revealed that the gendered nature of everyday language can affect our judgments, decisions, and behavior, shaping not only our self-perception but also our interactions with others.[112] In the workplace, gendered language can have a subtle yet significant influence.

Expressions like "grow a pair" and "man up" suggest that masculinity and toughness are required for success or compe-tence. Terms like "manpower" and "right-hand man" reinforce traditional gender roles, potentially excluding or marginalizing those who don't fit these stereotypes. Phrases such as "gentle-men's agreement" imply an exclusionary male-centric culture, while descriptors like "ballsy" equate bravery with masculine attributes.

The pejorative term "Karen," such as in the sentence, "Don't be a Karen," criticizes assertive or demanding behavior by rely-ing on sexist and ageist stereotypes to diminish women's voices and agency. Similarly, labels like "diva" and "drama queen" are often directed at women who exhibit confidence or express con-cerns, effectively silencing their perspectives and delegitimizing their emotions. These terms reinforce gender stereotypes and contribute to a hostile work environment by discouraging open communication.

It's not only gendered expressions and phrases. The tendency to refer to groups of men as "the accountants" while labeling women as "the girls in accounting" perpetuates gender bias and undermines professionalism by infantilizing women. Similarly, the term "IT guys" overlooks the presence and contributions of women in the field, reinforcing gender stereotypes and erasing their visibility. It's easy to fall into this habit without realizing it. I owned an IT company for fifteen years with a team of all men. I always referred to them as my "IT guys." Even now, when speak-ing about IT to a client, I catch myself saying "IT guys" out of habit and have to consciously replace it with "IT people." Breaking these habits takes ongoing, intentional effort.

As you become more mindful of the language you use, consider replacing these expressions with more neutral alternatives that promote inclusion. For example, instead of saying "grow a pair," try "stand your ground" or "assert yourself."

Honorific –A Dance of Politeness and Misogyny

Let me start this section with a confession: I am on a personal mission to stop the use of "sir" and "ma'am" with strangers. I'll explain why this matters so much.

Picture this: You're at a store, and the cashier cheerily says, "Thank you, ma'am!" Sounds polite, right? But let's peel back this layer of politeness.

During my workshops, I ask the women in the room, "Who here hates being called ma'am?" I witness not only hands in the air but eyerolls and groans in response. For many women, being called "ma'am" feels synonymous with "old." It stereotypes them based on someone else's perception of their appearance, suggesting they aren't young or pretty enough to be called miss. This is bias in a polite disguise.

The use of honorifics like "sir" and "ma'am" has a long history intertwined with gender stereotypes and societal expectations. Think about it: "miss" is for the young and presumably available, and as previously stated, "ma'am," as I mentioned, is for the . . . let's just say not-so-young. It's a linguistic dance around age, looks, and marital status, subtly reinforcing gender norms.

Gloria Steinem, a beacon of feminist thought, shared in a 2023 *CBS Sunday Morning* interview that *The New York Times* stubbornly clung to "miss," refusing to use "Ms." when referring to her. [113] Imagine that, "Miss Steinem of Ms. Magazine." If that isn't a glaring example of how entrenched these norms are, I don't know what is.

It's not all doom and gloom. We're learning, evolving. If a woman prefers "miss" and uses she/her pronouns, respect that choice. But let's not assume; let's ask. And for our nonbinary friends? "Mx." (pronounced *mix*) is a wonderful nod to inclusivity, acknowledging their identity respectfully.

Now, let's talk about the South. I spent two weeks in Mississippi in 2023 studying bias and came to appreciate the nuances of Southern politeness. "Miss FirstName" is a common term of endearment there, bridging the gap between formality and friendliness. It's respectful yet warm, like a verbal hug.

But here's the thing: Southern politeness often defaults to gendered honorifics based on how someone looks, which assumes there are only two genders. While "miss" works when you know someone's gender identity, what about when you don't? Here's where we can introduce a third option to the rules of Southern kindness: Mr., Miss, or Mx. This way, you have a respectful option to use until you know how someone identifies. "Mx. Amelia" is just as polite, offering the same warmth and respect while leaving space for someone's identity to shine through. We're not losing our manners; we're expanding them.

Yes, many of us were raised to believe that "sir" and "ma'am" are the pinnacle of politeness. But as we grow, so does our understanding. What was once polite can now be exclusive or even hurtful. Just like we've updated other parts of our language, we can modernize this too. Instead of defaulting to "sir," "ma'am," or even "miss," we can hold off on using any honorific until we know how someone identifies. Using a person's job title, like Doctor Brown, Professor Jones, or Engineer Smith, is another way to maintain respect while avoiding assumptions about gender. In situations where formality feels necessary, "Mx." is a respectful, gender-neutral alternative for everyone that avoids assumptions altogether. Let's be kind, inclusive, and, dare I say, authentic to the world as it is now. After all, isn't that what true politeness is all about?

Embracing Inclusivity in Familial Titles

The way we refer to family members often seeps into our professional conversations. It's in these seemingly mundane references where inclusivity can take a meaningful stand. Traditional familial titles can unintentionally exclude or misrepresent relationships. Let's take a closer look at how we can adapt these titles to honor every family structure and identity.

Navigating from what we've always known to what we aspire to become can be a journey of small yet significant steps. Here's a side-by-side comparison of traditional familial titles and their inclusive counterparts:

- Primary Family Members
  - Wife, Husband → Spouse or Partner: Suitable for any marital or committed relationship.
  - Mother, Father → Parent or Caregiver: "Parent" or "Caregiver" inclusively covers all bases.
  - Daughter, Son → Child: A simple and inclusive term for every family.
  - Sister, Brother → Sibling: Captures the bond without specifying gender.
- Extended Family Members
  - Grandmother, Grandfather → Grandparent
  - Granddaughter, Grandson → Grandchild
  - Aunt, Uncle → Parent's Sibling
  - Niece, Nephew → Sibling's Child (or Nibling, which is gaining traction)
- Relational Family Members
  - Mother-in-law, Father-in-law → Parent-in-law
  - Daughter-in-law, Son-in-law → Child-in-law
  - Sister-in-law, Brother-in-law → Sibling-in-law

- Complex Family Dynamic
  - Stepmother, Stepfather → Stepparent
  - Stepdaughter, Stepson → Stepchild
  - Stepsister, Stepbrother → Stepsibling
  - Half-sister, Half-brother → Half-sibling

Many nonbinary individuals, seeking to move beyond traditional gendered language, have crafted alternative family titles. These creative terms offer a way to honor familial bonds without relying on gender-specific or binary terminology.

The linguist Samuel Martin is credited with coining the gender-neutral term "nibling" in the 1950s to represent the gendered terms "niece" or "nephew." Nibling is derived from the word "sibling," with an *n* for niece or nephew.[114]

Likewise, the nonbinary version of aunt and uncle is "pibling," which is derived from sibling combined with the letter *p* for parent. Other nonbinary or gender-neutral names for aunt and uncle include:

- *titi*: derived from Spanish, *tía* and *tío*
- *zizi*: derived from Italian, *zia* and *zio*
- *nini*: similarly modeled on *titi* and *zizi*, with the *n* from *nonbinary*
- *bibi*: based on *titi* and *zizi*, with the *b* from *nonbinary*

There are also many nonbinary alternatives for mom and dad. Among the most common are "par," "ren," or "rent" as derived from the word "parent."

It is also quite common for people to develop their own unique nonbinary titles. In my family, "kidlet" is used as the nonbinary version of son or daughter, as "child" seemed to have an expiration date when it began to sound infantilizing.

Some titles develop over time and in the most unexpected ways. Shortly after I shared that I am nonbinary, one of my dear friends sent me a text that said, "Atta girl." She immediately realized and sent a corrected text that read, "Atta person." At least, that's what the text was supposed to say. Instead, her phone autocorrected it to, "Atta pesto." My immediate response to that was, "Oh, that's gonna stick!" And it did. I have been called Pesto by friends ever since. You're welcome to use it if it works for your pestos!

Addressing Groups

In our daily interactions, we often use gendered language to address groups without a second thought. We're now more aware than ever of the diverse spectrum of gender identities. So, let's talk about updating our group-address game. Remember, this isn't about policing your language with your inner circle but about being more inclusive around folks you might not know so well.

When we use inclusive language, we're saying, "Hey, I see you, I respect you, and you're welcome here." That's powerful, right? So, next time you're about to address a group, pause for a moment. Think about who is in the room (or the Zoom) and choose words that make everyone feel included. It's a small change in your speech that can make a big difference in creating an environment where everyone feels seen and valued.

And remember, it's okay to slip up sometimes. We're all learning. What matters is that we don't ignore these mistakes but work on correcting them. In the next chapter, we'll cover the best ways to address these slip-ups. For now, focus on making an effort to be inclusive and respectful. It's a journey, and each step counts toward creating a more welcoming environment for everyone.

Consider how often we use terms like "guys," "dude," and "man" to address groups. These words are ingrained in everyday language, but they inherently skew toward male identification.

While they may be acceptable with close friends or colleagues who you know are comfortable with them, in a diverse professional group, they can inadvertently exclude or misrepresent some individuals. Instead, consider using terms like "y'all," "everyone," "folks," or "friends" depending on the tone of your communication.

Save words like "dude" and "guys" for situations where you know everyone is comfortable with them. Asking a room of people, "I use 'dude' all the time; nobody here has a problem with that, right?" puts anyone who disagrees in an awkward position. While some may consider the term genderless, the reality is that some women, transgender or not, may not want to be called "dude."

When addressing a formal group, phrases like "ladies and gentlemen" have long been a staple, but this term excludes non-binary people. In formal settings, consider using "distinguished guests" or "esteemed guests" to add respectability without reinforcing the gender binary. In more casual settings, don't be afraid to have a little fun while staying inclusive. Phrases like "gentle-people," "friends," or even "gentlehumans" can lighten the mood while still making everyone feel welcome.

Finally, when describing individuals, take a moment to use more precise and inclusive language. Instead of saying "that man" or "that woman," try "the person in the yellow scarf" or "the person with the blue hat." This practice avoids assumptions and emphasizes the individual's presence over their presumed gender. It's a simple yet impactful shift that honors people for who they are, beyond just appearance.

Global Respect: Names and Pronouns in Multilingual Settings

In multicultural and multilingual workplaces, the challenge of fostering a gender-inclusive environment becomes even more nuanced. Many languages have gendered nouns and pronouns built into their grammatical structures, making it more complicated to adapt to gender-neutral language.

Begin by acknowledging that every language comes with its own set of rules and cultural contexts, which can make gender-neutral adaptations more complex. Respect linguistic diversity while simultaneously striving for inclusivity. Open dialogues with native speakers of the language in question can provide invaluable insights into potential workarounds or less-gendered alternatives.

For example, in languages like Spanish or French, which have gendered nouns, some progressive speakers are adopting "inclusive" forms of words. In Spanish, this might mean using "Latinx" or "Latine" instead of "Latino" or "Latina," or "todas" or "todes" instead of "todos" or "todas." However, not all individuals or communities accept these adaptations, so it's best to consult with people who speak these languages to learn more.

Likewise, the use of pronouns may differ substantially between languages. While English has adopted they/them as a singular gender-neutral pronoun, other languages may not have a widely accepted equivalent. Work closely with employees who are native speakers to understand how best to approach this in their language. Offer training sessions or workshops to discuss these language-specific challenges, and brainstorm solutions collectively.

Moreover, provide multilingual resources or training materials to assist in educating all employees, regardless of their linguistic background. Ensure that your commitment to gender inclusivity is as comprehensive as it is diverse. Written guides or online resources can be especially helpful for those who may not be fluent in the company's primary operating language, offering a point of reference that they can revisit as needed.

Overall, the goal is to approach the complexity of language with both sensitivity and a commitment to inclusion, recognizing that a one-size-fits-all solution may not be feasible. Instead, individualized, language-specific adaptations, developed in consultation with native speakers and experts, are more likely to be both respectful and effective.

CHAPTER 04

STRATEGIES FOR GENDER-INCLUSIVE COMMUNICATION

Beyond Words: Nonverbal Communication Strategies

Nonverbal cues form the silent yet powerful undercurrent of our interactions. They fill in the gaps, adding layers of meaning that words alone can't convey. This is particularly true in the context of gender inclusion. Whether it's the way you hold eye contact or the distance you maintain during a conversation, your nonverbal communication sends a message about your level of respect and openness toward all gender identities.

Nonverbal cues can either reinforce or undermine the verbal messages we send. For instance, you may say that you support gender inclusion, but if your body language signals discomfort or bias, your message will lose its credibility. It's not just what you say that matters, it's how you express it through your actions, gestures, and facial expressions that brings weight to your words.

When discussing gender inclusion, traditional norms often dictate how we use our body language. Men might be encouraged to use expansive gestures, while women may be socialized to take up less space. These ingrained habits can inadvertently perpetuate gender stereotypes and create barriers to true inclusion.

Your nonverbal cues act like the opening lines of a conversation, setting the tone for what's to follow. They can either prepare the ground for a meaningful dialogue about gender or establish a perimeter of exclusion. Being aware of the importance of your nonverbal communication cues is the first step toward fostering an environment that embraces diversity in all its forms.

Body language is a powerful tool for nonverbal communication that can either enhance or undermine your intentions. Often, microaggressions, those subtle, often unintentional slights, are conveyed through nonverbal cues like gestures, facial expressions, or the distance you maintain in a conversation. These behaviors are frequently one of the most unrealized ways biases can be communicated, especially when they contradict the inclusive messages we aim to send.

Consistency is key. While not everyone engages with nonverbal cues in the same way due to factors like ability, neurodiversity, or cultural background, it's important to apply these behaviors evenly. If you maintain eye contact, offer a firm handshake, or use open gestures with everyone except the one transgender or nonbinary person in the room, it can come across as a microaggression. Ensuring consistent nonverbal communication with all individuals helps create a more inclusive and respectful environment. Here are some common types of body language to consider:

- **Eye Contact:** Sustained, respectful eye contact shows engagement and validation. While avoiding eye contact can make some people feel ignored, remember that not everyone prefers direct eye contact. Many find that looking elsewhere helps them focus on listening.

- **Posture:** Standing or sitting up straight often indicates attentiveness and openness. Body posture can vary based on personal comfort or ability. Rather than focusing on perfect posture, the key is to ensure your body language communicates engagement and respect, as comfortably as you're able to manage.

- **Gestures:** Using open-hand gestures can signify inclusivity and openness, while pointing or using aggressive movements may seem confrontational.

- **Facial Expressions:** Your facial reactions to someone's statements can validate or invalidate their feelings. Aim for a consistently open and understanding expression, considering the overall context rather than focusing on any single reaction.

- **Personal Space:** Respecting someone's personal space can make them feel comfortable and valued. Understand that personal space preferences vary among individuals, and some may feel uncomfortable or overwhelmed if their space is invaded.

- **Handshakes:** Not everyone may be comfortable with handshakes at all due to personal, cultural, or physical reasons. When appropriate, aim for a consistent handshake for everyone, avoiding assumptions based on gender norms. My mother, a successful healthcare operations executive, always commented when someone shook her hand with a sort of gentility that made her feel like she wasn't worthy of a firm handshake because she was a woman: "It's like I'm shaking a dead fish."

- **Touch:** Touch is a tricky area that varies greatly among individuals. Always seek consent and be aware of cultural, personal, or sensory boundaries when considering any form of physical contact. For example, if you are culturally or socially inclined to hug someone, ask first rather than assuming they are comfortable with it.

Body language doesn't just come down to specific actions like eye contact or handshakes; it also includes the overall signals you send through positive or negative cues. The way you respond with your body can reinforce or undermine the messages you're trying to communicate. Here are some examples of positive and negative cues to keep in mind:

Positive Cues:

- Nodding in agreement or understanding
- Mirroring another's positive body language
- Leaning in slightly to show interest

Negative Cues:

- Eye-rolling
- Checking your watch or phone
- Sighing or showing impatience

Another crucial aspect of body language is facial expressions, which often convey more than words. Facial expressions serve as silent communicators of our thoughts and feelings, often more powerful than words. In a workplace striving for gender inclusion, these expressions can either invite a sense of belonging or perpetuate a feeling of exclusion.

For instance, a genuine smile when greeting everyone, regardless of their gender identity, fosters a feeling of warmth and acceptance. On the other hand, a look of surprise or discomfort when someone identifies with a pronoun or presents in a manner outside of traditional gender norms can send a disheartening message.

Being aware of your facial expressions is not about masking your true feelings but about cultivating a sense of empathy and understanding. It's easy to slip into subconscious expressions that might reflect societal biases or stereotypes about gender.

Your facial expression when you're listening to someone or how you react to new ideas can communicate varying levels of interest, agreement, and openness. In the interest of gender-inclusive communication, remember to:

- **Be Mindful:** Regularly check in with yourself during interactions. Do your expressions match your intentions?
- **Practice Empathy:** Understand the emotional context from which others are coming and let that guide your facial responses.
- **Be Consistent:** Aim for consistency in how you respond to everyone, regardless of their gender identity. A consistent facial expression can be a subtle yet strong indicator of an inclusive mindset.

By being mindful of your expressions, you can ensure everyone feels equally acknowledged. This is not policing or saying, "You should smile more, honey," but rather about recognizing how inconsistent expressions impact inclusivity in a diverse environment.

Even with the best of intentions, nonverbal cues can sometimes reinforce stereotypes or biases without us realizing it. Here are some common pitfalls to watch out for:

- **Ignoring Women and Nonbinary Employees During Eye Contact:** Let's say you're giving a presentation, and you find yourself only making eye contact with the men in the room. It may not be intentional, but you're sending a loud message to everyone else: their opinions or interests might not matter as much.
- **Closed-Off Body Language Around Nonbinary Coworkers:** Imagine a nonbinary colleague walks into a meeting and you unconsciously close yourself off; maybe you cross your arms or look away. This subtle act can have a

strong negative impact, making them feel unwelcome or marginalized.

- **Raising Eyebrows at Women Discussing Tech:** Suppose you're in a meeting and a female colleague starts discussing technical matters. If you react by raising your eyebrows, you're unintentionally reinforcing the stereotype that women are less tech-savvy.

- **Looking Confused or Uncomfortable:** One common pitfall is looking visibly confused or uncomfortable when encountering someone whose gender expression is unfamiliar to you. This seemingly innocuous reaction can send a strong message of exclusion and can make the other person feel that they don't belong or are not accepted.

- **Double-Taking at Transgender Colleagues:** The act of doing a double-take or visibly scrutinizing a transgender colleague can make them feel uncomfortable or singled out. Even if not intended to harm, these actions can perpetuate a sense of exclusion and are detrimental to a gender-inclusive workplace.

Creating an inclusive environment requires both individual awareness and collective effort. To ensure your workplace fosters respectful and gender-inclusive communication, consider these actionable steps that companies and employees can take:

- **Training:** Implement training sessions focused on nonverbal communication and its role in gender inclusion.

- **Feedback Mechanism:** Create anonymous channels where employees can report incidents of nonverbal microaggressions. This can help improve training programs.

- **Teams or Group Recognition:** Recognize teams or departments that excel in fostering an inclusive environment, including both verbal and nonverbal communication. Highlighting group efforts helps reinforce collective responsibility for maintaining an inclusive culture.

Inclusive Talk: Verbal Communication Strategies

Gender-inclusive communication hinges on the use of pronouns. Understanding and respecting pronouns is a sign of respect and acknowledgment of someone's identity. It is also a step toward dismantling gender bias and stereotypes.

Including pronouns in professional spaces, such as email signatures, website bios, and business cards, is a practice that normalizes gender. It's an invitation to openness, a nod to inclusivity, and a commitment to an environment where everyone, regardless of their gender identity or expression, feels acknowledged and respected. Let's delve into why this seemingly small act can make a significant impact:

- **Names and Gender:** Names alone do not reveal gender. Gender-neutral names like Morgan and nicknames like Sam (Samuel or Samantha) or Alex (Alexander or Alexandra/Alexandria/Alexa) can be misleading. In a culturally diverse workforce, it is entirely possible to encounter a name that is new to you, and without pronouns, you might find yourself in a guessing game when attempting to address a colleague respectfully.

- **Appearance vs. Identity:** Once we accept that gender expression does not equal gender identity, physical appearance stops becoming a reliable indicator of someone's pronouns.

- **Voice and Assumptions:** Assumptions based on the sound of someone's voice can lead to awkward or even disrespectful situations. Anyone can have a high or deep voice. On a video conference where names were visible, but cameras were off, I once heard someone say, "Why is your voice so deep when your name is Veronica?" As you might imagine, Veronica disconnected from the call.

- **Pronouns as Allyship:** For cisgender allies, sharing pronouns is a gesture of solidarity and support. It says, "I recognize the spectrum of gender identities, and I stand with everyone, regardless of where they are on that spectrum."

When a company or individual includes pronouns in professional spaces (email signatures, website bios, business cards, etc.), it sends a clear message of inclusivity. Seeing pronouns in your email signature can make a client or colleague feel more confident that they'll be respected and supported. It's a small gesture that communicates, "We support all people."

In a world where names, voices, and appearances can't tell the whole gender story, a well-placed pronoun is like a beacon of clarity in a sea of assumptions.

That said, sharing pronouns is not always appropriate, and it's essential to respect personal choice. A business should never mandate the use of pronouns. Deciding whether to display your pronouns in a professional context is a personal choice and one that requires thoughtful consideration.

Mandating that everyone lists pronouns forces individuals who may not be ready to share, or who do not feel safe doing so, into a position of discomfort. Not everyone in a company will be at the same place in their understanding of gender inclusion, and some may have personal beliefs that prevent them from fully embracing it. While it's essential for every employee to respect their colleagues, it's equally important that they aren't pressured to present themselves as allies when they aren't. Requiring pronouns from someone who harbors a conscious bias can be disingenuous at best, and harmful at worst. It's crucial that companies do not force individuals to advertise themselves as safe spaces if they are not truly supportive of transgender and nonbinary individuals.

On the flip side, prohibiting everyone from sharing their pronouns can send a different but equally damaging message: it suggests that your workplace is not a safe or welcoming environment for gender diversity. When companies or teams restrict the option to display pronouns, they can unintentionally communicate that gender inclusion isn't valued. If potential clients or new hires notice that no one in your organization shares their pronouns, they may assume that it's not a safe space for transgender and nonbinary individuals, even if many of your employees are inclusive and supportive.

Many businesses, especially in more traditional sectors, may worry that listing employee pronouns could deter potential clients or customers. This is a common concern in industries where some might assume clients prefer formality or conservatism. However, this assumption is increasingly outdated and often relies on stereotypes. Many potential clients are now the parents, grandparents, or relatives of transgender or nonbinary individuals. As a result, they can be highly attuned to inclusion signals and may be more likely to notice if pronouns are not listed than the business might expect. Assuming that clients will be uncomfortable with pronouns risks alienating those who value and seek out businesses that reflect respect and inclusivity.

There are many reasons an individual might not want to share their pronouns, even in an environment where doing so is encouraged:

- **Gender Questioning:** If you are questioning or contemplating a change in your own pronouns, being forced to share them might put undue pressure on you to reconcile your own identity. In such cases, prematurely declaring pronouns can feel like a forced outing, an experience that should be avoided at all costs. If you are stuck between the choice of coming out before you're ready or misgendering yourself, not listing pronouns might be the safest option.

- **Lack of Understanding:** If you are still in the process of learning about gender inclusion and don't feel fully prepared to communicate about gender with sensitivity and respect, it might be better to hold off on sharing your pronouns. Misleading others by sharing pronouns without the readiness to support and engage can inadvertently cause harm. If you are new to gender-inclusive concepts, I encourage you to read through this book in its entirety before jumping to share your pronouns with everyone. Understanding the nuances of gender-inclusive communication will allow you to make more informed, respectful choices.

- **Lack of Interest:** While respect for others is mandatory in any professional space, there are individuals who may not want to share their pronouns due to their personal beliefs or biases. While these individuals should be held to the same standards of respect and professionalism as anyone else, it's important that they are not forced to signal allyship if they do not genuinely embrace it. Forcing them to do so risks creating an environment of dishonesty and undermines the very inclusivity the policy aims to foster.

When I am asked to speak at a company on gender inclusion (or any topic), I often check their website to see if any team members list their pronouns in their bios. If no one does, I assume the business is not gender inclusive, whether or not that's the case. A potential client or customer could easily make the same assumption, thinking the company isn't a safe space for transgender or nonbinary people, even if several employees are personally inclusive. A total lack of pronouns suggests that either the company doesn't allow them or hasn't considered their importance.

If you decide to share your own pronouns, the following information will guide you on the "where" and "how" to make it happen.

Pronouns belong anywhere you would put your name: your email signature, social media profiles, video conference nameplates, business cards, and more. Each of these is a small but powerful way to announce not just who you are, but how you identify, and that you are welcoming of all identities.

Social media platforms vary in their support for pronouns. For instance, LinkedIn offers a dedicated space for pronouns, while on platforms like X (formerly Twitter), you might need to get creative, incorporating them into your profile description or last name.

When it comes to sharing your pronouns, think of it as leading by example. Let's say you're at a conference or a new team meeting. Instead of the old name and title introduction, consider demonstrating a new standard that includes your pronouns: "Hi, I'm Alex, and I use he/him pronouns." Simple, effective, and subtly powerful.

When you introduce yourself with your own pronouns, you are signaling to the other person that it's safe for them to share their own. I typically say, "Hi, I'm Amelia; they/them," which opens the door for the other person to respond with their name and pronouns, if they choose to.

Asking for someone else's pronouns should be treated as a choice. The reasons we've discussed for why you might not want to share your pronouns can apply to anyone. In a meeting, rather than instructing everyone to share their name and pronouns, consider saying something like, "When it's your turn to speak, please tell us your name and, if you're comfortable, your pronouns." This tiny tweak in phrasing can be the difference between inclusivity and pressure.

This approach also helps avoid the mistake of clocking, something we discussed in "Terminology" (Chapter 2). For example, walking up to the one person in the room whose gender expression confuses you and asking only them for their pronouns can inadvertently place an uncomfortable spotlight on them. If you are interested in someone's pronouns and have already established a trusting relationship, consider asking them privately in a respectful conversation. In public or group settings, everyone should feel comfortable and respected, regardless of whether they choose to share their pronouns.

Remember, consider using they/them for all individuals whose pronouns you do not know. While no gender-neutral pronoun is perfect, "they" is the most inclusive option we have among "he," "she," and "they." It again would be clocking to only use "they" for some people based on your interpretation of their presentation.

Practical Dos and Don'ts for Inclusive Communications

Navigating verbal communication in the workplace, particularly when it involves gender identity, requires sensitivity and awareness. Being both kind and educated means understanding the delivery and meaning behind our words. Sometimes, even well-intentioned remarks can be perceived differently, especially by transgender and nonbinary individuals who often encounter misunderstanding or insensitivity in their daily interactions.

There are two fundamental principles that should guide these interactions:

- **Respect Privacy:** Never disclose someone's transgender or nonbinary status, or any other personal information, without their explicit consent. Respect each person's right to decide if, when, and with whom to share details of their gender journey.

- **Honor Identities:** When someone shares their pronouns, accept and use them without hesitation. It's not our place to debate or scrutinize them. Delaying or questioning why they use those pronouns can feel like judgment or disapproval. Imagine how you would feel if an important part of your identity were dismissed or questioned, like saying to a chiropractor, "You're not a real doctor."

What Should I Do When Someone's Pronouns Change?

When someone shares that their pronouns have changed, think of it less like "coming out" and more like "letting you in." They're inviting you into their world, showing you who they really are. That's a big deal! Seeing it this way can shift your mindset from worrying about messing up to genuinely appreciating the trust they're placing in you. They've been on a journey to live authentically, and now they're sharing that with you. It's something to celebrate; so instead of stressing about mistakes, be happy for them.

Be mindful with apologies, especially if you're apologizing in advance. Over-apologizing or saying things like, "I'm so sorry if I get this wrong, I'll probably mess it up," can actually show discomfort or doubt. It may seem sweet to you, but what your colleague hears is more like, "I'll try, but I already see you a certain way, and I'm not sure I can change that." That's not what you want. A better way to respond is to simply acknowledge what they've shared and commit to using their pronouns moving forward.

Refrain from asking invasive questions. Asking about someone's surgical status or any other aspect of their physical transition is not only irrelevant but deeply intrusive. Respecting someone's gender identity isn't about their physical appearance or medical history; it's purely about acknowledging their expressed identity.

How Should I Respond When Someone Reveals They Are Transgender?

When someone casually mentions that they're transgender, it's a moment to practice subtlety and sensitivity. For example, say you're chatting about different experiences with a woman at work who mentions something about her childhood and reveals that she was raised as a boy. Don't overreact or make it a big deal; a simple acknowledgment is fine.

Saying something like, "Oh, I had no idea!" might seem supportive, but it can actually be overwhelming or even a bit invasive. It shifts the focus onto their appearance or how "passable" they are, and that's not what this is about. Treat the information like you would any other detail someone shares about their life. It's part of their story, nothing more, nothing less.

Lastly, do not make small talk about their gender journey. Even if your intention is to show interest or be supportive, asking personal questions like, "How did your family take it?" can potentially bring up painful memories. Many transgender and nonbinary people face tough challenges, including difficult or broken family relationships. What seems like a casual question can stir up emotions they weren't prepared to revisit.

What's the Best Way to Handle If I Misgender Someone?

Mistakes happen. We're all human, and we're going to mess up, especially when it comes to navigating gender identities. The real test isn't about getting it perfect every time; it's about how we bounce back when we slip up.

If you find yourself misgendering someone, don't panic. The most respectful thing you can do is correct yourself quickly, keep it simple, and move on. Something like, "He needs the report by tomorrow—sorry, I mean she needs the report by tomorrow," works perfectly. You've fixed it and kept the conversation rolling without making it a bigger deal than it needs to be.

Why does this matter? Over-apologizing or making a big deal out of the correction can actually make the person who was misgendered feel like they have to comfort you. Now, instead of just dealing with being misgendered, they're also navigating your emotions, which is not fair to them.

It might feel kinder to keep the conversation going and avoid acknowledging that you misgendered someone. Maybe it seems easier to let it pass. But trust me, they noticed. Misgendering doesn't go unnoticed and ignoring it can feel dismissive. A quick self-correction is far kinder than pretending it didn't happen.

The same goes for deadnaming. If you catch yourself about to use the wrong name, stop, correct it, and use their new name, even if they're not around to hear it. You're building new habits, so every time you slip up, just fix it and say the sentence again with the right name or pronoun.

If you're really struggling to get used to the change, here's a tip to practice in your everyday life. When you're at home, maybe doing laundry or dishes, talk out loud about your colleague. Something like, "Sarah was in the office yesterday in a new dress. Her outfit was cute. I don't remember if I told her . . ."

Here's another tip for getting used to using they/them pronouns: imagine the person has a little pet mouse in their pocket. Every time you talk about them, you're also talking about the mouse, since they're always together.

Mistakes don't only apply to names and pronouns. Other expressions or phrases might need to shift too. Let me share a story.

I met someone on LinkedIn, and we scheduled a virtual meeting to network. We hit it off instantly, and by the end, it felt like we'd been friends forever. He called me his "sister from another mister." I laughed and said, "I agree! But we need to come up with a new way to say it because I'm nonbinary so, not a sister."

His immediate response was, "Right! My bad. How's homie from another bromie?" I burst out laughing. We came up with a bunch of options, laughing harder with each new idea until we landed on "pal from another gal." Now, I'm his "pal from another gal," and he's my "brother from another mother."

This could have been awkward for us both, but instead, it was fun and lighthearted. The takeaway from this story:

- It's okay to mess up. What matters is how you respond.
- When you get it wrong, don't make it about you. My friend didn't get defensive; he just said, "My bad," and we moved forward together.

These moments don't have to be uncomfortable. Sometimes, they can even lead to a better connection. You might even come up with something fun, like, "pal from another gal."

If you want to practice getting more comfortable with different pronouns, check out Minus 18, an online network of LGBTQ+ youth in Australia that created an app where you can practice using different pronouns and neopronouns: https://www.minus18.org.au/pronouns-app.

How Do I Talk About a Transgender Colleague's Past?

This is one of the things I see people get wrong more often than anything else because most people don't know how to handle it. So, let's get it right. When you're talking about someone's past, especially if they're transgender, always use their current name and pronouns, no exceptions.

Take the example of Sarah, a transgender woman who transitioned last year and has been with the company for five years. If a colleague, Rick, is telling a story from four years ago, he should still say, "Sarah did this," and use she/her pronouns. Now, I know this can feel counterintuitive at first; Sarah wasn't using her current name and pronouns at that time. But remember, if you think of Sarah "sharing her truth" (the truth she always had) instead of "coming out," it might be easier to realize that Sarah has always been Sarah, even if she wasn't publicly living that truth yet.

Where things usually go off the rails is when Rick stops mid-story, hand raised as if he is about to make a big announcement, and says something like, "I'm going to say [deadname] because that's who [wrong pronoun] was back then." If you have to explain why you're about to misgender or deadname someone *while you're doing it*, that's your cue that you know it's wrong on some level. Stopping to explain or justify it not only makes it worse but also reinforces the harm.

Side note: If I were telling this story out loud, I would say "deadname" and "wrong pronoun" instead of using Sarah's actual deadname or misgendering her, to avoid causing harm.

Deadnaming or misgendering someone, even in a story from the past, invalidates their identity. It's not harmless, and it's not "just semantics;" it can be hurtful.

How Do I Handle Questions About Restrooms Inclusively?

This might seem insignificant, but how you respond to simple questions about restrooms can make a big difference in creating an inclusive workplace. Here's how to approach it with sensitivity:

When someone asks where the restrooms are, give clear, neutral directions. If the restrooms are close together, just point and say, "The restrooms are over there." This is straightforward—no need to put extra emphasis on gender.

If the restrooms are in separate locations, it's fine to specify with, "The men's room is this way, and the women's room is that way." Keep in mind that the person asking might be doing so for someone else, so make sure your directions cover all bases without making assumptions.

There is no need to launch into a speech about your company's inclusion policies. Over-explaining can feel performative or insincere, and the person who asked could feel clocked or outed. A simple, direct answer respects the person's privacy and shows that inclusion is just part of how things are done around here.

Is It Okay to Ask Why Someone Uses Certain Pronouns?

It's natural to want to understand more about someone, especially when you're learning something new. But before anything else, remember this fundamental rule: once someone tells you their pronouns, your priority is to use them. Your first responsibility is to respect and honor their identity.

This kind of situation calls for discernment. Ask yourself: Why do I want to know? Is it coming from a place of genuine interest and connection, or is it rooted in judgment or unhelpful curiosity? Am I making this about me, or am I truly focused on them?

If you decide that asking is appropriate, here are some ground rules to guide you:

- **Always wait:** Don't ask anything until you've been using their pronouns for a while. Immediate questions never feel like caring; they feel like judgment, as if your approval is required before you'll respect their pronouns.

- **Ask privately and thoughtfully:** A private conversation is more respectful than putting someone on the spot in public. You could begin by asking them if they are okay with being asked questions; some people are, and some are not.

How Can I Support My Trans or Nonbinary Colleague in Unfamiliar Settings?

When you and your colleague or friend are in a new environment, whether it's a business meeting, event, or social gathering, they might feel anxious about being misgendered. You want to offer support without making them feel uncomfortable or drawing unnecessary attention to their gender identity.

One simple and effective way to help is by naturally using their correct pronouns during introductions or conversations. For example, at a networking or social event, you might say something like, "[Their name] and I were just talking about that, and he mentioned . . ." In a business meeting or event, you could make an introduction with, "This is [Their name]. They're leading the initiative on [project]." This subtly signals to others which pronouns to use without making it the focus of the interaction. It's a non-intrusive way to lead by example and can help others pick up on the correct pronouns without putting your colleague on the spot.

Another tip is to have a private conversation with your colleague ahead of time to understand their preferences. Some people prefer that you correct others directly, some prefer to handle it themselves without outside intervention, and others may not want any attention drawn to it at all. By discussing this beforehand, you can better support your colleague based on their comfort level.

What Should I Do if I Witness Someone Being Misgendered or Deadnamed?

Addressing situations where someone else is being misgendered can be challenging, especially when it happens in real time, and there's no explicit guidance on how to handle it. This is typically referred to as "bystander intervention," where someone steps in to address a harmful situation affecting another person. So how should one react when witnessing misgendering?

Let's say your colleague, Rick, misgenders Sarah, a transgender colleague who uses she/her pronouns, by saying, "Sarah takes his coffee with sugar," and you're unsure how Sarah would like it handled. One straightforward approach is to gently correct Rick by stating the correct pronoun: simply interject with "her," and nothing more. This method allows Rick to then self-correct and acknowledge his mistake without escalating the situation.

However, your safety and well-being should always be a priority. If you feel that correcting Rick, regardless of whether he is in a position of authority, might jeopardize your workplace relationships or position, consider the risks first.

For a subtler approach, especially in cases where direct correction might be uncomfortable, you can continue the conversation using the correct pronoun. Using the earlier example, after Rick says, "Sarah takes his coffee with sugar," follow with a response such as, "Yes, she told me once she used to drink it black but found it a bit too strong." This indirect method subtly informs Rick of his mistake without directly correcting him in front of anyone. This technique can be less confrontational, reinforcing the correct pronoun usage in a natural way. This method also works when someone is deadnamed by using their name instead of their pronoun in a follow-up sentence.

Bystander intervention isn't just limited to moments when someone is misgendered or deadnamed. It can extend to other problematic situations, like when someone makes a joke about pronouns or gender identity or makes disparaging comments about using inclusive language. In these situations, keep the following in mind:

- **Safety First:** Your safety is your top priority. Don't intervene if it puts you at risk.

- **Stay Calm:** Avoid escalating the situation. Getting emotional can shift the focus away from the issue at hand and make it harder to resolve.

- **Lead by Example:** As with the techniques we discussed, sometimes simply modeling the right behavior can be enough to shift the tone of the conversation without confrontation.

- **Support the Affected Person:** After the incident, check in with anyone who may have been affected by the event.

- **Notify HR (with consent):** With the affected person's consent, inform HR if a colleague has made a disparaging remark about transgender or nonbinary people. This ensures HR can support inclusion in the workplace while respecting privacy.

We'll dive deeper into bystander intervention and how to handle these situations in "Human Resources: Fostering an Inclusive

Culture" (Chapter 6), where we'll also discuss how companies can support transgender employees during their transitions.

Writing with Respect: Written Communication Strategies

A common misunderstanding about gender-neutral documents is that it does not mean devoid of any gender-specific language. Think of "gender-neutral" as "gender-accurate." When you know the gender of the person you're addressing, use the appropriate gendered terms. Neutrality only matters when the reader is unknown, or the document addresses a broad audience.

There are several methods to employ when rendering a document gender-neutral; each can be applicable in different contexts.

- **Expand Third-Person Language:** Modify sentences to include a broader range of pronouns. Example: Change "The applicant should submit his/her resume by May 15," to "The applicant should submit his/her/their resume by May 15."

- **Use Second-Person Focus:** Shift from third to second person to avoid gendered pronouns. Example: Change "The applicant should submit his/her application," to "Submit your application by the deadline."

- **Opt for Plural Nouns:** Use plural nouns to create natural gender neutrality. Example: Rather than using "Each applicant must send his or her application," use "All applicants must send their applications."

- **Eliminate Pronouns:** Where possible, remove pronouns entirely. Example: "Submit applications by the due date."

- **Repeat Nouns:** Use repeated nouns to avoid pronouns. Example: "A teacher provides instruction to students beyond official class hours."

- **Employ Singular "They":** The singular "they" is increasingly accepted and can be used for inclusivity. Example: Change "Everyone has his or her favorites," to "Everyone has their favorites."

These methods enhance the clarity and inclusivity of written documents and reflect a conscious effort to embrace diversity and respect in professional communication.

Forms

Inclusive forms design involves reconsidering how we inquire about gender and offers respectful ways for individuals to share this information. This section will explore strategies for making forms gender inclusive and respectful. To create a sense of trust and transparency, consider the following practices:

- **Explain the Purpose:** Include a brief explanation of why gender information is being collected and how it will be used. This transparency helps users make an informed decision about whether to provide this information.
- **Ensure Confidentiality:** Assure users that, if provided, their gender information will be handled with confidentiality and respect and used solely for the purposes outlined. This assurance can encourage voluntary disclosure.

Inclusive forms design involves reconsidering how we inquire about gender and offers respectful ways for individuals to share this information. This can be done by rethinking the need for gender-related questions and offering inclusive options. Here are some ways to ensure you're collecting gender information in a respectful and thoughtful manner:

- **Pronouns vs. Gender:** Before adding a gender question to a form, consider if the question is absolutely necessary.

In many cases, asking for pronouns may be more relevant than asking for someone's gender.

- **Gender Options:** When gender information is needed, offer a range of options that go beyond the binary choices of male and female. This can include options such as nonbinary, genderqueer, and genderfluid. This applies to honorifics or title fields as well.

- **Opt-in Disclosure:** In addition to a range of gender options, the form can include an option for "Prefer Not to Say" or even a setup where the question can be skipped entirely without impeding the completion of the form.

- **Self-Identification:** Depending on the purpose of the form, a text box may not be feasible. However, when possible, providing a text box allows individuals to self-describe their gender if the existing options don't fully represent their identity.

Inclusive forms should also be mindful of the language used around names and pronouns. While it's common to ask for a "Preferred Name" on forms, which is both thoughtful and practical, the term "preferred pronouns" falls short for important reasons.

As we discussed in Chapter 2, asking for a "Preferred Name" is valuable because many individuals, including but not limited to transgender people, use names different from their legal ones. This practice accommodates people who go by a nickname or choose a name that reflects their identity, allowing everyone to be addressed in a way that resonates with them. For example, someone named Samantha may prefer "Sam."

However, the term "preferred pronouns" implies that pronouns are a matter of preference, rather than an essential part of someone's identity. It suggests, "I know what your pronouns should be, but what would you prefer instead?" To be more respectful and accurate, update any outdated language on forms by simply asking for "pronouns" rather than "preferred pronouns."

Building on this commitment to gender inclusivity, there are several additional ways to ensure that written communication is more gender inclusive. Here are some practical tools you can employ:

When it comes to addressing envelopes and letterhead, consider modern, inclusive practices that embrace simplicity and gender neutrality:

- **Modernizing Address Formats:** The traditional practice of including titles in addresses is becoming outdated. For example, instead of "Ms. Amelia Michael," using "Amelia Michael" or "A. Michael" is now widely acceptable. This approach not only embraces gender neutrality but also aligns with contemporary preferences for simplicity and informality. It is still acceptable to use the traditional honorific, however, only when you know the pronouns of the recipient.

- **Family Correspondence:** Instead of "Mr. and Mrs. Michael and Family," a more inclusive approach would be "The Michael Family." This format removes unnecessary emphasis on marital status and gender.

- **Inclusive Family Names**: When family members have different last names, opt for a format like "The Michael and Smith Family." This approach respects each individual's name without assuming shared last names, maintaining inclusivity across various family structures.

In written communication, such as letters and emails, inclusive language can create a more welcoming environment:

- **Evolving Beyond Courtesy Titles:** The conventional "Dear [Courtesy Title] [Last Name]" format is giving way to more inclusive approaches. For known recipients, if their preferred title is known (Mr., Mrs., Miss, Ms., Mx.), it can be used. However, for unknown recipients, use more broad terms like "To Whom It May Concern" or "To Our Trusted Clients."

- **Email Etiquette:** The formal "Dear" in emails is increasingly being replaced by a friendlier and more casual "Hello," which sidesteps the need for gender-specific titles altogether. This shift not only caters to the trend of less formal electronic communication but also inadvertently aids in gender-neutral communication. If the formal "Dear" is still desired, addressing their role (e.g., Dear Taxpayer, Dear Homeowner) can be more appropriate.

Use gender-neutral language when sending invitations for company events. Instead of addressing invitations to "Mr. and Mrs.," use the full names of the invitees without gendered titles, such as "Amelia Michael and Partner." This ensures inclusivity and respects the identities of all guests.

Traditional titles such as Mrs., Miss, and Ms. have long been a focal point in discussions about gender and feminism. Each of these titles carries its own set of implications and societal expectations, often rooted in marital status and gender norms. For example:

- **Mrs.:** Historically used to indicate a married woman, often linked to her husband's identity (e.g., Mrs. John Smith). This can imply a woman's identity is tied to her marital status and her husband's name.

- **Miss:** Traditionally used for unmarried women, which can undesirably highlight their marital status.

- **Ms.:** Emerged as a feminist response to the marital status implications of Mrs. and Miss. It's used regardless of marital status, offering women a title that parallels the male "Mr.," which isn't indicative of marital status.

In the context of feminism, these titles have been debated and discussed extensively. Feminists have advocated for the use of titles that do not segregate women based on marital status or define them in relation to men. The introduction of "Ms." was a significant step in this direction, offering a more neutral option.

As society's understanding of gender evolves, the limitations of binary gender titles like Mrs., Miss, and Ms. have become more apparent. There is growing recognition that these titles don't fully accommodate the diversity of gender identities. Two common alternatives are emerging in professional and social settings:

- **First-Name Basis:** One increasingly popular option is to forego honorifics altogether and use first names. This approach removes the need for gender-specific titles, breaks down formal barriers, and promotes equality and individuality. It can also make interactions feel more personal and less bound by traditional hierarchies. Many businesses and institutions are embracing this option for its simplicity and inclusivity.

- **Gender-Neutral Honorifics:** For businesses that prefer to maintain formal titles, Mx. offers an inclusive option. The use of "Mx." as a default honorific signals an acknowledgment of diverse gender identities and is particularly useful in environments where formality is still expected. Though this might feel new or unfamiliar to some, it allows organizations to move away from the outdated implications of gendered titles.

Case Study: Gender Neutrality in the 117th Congressional Rules Package

The 117th Congressional Rules Package marked a significant milestone as the first completely gender-neutral document in the context of US government proceedings. This groundbreaking document was designed to serve as a comprehensive guide for the operational and procedural norms for Congress in the ensuing year.

The Congressional Rules Package is a collection of regulations and guidelines that govern the functioning of the US Congress. It sets the framework for everything from legislative procedures to the ethical guidelines to which members and employees must adhere. The intended audience for this document is vast, encompassing not only members of Congress and their staff but also the wider public who engage with legislative affairs.

Prior to this iteration, the Rules Package often employed gender-specific language to outline various regulations. For instance, it detailed employment restrictions concerning relations to members of Congress using terms like "mothers," "fathers," "sisters," "brothers," "aunts," and "uncles." The 117th package transitioned to using gender-neutral terms like "parents" and "siblings." This shift reflects a conscious effort to acknowledge and respect the diversity of gender identities, ensuring the language used is inclusive and representative of all individuals.

Despite its progressive nature, the gender-neutral stance of the Rules Package did not escape controversy. Conservatives such as then House Minority Leader Kevin McCarthy and news outlets such as Fox News claimed a rules change banned US House members from using any gendered language.[115] Speaker

Nancy Pelosi referred to herself as a grandmother in a social media post, and critics argued that her use of a gender-specific title broke this rule.[116]

This incident highlights the importance of education surrounding gender neutrality, especially in public and political spheres. The 117th Congressional Rules Package is gender inclusive because the audience for the document is broad and unspecific. Nancy Pelosi referring to herself as a grandmother is gender accurate and entirely separate from understanding the importance of gender neutrality when writing to a diverse audience.

Shortly after this, the California code was amended to remove gender-specific language from legislative positions and titles after the first woman was appointed CHP Commissioner, which was previously described with only masculine terms.[117] Since then, the rules have remained gender-neutral, and several states, including Minnesota, New Mexico, Ohio, Oregon, Washington, and Wisconsin, have passed legislation to remove gendered language from legal code.[118]

The case study on the 117th Congressional Rules Package illustrates how gender neutrality can be implemented in a formal setting. This shift, while not without controversy, serves as an example of how thoughtful language changes can promote inclusivity and respect for diverse identities.

Unfortunately, the progress made in 2021 with the 117th Congressional Rules Package was short-lived. In 2025, the 119th Congress, led by House Republicans, chose to replace gender-neutral terms such as "parent" and "child" with gender-specific terms like "mother" and "son" under the guise of restoring "family-centric" language. This change was framed as a return to tradition, but critics, including members of the Congressional Equality Caucus, have highlighted how this shift excludes

LGBTQ+ individuals and erases the intentional inclusivity introduced in prior years.[119]

The 117th Rules Package illustrated how thoughtful, inclusive language can serve a broad audience with respect and dignity. Even when progress is temporarily reversed, these examples remind us that inclusivity is a choice—a choice that can, and must, be made again.

PART THREE:

Implementing Gender Inclusion at Work

This section of the book focuses on practical strategies for embedding gender inclusion within each department of your organization. While leadership may set the tone, real progress requires buy-in and engagement from every department. Gender inclusion is a shared responsibility, with each department making a unique contribution to the overall effort.

The current political climate in the US presents unprecedented challenges for DEI efforts. At the time of this writing, the 2025 US administration is using executive orders and Department of Justice (DOJ) investigations to dismantle Diversity, Equity, and Inclusion (DEI) efforts and erase gender identity protections. In a shocking escalation, the Department of Justice, under Attorney General Pam Bondi, has even announced criminal investigations into private businesses that maintain DEI programs.[120] The administration has framed DEI as illegal discrimination and, in some cases, even absurdly blamed diversity initiatives for unrelated tragedies, such as a commercial plane crash.[121]

This baseless attack on DEI escalated when President Trump suggested, without any evidence, that hiring practices under the Federal Aviation Administration's diversity program contributed to a deadly collision between a passenger plane and an Army helicopter. His administration quickly seized the moment to justify eliminating DEI in aviation, even though experts, including the FAA and air traffic controllers' union, have confirmed that all hires must meet rigorous qualifications.[122]

Despite these aggressive political attacks, it's critical to understand what is and isn't legally enforceable. Gender remains a protected class under federal law, and businesses are not legally required to comply with anti-DEI political pressure. The DOJ's overreach is already being challenged in court, and federal judges—including Judge John Cronin, a Trump appointee—have ruled that banning DEI in private workplaces would violate the First Amendment.[123]

Businesses must recognize that their DEI strategies remain both lawful and necessary. While the administration attempts to create fear and uncertainty, no federal law currently prohibits private companies from fostering inclusion. Until the Supreme Court makes a final ruling that undermines the First Amendment, organizations should remain steadfast in their commitments to equity. No matter the political climate, workplaces are responsible for creating fair and equitable environments—making proactive ownership of inclusion strategies more critical than ever.

The chapters follow a deliberate order, starting with Leadership and HR, and progressing through departments such as legal, IT, marketing, and sales. This structure illustrates how inclusion can be integrated into your organization's policies, systems, and physical spaces.

That said, this book is designed for flexibility. If your immediate needs are department-specific, feel free to jump directly to the chapters that are most relevant. Whether you're a department head, manager, or individual contributor, the content is organized to provide tailored solutions for your role while encouraging exploration of the broader picture of gender inclusion across all departments.

This section concludes with Chapter 15, which showcases real-life examples of businesses and municipalities that have successfully implemented gender-inclusive practices. These case studies provide valuable insights and actionable inspiration from companies that are leading the way in their industries, offering a roadmap for your own organization to follow.

CHAPTER 05

LEADERSHIP: SETTING
THE TONE FOR INCLUSION

In any organization, leadership is the compass that guides culture. When it comes to gender inclusion, leaders are the ones who set the tone, influencing everything from daily interactions to the core values that shape an employee's experience. Employees look to leaders to see if inclusion is just a buzzword or a genuine priority.

The ripple effect of leadership's actions can't be overstated. When senior leaders visibly commit to Diversity, Equity, and Inclusion (DEI), they make inclusion a foundational value of the organization. This commitment has a real impact: in workplaces where leaders champion DEI, a remarkable 84% of employees feel valued and respected. But when leaders show little or no commitment, that sense of value drops sharply: down to 44% in companies with weak leadership support, and only 16% when employees see no commitment from leadership at all.[124] Leadership's visible commitment to equity remains one of the most powerful factors in building a thriving, resilient workforce.

It's not just marginalized groups who benefit from these initiatives. DEI efforts create a happier workplace for everyone. For instance, in companies where leaders are known to support DEI, 84% of straight, cisgender men report feeling happy at work. That number falls to 47% without this commitment.[125] Everyone, regardless of identity, feels the positive impact when DEI is genuinely prioritized by leadership.

Leaders shape the workplace by modeling the behaviors they want to see at every level. From the C-suite to department heads and team leads, when they champion authenticity and inclusion, it cascades through the organization, inspiring others to follow.

Building Blocks of Inclusive Leadership

Inclusive leadership requires that leaders model and promote inclusive practices throughout their organizations. This is particularly important in industries like healthcare, where patient care involves highly personal interactions and serious missteps could lead to patients refusing future care. By setting an example, leaders foster a culture of respect and safety. These principles apply across all industries, where leadership's commitment to inclusion shapes the organizational culture and influences how employees interact with clients, customers, and one another.

Traits of Inclusive Leaders

Inclusive leadership is characterized by various traits that foster Diversity, Equity, and Inclusion in the workplace. According to a Deloitte University Press report called "The Six Signature Traits of Inclusive Leadership: Thriving in a Diverse New World," Bernadette Dillon and Juliet Bourke detail the traits that stand out as elements of inclusive leadership, and the actions leaders can take to build these skills. By embodying these qualities, leaders can create a workplace environment where all team members feel valued and respected.[126]

Six Signature Traits of Inclusive Leaders

1. **Commitment:**
   - **Personal Values:**
     - o Treat all team members with fairness and respect.
     - o Understand the uniqueness of each team member.
     - o Ensure each team member feels connected to the group/organization.
     - o Proactively adapt work practices to meet the needs of others.
   - **Belief in the Business Case:**
     - o Treat diversity and inclusion as a business priority.
     - o Take personal responsibility for diversity and inclusion outcomes.
     - o Clearly and authentically articulate the value of diversity and inclusion.
     - o Allocate resources toward improving diversity and inclusion within the workplace.

2. **Courage:**
   - **Humility:**
     - o Acknowledge personal limitations and weaknesses.
     - o Seek contributions from others to overcome personal limitations.
     - o Admit mistakes when made.
   - **Bravery:**
     - o Approach diversity and inclusion wholeheartedly.
     - o Challenge entrenched organizational attitudes and practices that promote homogeneity.
     - o Hold others accountable for non-inclusive behaviors.

3. **Cognizance of Bias:**
   - **Self-Regulation:**
     - Learn about personal biases, including through feedback.
     - Follow processes to ensure personal biases do not influence decisions about others.
     - Identify and address organizational processes inconsistent with merit.
   - **Fair Play:**
     - Make fair and merit-based decisions about talent (e.g., promotions, rewards, task allocations).
     - Employ transparent, consistent, and informed decision-making processes about talent.
     - Provide clear explanations of processes applied and reasons for decisions made to those affected.

4. **Curiosity:**
   - **Openness:**
     - Demonstrate a desire for continued learning.
     - Actively seek the perspectives of diverse others in ideation and decision-making.
     - Withhold fast judgment when engaging with diverse others.
   - **Perspective-Taking:**
     - Listen attentively when another person is voicing a point of view.
     - Engage in respectful and curious questioning to better understand others' viewpoints.
     - Demonstrate the ability to see things from others' viewpoints.

- **Coping with Ambiguity and Uncertainty:**
  - o Be flexible and adapt quickly to new or unexpected situations.
  - o Demonstrate and encourage divergent thinking.
  - o Seek opportunities to connect with a diverse range of people.

5. **Cultural Intelligence:**
   - **Drive:**
     - o Take an active interest in learning about other cultures.
     - o Seek out opportunities to experience culturally diverse environments.
     - o Be confident in leading cross-cultural teams.
   - **Knowledge:**
     - o Seek information on the local context (e.g., politics, ways of working).
   - **Adaptability:**
     - o Develop the ability to collaborate with people from diverse cultural backgrounds.
     - o Change style appropriately when a cross-cultural encounter requires it.
     - o Use appropriate verbal and nonverbal behavior in cross-cultural encounters.

6. **Collaboration:**
   - **Empowerment:**
     - o Give team members the freedom to handle difficult situations.
     - o Empower team members to make decisions about issues impacting their work.

- o Hold team members accountable for performance they can control.
- **Teaming:**
  - o Assemble teams that are diverse in thinking.
  - o Ensure team members respect each other and prevent out-groups within the team.
  - o Anticipate and address team conflicts when they occur.
- **Voice:**
  - o Create a safe environment where people feel comfortable speaking up.
  - o Explicitly include all team members in discussions.
  - o Ask follow-up questions.

Inclusive leadership isn't just about having a set of skills; it's about how leaders consistently show up for their teams. Beyond the core traits we've explored, inclusive leaders exhibit a range of behaviors that further create a culture of trust, respect, and belonging. Some of these additional behaviors include:

- **Active Listening:** Inclusive leaders are excellent listeners. They pay close attention to both what is said and what is not said to understand the underlying concerns and aspirations of their team members.

- **Encouraging Participation:** Leaders encourage participation from all team members, especially those who may be hesitant to speak up. This might involve direct solicitation of opinions from quieter team members during meetings or creating alternative channels for them to voice their thoughts and ideas.

- **Emphasizing Empathy:** By showing empathy, leaders acknowledge the unique challenges and experiences of their team members. This doesn't just mean understanding where others are coming from but also showing genuine concern and a willingness to act to support them.

- **Demonstrating Cultural Intelligence:** Inclusive leaders are culturally intelligent. They are aware of diverse cultural norms and understand how these can affect workplace dynamics. They respect these differences and leverage them to build a stronger team.

- **Mitigating Bias:** Leaders are proactive in identifying and mitigating their own biases and those within their teams. This involves regular training and open discussions about unconscious bias, ensuring that decisions are fair and based on merit.

- **Transparent Communication:** Leaders communicate transparently, sharing their rationale behind decisions and policies, thereby building trust and clarity among team members.

- **Advocating for Diversity:** Inclusive leaders not only support diversity initiatives but also advocate for them. They understand the strategic importance of diversity and are vocal about its benefits to the organization as a whole.

By embodying these behaviors, leaders not only set the tone for a more inclusive workplace but also inspire others to follow suit, fostering an environment where every voice is heard, valued, and considered in shaping the future of the organization.

The goal isn't to master all these behaviors overnight. Becoming an inclusive leader is a gradual process, one that involves adapting behavior step by step. It's important to reflect regularly, returning to these principles as a guide, and focusing on making small but impactful changes. By coming back to these pages, you'll remind yourself of what to focus on and how to ensure that every voice is heard, valued, and considered in shaping the future of the organization.

Leading with Inclusivity

Diverse teams thrive in environments where every voice, regardless of background or identity, is valued and heard. Without diverse leadership, unique and innovative ideas from minority groups, including women and LGBTQ+ individuals, often get overlooked. This not only stifles innovation but also leads to missed market opportunities. To foster this inclusivity, leaders should cultivate a "speak-up" culture by implementing six behaviors: [127]

- **Ensure all team members have a voice:** Make it clear that everyone's input is valued.

- **Create a safe space for innovative ideas:** Encourage creative thinking without fear of judgment.

- **Delegate decision-making authority:** Empower your team to make decisions.

- **Share successes:** Celebrate the wins together.

- **Offer constructive feedback:** Provide feedback that helps your team grow.

- **Act on team input:** Show that you value their ideas by taking action.

This approach not only sparks innovation but also enhances employee satisfaction and retention. It ensures that decision-making processes benefit from a variety of perspectives, enriching the company's strategic approach and fostering a truly inclusive workplace environment.

Creating Safe Spaces: Nurturing Creativity and Openness

Creating safe spaces goes beyond physical areas. Cultivate a culture where everyone feels comfortable and empowered to share their ideas and perspectives. These spaces promote psychological safety and openness, celebrating diversity of thought.

Safe spaces enhance engagement, foster innovation, and support mental health in an increasingly diverse workforce. It allows different perspectives to flourish, enabling individuals from various backgrounds to express themselves without fear of judgment or retribution. This is especially crucial for minority groups who might otherwise feel marginalized or unheard.

Creating an inclusive and safe environment means making sure everyone feels comfortable expressing their true selves. Here are some practical ways to achieve that in your workplace:[128]

- **Non-Judgmental Listening Sessions:** Set up regular sessions where employees can share their thoughts and experiences without fear of judgment. Make sure these sessions are facilitated in a way that values everyone's input equally.

- **Feedback Mechanisms:** Establish anonymous feedback systems to help employees voice concerns or suggestions they might not feel comfortable sharing openly. Take this feedback seriously and act on it whenever possible.

- **Inclusive Team Meetings:** Structure meetings so everyone has a chance to contribute. Rotate meeting leadership or set clear agendas that include time for each member to speak.

- **Training and Workshops:** Conduct regular training sessions and workshops on Diversity, Equity, and Inclusion to create a shared understanding and promote a more inclusive culture.

Here are some examples of organizations with successful inclusive communication practices:

- **Google:** As of January 2025, Google's Psychological Safety program focuses on creating a work environment where everyone feels safe to take risks and share innovative ideas. Their program involves encouraging employees to spend 20% of their time on projects of personal interest, offering feedback forums to promote transparency and training on communication skills like active listening and empathy.[129] However, in February 2025, Google significantly scaled back its DEI efforts, including removing Pride Month and Black History Month from shared company calendars.[130] While this is still a good example of upholding psychological safety, recent moves suggest that these protections may not be extended equally to all employees moving forward.

- **Salesforce:** Salesforce leadership has implemented Equality Circles, which are internal employee gatherings to share, process, and support one another during times of crisis. This initiative fosters a supportive and inclusive environment for all employees.[131]

- **Accenture:** Accenture's Psychological Safety program focuses on fostering a work environment where trust, openness, and transparency are prioritized, ensuring that employees feel safe to express themselves and contribute ideas without fear of negative consequences. They use a tool called InsightScan to assess team dynamics, determining levels of engagement and psychological safety. Accenture emphasized the importance of empathetic leadership, encouraging transparency in handling conflict, and training teams for both immediate and long-term psychological safety in diverse in-person and virtual work environments.[132] In February 2025, Accenture announced it would be "sunsetting" its diversity goals and career development programs for underrepresented groups, citing recent executive orders and shifting political pressures.[133] It is unclear how this will impact their psychological safety program, but it remains a strong example of how to foster psychological safety at work.

Supporting Transitions

Leaders should foster a workplace where gender transitions are genuinely supported, not merely accommodated. When employees undergo gender transitions (or other significant life changes), how leaders respond can significantly impact the employee's experience and overall workplace inclusivity. Research shows that senior leaders who consistently model trans-inclusive behaviors help create a supportive environment for transgender and nonbinary employees.[134]

Leadership support during transitions is crucial. Individuals contemplating or undergoing gender transitions often face anxiety about colleagues' and superiors' reactions. Visible support from top leaders sets the tone for acceptance and inclusion throughout the organization.

Here are some ways leadership can support gender transitions:[135]

- **Model Trans-Inclusive Behaviors:** Demonstrate trans-inclusive behaviors, such as using correct names and pronouns, supporting gender-inclusive dress codes, and advocating for gender-neutral restrooms.

- **Participate in Trans-Specific Initiatives:** Engage in trans-specific initiatives by attending or presenting at conferences and events focused on transgender issues, showing your commitment to understanding and addressing these challenges.

- **Publicly Champion Inclusivity:** Public statements from top leaders that champion inclusion and diversity, including gender diversity, send a powerful message throughout the organization. Use your platform to advocate for inclusive policies, promote diversity and inclusion training, and encourage a culture of respect.

- **Provide Practical Support:** Ensure that practical measures are in place to assist employees during transitions. This may involve working with various departments to create clear guidelines on items such as restroom usage, name changes in systems and records, security badges, healthcare, and dress code modifications.

- **Offer Guidance and Resources:** Offer guidance and direct employees undergoing transitions to relevant resources, support groups, and networks. This proactive approach ensures that employees have access to any assistance they may need.

Promoting Allyship and Inclusivity Within the Workplace

Allyship involves advocating for and supporting transgender and nonbinary individuals, along with others who belong to marginalized or underrepresented groups. Being an ally means recognizing that every employee, regardless of their gender identity, deserves respect, understanding, and validation. Fostering allyship means using your privilege to uplift others and create a more equitable and welcoming environment. Here are some strategies for promoting allyship within your organization:

- **Workshops and Training:** Organizations can hold sessions to educate employees on allyship and becoming effective allies. These sessions can help individuals understand gender diversity, address unconscious biases, and provide tools and recommendations for supportive actions.

- **Mentorship Programs:** Pairing employees from diverse backgrounds with supportive managers or leaders provides guidance on workplace dynamics while fostering an environment where individuals feel comfortable being authentic. This relationship allows allies in leadership positions to advocate for, support, and elevate underrepresented individuals, contributing to a more inclusive and supportive organizational culture.

- **Resource Sharing:** Provide accessible resources, such as articles, videos, and webinars to help employees learn more about gender identity and inclusive practices. These resources empower individuals to educate themselves and engage in meaningful conversations.

- **Allyship in Action:** Lead by example to encourage employees to visibly show their allyship where possible—whether by incorporating pronouns in their email signatures, ID badges, or virtual communication platforms, or by consistently using correct pronouns in conversations. This simple gesture creates an atmosphere of inclusivity and safety.

- **Normalizing Pronoun Usage and Inclusive Language:** Use correct pronouns and inclusive language in daily interactions to affirm and support transgender and nonbinary employees.

- **Leadership Support for Transitioning Employees:** Leaders should support employees through their transition journey by engaging in empathetic and informed conversations, using inclusive language, and assisting with workplace adjustments such as name changes and healthcare benefits. Understanding that transitioning is a deeply personal and nuanced experience, leaders should validate employees' gender identities, help create a supportive plan for their transition at work, and advocate for their needs.[136]

- **Supportive Supervisor Responses to Identity Disclosure:** Supervisors' responses to employees disclosing a stigmatized identity, like being transgender, shape the employee's job satisfaction and overall well-being. Positive and empathetic responses can significantly impact these individuals' work experience and feelings of inclusion.[137] Leaders should be trained and prepared to respond supportively to disclosures of gender identity, ensuring that transgender employees feel respected, valued, and understood in their work environment.

Personal Story: The Importance of Allyship

During a networking event, I encountered a situation that underscored the importance of allyship and gender-inclusive practices. At the time, though, I was just quietly miserable, feeling the tension of not wanting to stand out.

The event name badges didn't have a designated space for pronouns, which posed a challenge for me, and likely for others who didn't want to be misgendered.

I decided not to add my pronouns to my badge. It wasn't because I didn't want to, but because no one else had their pronouns listed; I didn't want to be "that person" with "they/them" scribbled in by hand. Marginalized people don't always want to stand out. If even one cisgender person had listed their pronouns, it would have signaled to me that someone in the room was safe. It would've given me the confidence to list mine.

Initially, I made the decision whether to correct someone who misgendered me based on each individual interaction. But as the event went on, some people I knew made a point of using my pronouns in front of others, which eased the pressure on me and made me feel less alone. Without them, I probably would have left early. Their presence provided a sense of belonging and allowed me a little more room to be myself, even in a setting that wasn't explicitly inclusive.

Small actions, like listing pronouns and gendering me correctly in front of others, create an atmosphere where people feel safe being their true selves. When that's missing, it creates a barrier, albeit possibly unintentional. Allies can break down that barrier just by showing up and being visible in their support.

Using privilege to help those without it gives us all a voice.

Cultivating Continuous Learning and Growth

Leaders should focus on designing and implementing training programs that address the nuances of gender diversity. This involves:

- **Tailoring Content:** Ensure that the training content is relevant, engaging, and updated regularly to reflect the latest insights and best practices in gender inclusion.

- **Mandatory Participation:** Make inclusion training mandatory to underscore its importance and ensure uniform exposure across the organization.

- **Frequency and Consistency:** Regular training sessions or workshops help keep the conversation on inclusivity alive and relevant.

- **Empowering Through Knowledge**
  - **Expanding Scope:** Gender inclusion should be part of a broader discussion on diversity and inclusion, preventing singling out and normalizing the importance of understanding all aspects of diversity.

- o **Interactive and Engaging Sessions:** Use interactive formats like workshops, role-playing, and group discussions to make training programs more impactful and memorable. I typically find that starting with low-pressure activities in early sessions helps avoid putting participants on the spot. As they become more comfortable, interactive elements like role-playing can be introduced.

- **Measuring Impact and Feedback**
  - o **Feedback Mechanisms:** Implement feedback channels to gather insights from employees on the effectiveness of training programs. This feedback can guide future training and policy adjustments.
  - o **Tracking Progress:** Regularly assess the impact of these training sessions through surveys and discussions to understand their effectiveness and areas for improvement.

Leaders must recognize that training and awareness programs are not one-time events but ongoing processes that evolve with our understanding of gender diversity and inclusion.

Case Study: Marc Benioff and Salesforce: A Leadership Blueprint

Marc Benioff, Chair, CEO, and Co-Founder of Salesforce, leads one of the world's largest enterprise software companies, a Fortune 150 firm with over 70,000 employees. Under his leadership, Salesforce is guided by five core values, trust, customer success, innovation, equality, and sustainability, demonstrating a commitment to both business growth and social responsibility.

Benioff's stance on equality has made headlines. In 2015, he canceled Salesforce events in Indiana after the state passed a law allowing businesses to refuse service to LGBTQ+ customers. The following year, despite Salesforce having no major presence in North Carolina, he publicly condemned North Carolina's HB2 Bathroom Law—which required individuals to use bathrooms that corresponded with the gender assigned at birth—and urged other CEOs to speak out.[138]

Beyond advocacy, Salesforce has implemented many gender-inclusive benefits for its employees, including reimbursement for gender-affirming medical services, recovery leave, legal fee support, wardrobe reimbursement, counseling services, and more. Benioff's commitment extends beyond rhetoric, ensuring that transgender and nonbinary employees in all Salesforce global locations are supported throughout their transition journeys.[139] More recently, Benioff announced that Salesforce would pay to relocate employees who feel unsafe in their current city or state due to political conditions, framing this as a common-sense business practice.[140]

Benioff's leadership exemplifies how business leaders can drive change by aligning corporate values with tangible actions. He consistently uses social media and public platforms to advocate for LGBTQ+ rights, reinforcing the message that inclusion is not just a policy but a fundamental value at Salesforce. This commitment to equality benefits Salesforce in many ways: boosting recruitment, morale, and even sales. As Benioff himself has said, "Our employees come here knowing that this is something that is extremely important to us. Business is the greatest platform for affecting change."[141]

While Benioff has long been a champion for equality, leadership legacies are never static. Recent reports suggest that Benioff may be warming to President Trump, raising questions about whether his actions reflect a pragmatic effort to safeguard Salesforce under an administration openly hostile to DEI efforts or indicate a broader shift in priorities.[142] At the time of this writing, it is unclear whether these decisions are strategic responses to political pressures or signal a deeper change in values. Whatever the future holds, Salesforce's previous commitments set a high bar for inclusion in the workplace.

In the years leading up to this moment, Benioff's leadership exemplified how business leaders could align corporate values with tangible actions to drive meaningful change. From championing LGBTQ+ rights to implementing groundbreaking gender-inclusive practices, Benioff's actions, particularly in standing up for transgender and nonbinary people both inside and outside Salesforce, offered a powerful blueprint for fostering equity and belonging. Whatever the future holds, his legacy as a vocal advocate during this period of his career remains an enduring example of how businesses can lead the charge for inclusion.

Addressing Resistance from Leaders and External Stakeholders

I'll be honest, I didn't want to write about this at all. I wish this wasn't an issue we had to face, but the reality is too important to ignore: resistance to transgender rights and challenges to gender inclusion at work are inevitable. Resistance to gender inclusion isn't happening in a vacuum—it's fueled by broader cultural and political movements. When political leaders dismantle DEI efforts and attempt to erase transgender and nonbinary people, it spreads anti-trans rhetoric that seeps into workplaces, emboldening opposition to inclusive practices. These actions encourage stakeholders to push back against inclusion, whether overtly or through passive discomfort shaped by misinformation. Acknowledging these influences doesn't excuse resistance—it creates space to understand the context so we can address it effectively.

You're here because you're ready to move forward, but not everyone is on the same page. Resistance from other leaders or external stakeholders such as vendors, business partners, or investors, often arises from discomfort or uncertainty. In my workshops, I make a point to acknowledge that this topic can be uncomfortable; it helps put people at ease because it's an honest recognition of their feelings.

By 2024, the US had broken its record for the fifth consecutive year, with hundreds of anti-trans bills considered across forty-three states.[143] The inauguration of the 2025 administration has intensified these efforts, with federal DEI rollbacks and public endorsements of anti-trans rhetoric emboldening similar state-level initiatives. Although many of these bills do not gather enough support to pass, the disinformation fueling them has a profound effect on public opinion. Large-scale disinformation campaigns, such as the twenty-million-dollar anti-trans ad blitz during the 2024 presidential campaign, continue to shape public discourse. Research shows that, even when these ads fail politically, they contribute to reduced public acceptance of trans people, spreading harmful misinformation that amplifies resistance.[144]

The same holds true in workplaces: resistance doesn't always stem from outright opposition but often comes from confusion and discomfort, shaped by the same misinformation driving anti-trans legislative efforts. Even in states actively securing protections for trans rights, resistance and discomfort can arise. Beyond the US, many countries also face legal and social restrictions on LGBTQ+ rights, adding further barriers to gender inclusion. No matter where your organization is located, fostering an inclusive, respectful workplace remains both essential and achievable.

Acknowledging these realities is critical to understanding the barriers you may face, but it doesn't change the ultimate goal of creating an environment where everyone feels respected and included.

Addressing resistance from leaders and external stakeholders involves a three-step approach: understanding the root of the resistance, addressing concerns and fears through education, and defining and upholding your company's inclusive practices. Each instance of resistance should cover all three steps to ensure a comprehensive response that meets concerns on both sides. That said, each situation will be unique; sometimes it's worth investing time in bringing someone along, and other times, walking away is the best option.

- **Understand the Root of Resistance:** The first step is to explore where resistance is coming from, shaped by personal, cultural, or professional factors. Create a non-judgmental space that acknowledges discomfort and encourages open dialogue. Each instance of resistance is unique. In the following chapter (Chapter 6), the section "Addressing Resistance from Employees" examines specific types of resistance and how to apply proactive or reactive strategies to address each effectively.

  o **Acknowledge Discomfort:** Recognize that discomfort is a natural response to discussions around gender inclusion and gender identity, especially if someone is engaging with the topic for the first time. Acknowledging the discomfort with them lets them feel safe to share more with you.

  o **Be Curious and Convey Understanding:** Ask open-ended questions to invite individuals to share their concerns and perspectives. For example, you could ask, "Are there any aspects of this initiative that you're unsure about?"

  o **Actively Listen and Avoid Assumptions:** Allow them space to articulate their concerns without jumping to conclusions. Active listening means focusing on their words without being distracted, avoiding interruptions, and paraphrasing or asking clarifying questions to show them that you hear their concerns. Use verbal affirmations, such as, "I see," or "I understand."

- **Address Concerns with Awareness and Education:** Once the root causes of resistance are identified, the next step is to present facts and educate in a way that fosters empathy. Use personal stories, real-world examples, and relevant data to humanize the issue and address specific concerns, without conveying judgment. By offering clear explanations and evidence, you can help leaders and stakeholders better understand the importance of gender inclusion in both human and business terms.

  o **Build Empathy Through Stories:** Share real-life examples to humanize gender inclusion and create emotional connections. For example, you might share a case study of a company that successfully implemented inclusive practices and saw improvements as a result. For example, refer to the case study on Caroline Farberger in "Why Gender Inclusion at Work Matters" (Chapter 1).

  o **Explain the Business Case:** Demonstrate how gender inclusion positively impacts business outcomes. Many leaders are more likely to support these initiatives if they understand the financial benefits. For instance, you could reference the data showing that inclusive workplaces experience higher employee satisfaction, retention, and profitability. Refer to "Why Gender Inclusion at Work Matters" (Chapter 1) for the economic advantages of inclusion, innovation, and the cost of exclusion.

- o **Highlight Cultural and Social Awareness:** Highlight how gender inclusion is part of a larger cultural shift. Organizations that fall behind on inclusion risk damaging their public image and missing out on talent. For example, you can point out that younger, socially conscious consumers tend to favor brands and work for companies that embrace diversity and inclusion. "Why Gender Inclusion at Work Matters" (Chapter 1) includes information on the growing influence of Generation Z and improving corporate image.

- o **Define Terminology:** Some resistance comes from a lack of understanding of gender-related terms. Explain concepts like "nonbinary," "cisgender," and "gender identity." Bust myths about transgender and nonbinary people as they arise. Correct information, such as the misunderstanding that "they/them" is not a grammatically correct singular pronoun. See "Terminology" (Chapter 2) for useful information.

- o **Reinforce That This Is a Journey:** It's important to reassure those you are speaking with that inclusion is a long-term effort, and they aren't expected to master everything immediately. Offer support, training, and resources to help them along the way.

- **Define and Uphold Inclusive Practices:** Once you have identified the root of resistance and educated them on the impact of inclusion from both a human and business perspective, the last step is to clearly outline your company's gender-inclusive practices and policies. This reinforces your transparency and sets expectations for how to move forward.

  - o **Provide Basic Communication Strategies:** Outline practical, inclusive communication practices, such as using gender-neutral language, respecting pronouns, and practicing inclusive non-verbal communication. Refer to "Principles of Gender-Neutral Communication" (Chapter 3) and "Strategies for Gender-Inclusive Communication" (Chapter 4) for effective communication strategies.

o **Detail Relevant Policies:** Share the specific gender-inclusive policies relevant to the leader's department or stakeholder's area of responsibility. Provide concrete examples or guidelines, such as inclusive hiring practices, HR benefits, or gender-neutral marketing and branding. Refer to the relevant chapters in this book for additional guidance tailored to specific departments.

o **Offer Support and Resources:** Assure leaders or stakeholders that they'll receive support throughout the process. Offer them a roadmap, such as an internal DEI team, an HR contact, or even this book as a guide to help them work through the ongoing implementation.

o **Set Clear Expectations:** State that inclusion is a non-negotiable part of the organization's core values. Make it clear that feedback is valued, but inclusivity must be upheld across all departments.

o **Stay Resilient Amid External Pressures:** Even in a polarized climate, staying aligned with core organizational values is critical. While external pressures, including political shifts, may encourage some stakeholders to backtrack, companies that uphold their inclusive practices not only protect their employees but also strengthen their credibility and resilience. Inclusion is not a trend; it's a long-term commitment to equity and belonging that can't waver with political tides.

○ **Explain Consequences of Non-Compliance:** For external stakeholders or resistant leaders, set boundaries by explaining that failing to support inclusive values may impact ongoing partnerships. Framing this as a boundary rather than a threat reinforces that it's about alignment with the company's core mission.

If resistance persists despite efforts to educate and engage, it may be necessary to reconsider relationships with stakeholders or leaders who do not align with the company's inclusive values. While the goal is always to bring others along, sometimes staying true to your core values means making hard calls about who remains part of your network.

Summary Checklist for Leadership

Building Blocks of Inclusive Leadership

- ☐ Exhibit commitment to diversity and inclusion.
- ☐ Demonstrate awareness of personal and organizational biases.
- ☐ Show humility and seek input from others.
- ☐ Encourage diverse perspectives in decision-making.

Inclusive Leadership Behaviors

- ☐ Practice active listening and empathy.
- ☐ Encourage participation from all team members.
- ☐ Communicate transparently and advocate for diversity.
- ☐ Mitigate bias in team decisions and actions.

Empowering Voices for Inclusive Leadership

- ☐ Ensure all team members have a voice and create a safe space for innovation.
- ☐ Share successes and offer constructive feedback.
- ☐ Act on team input and delegate decision-making authority.

Creating Safe Spaces

- ☐ Establish non-judgmental listening sessions.
- ☐ Implement anonymous feedback mechanisms.
- ☐ Structure inclusive team meetings and provide diversity training.

Supporting Transitions

- ☐ Model trans-inclusive behaviors.
- ☐ Engage in trans-specific initiatives.
- ☐ Provide practical support and resources for transitioning employees.

Promoting Allyship and Inclusivity

☐ Offer workshops and training on allyship.

☐ Implement mentorship programs and share educational resources.

☐ Encourage pronoun usage and inclusive language.

Cultivating Continuous Learning

☐ Design and implement regular gender-inclusion training programs.

☐ Tailor content and ensure mandatory participation.

☐ Use interactive and engaging formats for training.

☐ Implement feedback channels and track progress.

Addressing Resistance

☐ Understand the root of resistance.

☐ Address concerns with awareness and education.

☐ Define and uphold inclusive practices.

CHAPTER 06

HUMAN RESOURCES:
FOSTERING AN INCLUSIVE CULTURE

In its early days, the "Personnel Department" was created to manage the basics: hiring, firing, and keeping employees productive. It wasn't a department known for driving change. But in the 1950s and 60s, things began to shift. With the rise of industrial psychology and a focus on employee well-being, HR started to evolve. Companies began to see that taking care of employees was good for business.

By the 1970s, HR was on the frontlines of social change, implementing anti-discrimination policies born out of the Civil Rights Act of 1964 and the Women's rights movement. Women finally gained the right to refuse sexual advances from their bosses without fear of being fired and could no longer be terminated for being pregnant. These victories were hard-won and long overdue, but it's important to remember that the fight for gender equality didn't, and shouldn't, end there.

My point? Feminism isn't just for women. As Jane Fonda said, "Feminism is not gender-specific." It's about believing and supporting that "every human being, no matter what the gender, has a right to opportunity, to chances, to equality, to fairness."[145]

That means recognizing that trans men, nonbinary employees, and anyone who doesn't fit into traditional gender categories deserves the same protections and opportunities that women continue to fight for. HR is the champion of this inclusivity, driving the changes that ensure everyone is treated fairly.

The evolution of HR from "Personnel" to a key driver of Diversity, Equity, and Inclusion (DEI) has been decades in the making, but its mission is clear: to create workplaces where everyone can thrive.

Advocating for Inclusivity

A comprehensive DEI strategy is critical for promoting a safer and more inclusive environment, especially for trans and nonbinary employees. HR departments play a central role in designing and delivering this training across the organization.

- **Identify the Need for DEI Education:** Recognize and demonstrate the need for DEI training within the organization. Gather data, highlight industry trends, and present case studies to illustrate the tangible benefits of such training to leadership and decision-makers.

- **Select Comprehensive DEI Programs:** Once the need is established and approved, identify and select comprehensive training programs that cover a wide range of DEI topics, including gender inclusion, cultural competency, unconscious bias, and more. Develop programs that are engaging, relevant, and applicable to everyday work scenarios.

- **Customize Training to Organizational Needs:** Every organization is unique, and DEI training should reflect this. Tailor these programs to suit your specific organizational culture, addressing the challenges and opportunities within your workforce. Each department and profession within an organization may have unique DEI training needs. For example:

o **Recruitment Teams:** Recruitment teams must be particularly vigilant during interviews, ensuring that questions and conversations reflect inclusion. They must also be skilled in reading nonverbal cues that may reveal anti-inclusion biases in candidates. This will help mitigate the risk of hiring individuals whose attitudes might clash with the organization's commitment to diversity. We will explore recruitment strategies in more detail later in this chapter.

o **Law Firms:** Certain practice areas like elder law, family law, and trusts and estates require extra sensitivity to avoid reinforcing harmful family dynamics or microaggressions. Additionally, lawyers and paralegals who draft legal documents must be well-versed in inclusive writing for court documents and other legal proceedings. For more on this topic, refer to "Legal: Advocating for Inclusion" (Chapter 7).

o **Patient Care Providers:** Healthcare workers, especially in patient-facing roles like doctors, nurses, and therapists, must be trained to provide gender-affirming care. Even if they are not directly involved in providing these services, they need to understand the unique experiences and healthcare needs of their transgender and nonbinary patients.

o **Substance Use Treatment Providers:** Providers in substance use treatment need training to understand the higher rates of substance use disorders and the specific stressors that may contribute to these issues. Training in these areas will allow substance use treatment providers to offer more effective and compassionate care.

- **Implement Training Across Levels:** Inclusivity is every-one's responsibility. Ensure that training is offered to all employees, from executives to entry-level positions, even those that might be considered outside the core focus of the business. Every role in an organization contributes to the culture of inclusivity. For example:

  o **Custodial Services:** These employees are often assumed to have little interaction with customers or clients, but that's rarely the case. Custodial staff fre-quently interact with both employees and visitors (or patients, in the case of healthcare), and their presence contributes to the overall environment and experience.

  o **Administrative Support:** Receptionists and clerks are often the first point of contact for customers, clients, or patients, and their behavior sets the tone for inclusion.

  o **Security Personnel:** Security teams frequently interact with employees and visitors, so they should be trained to manage sensitive situations inclusively. Refer to "Security and Safety Services: Protecting with Inclusive Awareness" for more information on this.

- **Offer Multiple Training Formats:** Training must be acces-sible to all employees by offering a variety of formats and accommodating different needs. This includes scheduling multiple sessions to accommodate shift workers, offering e-learning or online modules for flexibility, and providing private or small group training sessions in organizations with clear leadership hierarchies where employees may feel hesitant to ask questions in front of their boss.

- **Follow-Up and Reinforcement:** Post-training, estab-lish mechanisms for follow-up and reinforcement of the training content. This could be through periodic refreshers, integrating DEI discussions in regular meetings, or even incorporating DEI metrics in performance evaluations to encourage ongoing engagement.

- **Ongoing Training and Education Within HR:** Continuous education and training in diversity and inclusivity are both beneficial and necessary. The dynamics of gender identity and inclusivity evolve rapidly; it's important to keep all employees informed. For example, years ago, "preferred pronouns" was considered an appropriate term and today, we know it isn't. Some effective education methods include:

    o **Regular Workshops and Seminars:** Schedule regular sessions on the latest in diversity and inclusivity, covering everything from basic gender identity concepts to complex discussions about intersectionality and systemic biases.

    o **Collaboration with Experts:** Partner with diversity and inclusion experts or specialized organizations to gain valuable insights and up-to-date information.

    o **Interactive Learning Modules:** Develop or use interactive online training modules that mix videos, quizzes, and discussion forums, allowing HR professionals to learn at their own pace while staying engaged.

- **Create an Open Dialogue:** Facilitate an open dialogue around DEI issues, encouraging employees to share their experiences and perspectives. This not only helps reinforce training but also contributes to a culture where diversity and inclusion are ongoing conversations rather than one-time training topics.

- **Creating Spaces for Private or Anonymous Questions:** Employees must feel safe to ask questions, especially those they might find embarrassing or sensitive. Anonymous questions ensure that everyone's concerns are addressed without fear of judgment, increasing engagement and enhancing the effectiveness of inclusivity training.

- o **Online Sessions:** To encourage participation from those who may be hesitant to speak up publicly, I always have a second host who will receive direct questions and read them anonymously. This co-host can decide if the question is best to ask in the moment or saved until later.

- o **In-Person Sessions:** Provide a system where attendees can submit written questions during breaks. I use 3x5 cards that are distributed to all attendees, collected after the break, and addressed at the end of the session.

- o **Offline Mechanisms:** Implement methods for employees to ask questions or provide feedback anonymously outside of training sessions. This can include suggestion boxes, anonymous email submissions, or online portals. This information can help HR determine what topics need more attention in future training sessions.

- **Evaluate and Evolve Training Programs:** Continuously evaluate the effectiveness of training programs. Gather feedback from employees, analyze how training impacts workplace culture, and stay up to date with DEI best practices to refine and adapt the content.

- **Inclusive Policy Review:** In addition to evaluating training, regularly review and update organizational policies to ensure they reflect the latest understanding and practices in gender inclusion. This should be a collaborative process involving input from diverse employees, department leaders, and external experts. The next section in this document will review details about crafting inclusive policies and practices.

By playing this proactive and central role in DEI education, Human Resources helps organizations meet legal standards while creating a safe and affirming space for transgender and nonbinary employees. It's more than respecting pronouns or identities; it's about actively dismantling barriers that prevent these employees from feeling fully included and supported in their workplace. A DEI approach rooted in understanding the unique challenges of trans and nonbinary individuals fosters a culture of true belonging, where they can contribute fully and authentically, ultimately enhancing both individual well-being and organizational success.

To effectively lead inclusion efforts, HR professionals must continually educate themselves on gender identity and inclusion. Some of the best methods for this are as follows:

- **Subscriptions to Relevant Publications:** Stay abreast of new findings and evolving best practices. Subscribe to journals, magazines, and online platforms that regularly publish articles and research on gender identity and inclusion.

- **Networking and Professional Groups:** Participate in professional groups or networks that focus on diversity and inclusion. Networking with peers from other organizations can provide fresh perspectives and shared learning opportunities.

- **Attending Conferences:** Attend national or international conferences on diversity and inclusion. These events are not only educational but also provide opportunities to learn about the challenges and successes of other organizations.

- **Feedback and Reflection Sessions:** Organize internal feedback sessions where HR professionals can share what they learn and discuss how to apply new knowledge in their daily practices. These sessions can also serve as a platform for reflecting on current policies and brainstorming improvements.

By prioritizing training and continuous learning, HR can effectively guide their organizations through the complexities of gender identity and inclusion, ensuring a respectful and welcoming environment for all employees.

To effectively demonstrate inclusive behavior, HR professionals can implement the following strategies:

- **Active Listening and Open Communication:** Practice active listening, creating a safe space where employees feel heard and respected. Be attentive, empathetic, and understand issues from different perspectives, especially those different from your own.

- **Continuous Education:** Continuously educate yourself on gender diversity and inclusivity. Attend workshops, participate in webinars, and stay updated with the latest research and best practices. This ongoing learning helps you address gender identity issues sensitively and knowledgeably.

- **Inclusive Language:** Use inclusive language in all HR communications. This means using gender-neutral terms, respecting pronouns, and acknowledging the diverse spectrum of gender identities. The language HR uses can set the tone for the entire organization.

- **Fair and Inclusive Decision-Making:** Make decisions with inclusivity in mind, whether in hiring, promotions, or conflict resolution. Recognize unconscious biases and consider diverse perspectives. Strategies that aim to acknowledge underrepresented employees should be sincere and meaningful, avoiding the pitfall of tokenization. Tokenization occurs when individuals from underrepresented groups are only recognized or valued to fulfill a diversity quota rather than for their actual contributions and expertise. Celebrate the unique talents and perspectives of every team member genuinely.

- **Visibility and Advocacy:** Visibly advocate for gender inclusivity. Support inclusion initiatives, participate in diversity and inclusion forums, and openly celebrate a variety of gender-related events beyond Pride Month, such as International Pronouns Day or Transgender Day of Visibility. Rather than sending a simple email blast, organize a fundraiser or participate in community events to demonstrate the organization's commitment. By recognizing and celebrating these important milestones, HR can foster awareness and solidarity across the organization.

- **Feedback and Improvement:** Regularly seek feedback on inclusivity efforts through surveys, suggestion boxes, or check-ins with staff. Be open to feedback and ready to adjust strategies as needed.

Creating an inclusive workplace is a team effort, requiring HR, leadership, and various departments to work together. HR professionals serve as the linchpin in these collaborations, working closely with leaders and department heads to turn inclusion from policy into reality. This means actively engaging leadership to shape policies and guide the implementation of inclusive practices.

- **Initiating Cross-Departmental Dialogues:** Initiate and facilitate discussions on inclusion across departments. This involves organizing workshops, roundtable discussions, or informal gatherings where employees from different levels and functions come together to share perspectives, challenges, and ideas. These conversations help departments learn from each other and understand their colleagues' diverse needs.

- **Driving Inclusive Initiatives:** Spearhead initiatives that promote inclusivity, such as joint training programs or collaborative projects aimed at enhancing workplace diversity. By involving various departments in these initiatives, these efforts have a broader reach and deeper impact.

- **Supporting Departments in Implementation:** Beyond initiating discussions and programs, support departments as they implement inclusive practices. This can include providing resources, sharing best practices, or offering guidance on navigating complex situations related to inclusivity.

- **Ensuring Consistency Across the Organization:** Ensure that the inclusivity ethos is uniformly understood and applied, from the way meetings are conducted to how decisions are made. This uniform approach prevents silos and ensures that inclusivity is a shared responsibility across the organization.

Human Resource Information Systems (HRIS) and Payroll services should support tracking preferred names and pronouns, and ensure employees are not deadnamed. Work with IT to ensure that systems are effectively implemented. Additionally, be certain that any third-party software has pronouns and preferred name fields visible to all departments that access records. Refer to "IT: Ensuring Inclusive Systems and Networks" (Chapter 8) for more information on IT's role when integrating third-party solutions.

Key Features of Inclusive HRIS Systems:

- **Tracking Preferred Names and Pronouns:** Ensure the HRIS system has fields for both legal names and preferred names. Preferred names should be visible to all employees interacting with the system, while legal names are used only for official documentation and processes. Include a field for pronouns to ensure proper and respectful communication.

- **Handling Sex Assigned at Birth:** For benefits and compliance purposes, some systems may require information on sex assigned at birth. Ensure this information is handled sensitively and is not visible to all users.

- **Ensuring Continuity Across Departments:** Implement a system that ensures continuity in the use of preferred names across all departments. This prevents instances where different departments, like marketing and housing, might use different names for the same person.

Coworkers are key players in creating an inclusive workplace, especially when it comes to supporting transgender colleagues through their transitions. When coworkers show up with understanding and respect, it makes a world of difference in a transgender employee's job satisfaction and sense of belonging, helping create a space where everyone feels they fit in.

- **Understanding the Influence of Coworker Support:** Recent studies underscore that the satisfaction and comfort that transgender employees feel at work are significantly influenced not just by their ability to express their gender identity (known as action authenticity) but by their coworkers' understanding and acceptance of their gender identity (known as relational authenticity). This dual aspect of authenticity, being true to oneself and being recognized as such by others, is a cornerstone of a supportive work environment.[146]

- **Real-World Impact of Coworker Acceptance:** Stories from various workplace settings reveal the transformative power of coworker support. For instance, a transgender man working as a museum curator felt truly accepted when his colleagues included him as "one of the guys," marking a significant increase in his sense of belonging and job satisfaction. Another moving instance involved a trans woman in manufacturing who felt profound acceptance when a coworker invited her to dance, her first time in a dress at a company function, publicly acknowledging and supporting her identity. "His courage in accepting who I was in front of all our coworkers can bring me to tears to this day," she said. [147]

- **Promoting an Environment of Support and Inclusivity:** By creating a culture where every employee feels valued for who they are, businesses can foster an environment where transitions are smoother and transgender employees can thrive. Johnson & Johnson not only assists transitioning employees but also educates managers and coworkers to increase awareness and acceptance.[148]

Balancing State Laws and Federal Guidelines

In 2023, nine states passed laws restricting how pronouns were used in K-12 schools, preventing students and teachers from using language that didn't align with a person's assigned sex at birth. [149] At the time, these laws were largely limited to education settings, but advocates warned that this was just the beginning—that these restrictions could extend beyond schools and into broader workplace policies.

That warning became reality in 2025. The federal government implemented sweeping rollbacks that banned federal agencies from enforcing DEI-related workplace policies and introduced multiple executive orders aimed at eliminating legal recognition and protections for transgender people.[150] These orders included prohibiting gender-affirming care for minors,[151] banning transgender service members from the military,[152] and blocking transgender athletes from competing in sports.[153] In the wake of these directives, some states moved aggressively to further restrict trans rights in all areas of life. Alabama's SB79, for example, legally defines sex as strictly male or female and eliminates recognition of transgender and nonbinary identities in state records.[154]

These federal and state attacks directly contradict existing legal protections under Title VII of the Civil Rights Act, which prohibits sex-based workplace discrimination. The Equal Employment Opportunity Commission (EEOC) reinforced this in its 2024 workplace harassment guidance, stating that intentional misgendering could contribute to a hostile work environment.[155] Despite this, the administration is pressuring agencies to ignore long-standing protections—and some businesses are panicking, prematurely dismantling their own DEI initiatives.

So where does that leave HR? While the legal landscape is shifting, some things have not changed: Title VII still protects transgender employees, and courts are already blocking parts of the administration's anti-DEI orders.[156] It's critical that HR departments stay informed, hold firm to inclusion commitments, and avoid making hasty changes that could harm employees and weaken workplace culture.

Here are some strategies for HR:

- **Understand the Current Legal Landscape:** Gender identity remains a protected class under Title VII, and erasing or disregarding transgender employees' rights is both unethical and unlawful. While federal and state governments are attempting to roll back protections, businesses are not obligated to comply with policies that contradict established case law. HR professionals must be well-versed in both federal and state-level restrictions, as well as any remaining legal protections, to ensure that workplace policies align with civil rights laws rather than shifting political agendas. A proactive approach to workplace inclusivity is more critical than ever.

- **Stay Vigilant When Vetting Resources:** Historically, organizations such as the EEOC and SHRM have been strong advocates for workplace inclusion. However, in the current political climate, some professional groups have begun shifting their guidance to align with federal rollbacks rather than existing legal protections. In February 2025, the EEOC took an unprecedented step by moving to drop active gender discrimination cases, signaling a complete reversal in its enforcement of workplace protections.[157] Likewise, SHRM has begun advising early compliance with restrictive state laws rather than supporting HR leaders in maintaining inclusive policies.[158] These shifts make it essential for HR professionals to critically assess workplace guidance from external organizations and stay informed through independent legal experts and civil rights groups rather than relying on institutions that may be prioritizing political expediency over employee rights.

- **Consult Employment Law Experts and Civil Rights Organizations:** With ongoing lawsuits challenging these rollbacks, HR should work with employment law experts and civil rights organizations to determine the best course of action for their organization. If an employer faces legal threats—such as the potential loss of federal funding for maintaining inclusion policies—consulting state or local resources can provide avenues for legal recourse. Businesses do not have to comply early with unlawful mandates and may have grounds to challenge them in court.

- **Monitor Lawsuits That Could Reinstate Protections:** Multiple lawsuits are challenging these rollbacks in federal courts, and businesses must be prepared to adjust policies if legal protections are reinstated. Employers who prematurely eliminate inclusion policies may face backlash or be forced to reverse course later, damaging employee retention and recruitment as well as brand reputation. Staying informed on court rulings ensures that HR can navigate these changes strategically while maintaining consistency in their inclusion commitments.

- **Develop State-Specific Risk Mitigation Strategies:** Organizations operating in multiple states must develop location-specific policies that uphold their commitment to inclusion while accounting for legal risks. Some companies may choose to maintain consistent inclusion policies across all locations, while others may adapt state-by-state strategies based on evolving legal challenges. Regardless of approach, employers should not preemptively weaken protections out of fear of legal repercussions. Instead, they should resist unnecessary rollbacks and allow the legal process to play out.

- **Prepare for Internal Conflicts Over Pronoun Policies:** With anti-DEI rhetoric on the rise, some employees may feel emboldened to challenge workplace inclusion policies.

HR should proactively reinforce that respectful workplace policies apply to all employees, regardless of personal beliefs. Managers must be trained to de-escalate pronoun-related conflicts before they become workplace disruptions and to handle noncompliance in a way that aligns with company values and legal protections. Refer to the "Addressing Resistance from Employees" section of this chapter for specific strategies on managing internal resistance effectively.

- **Protect Transgender and Nonbinary Employees:** As the federal government dismantles DEI initiatives and wages a systematic attempt to erase transgender people from public life, transgender and nonbinary employees face increased risks—not only in the workplace but also to their overall well-being. HR must take proactive steps to support these employees, recognizing that inaction contributes to harm. Organizations should explore all available options to provide gender-affirming healthcare, offer legal resources for ID and name changes, and establish safe internal reporting channels for discrimination concerns. Failing to act not only exposes businesses to potential legal consequences but also damages employee morale, retention, and overall workplace culture.

The fight for transgender workplace protections is far from over. The courts, political shifts, and corporate responses will continue shaping the landscape in unpredictable ways. While businesses cannot control federal or state policies, they *can* control how they support employees and uphold their values. The choices made now—whether to resist or comply with these rollbacks—will define workplace culture and shape the future of inclusion for years to come.

Workplace Policies and Practices

Creating a truly inclusive workplace starts with inclusive language and policies. As our understanding of gender diversity grows, so should our approach to inclusion. Workplace policies aren't set in stone; they're living practices that need regular updates to stay in tune with evolving insights.

Recognizing and Using Neopronouns

As discussed in "Why Gender Inclusion at Work Matters" (Chapter 1), Generation Z is an essential talent pool for today's workforce. With a fresh, often more fluid understanding of gender identity, Gen Z is helping to bring neopronouns into everyday language and workplace culture. By using neopronouns, HR professionals demonstrate a strong commitment to respect and inclusivity, which is vital for attracting and retaining a diverse workforce.

In addition to adopting neopronouns, HR plays a key role in educating the broader workforce about their significance. Through training sessions, workshops, and daily interactions, HR can lead by example, reinforcing the importance of embracing diverse gender identities in the workplace. This not only supports employees who use neopronouns but also fosters an environment where everyone feels valued and included.

Employee Handbook and Policy Documents

Effective workplace communication relies on clear, unambiguous language to shape interactions and cultivate success. Employee handbooks, policy documents, and other written materials should be carefully crafted to use gender-neutral language. This approach not only ensures clarity but also affirms the diverse range of gender identities present within the organization.

- **Gender-Neutral Pronouns:** There are so many ways to rewrite an employee handbook to remove gendered pronouns. Refer to the section "Writing with Respect: Written Communication Strategies" in "Strategies for Gender-Inclusive Communication" (Chapter 4) for examples.

- **Language around Pregnancy and Parental Leave:** Terms like "pregnant person" instead of "pregnant woman" or "parental/family leave" instead of "maternity/paternity leave" can be used universally.

- **Healthcare Terms:** In medical settings, using terms like "internal reproductive organs" instead of "female organs" or "chest" instead of "breasts" for transgender individuals can make healthcare more inclusive.

- **Familial Relationships:** Use gender-neutral family titles, such as "sibling" instead of "brother" or "sister." Refer to the section on "Words for Everyone: Universal Terminology" in "Principles of Gender-Neutral Communication" (Chapter 3) for detailed information.

- **Job Titles:** Use job titles that are free of gender connotations, such as "firefighter" instead of "fireman." The previously mentioned section on "Words for Everyone: Universal Terminology" in "Principles of Gender-Neutral Communication" (Chapter 3) covers more detailed information on job titles.

- **Spousal Benefits:** Refer to spousal or partner benefits inclusively, allowing employees with nonbinary partners to feel included.

Dress codes often contain references that are inadvertently gender-specific. To embrace diversity, review and revise dress codes to eliminate any gendered language or expectations. By adopting gender-neutral guidelines, companies not only promote inclusivity but also respect individual self-expression.

Instead of specifying attire based on traditional gender roles (e.g., men should wear suits, women should wear skirts or dresses), use terms that describe the clothing itself, like "business professional" or "business casual," followed by examples that are not gender-specific.

While preparing for my keynote at a very traditional club in Philadelphia, I received an email the day before the event reminding attendees of the dress code. It specified clothing options based on gender: men were expected to wear collared shirts or turtlenecks with slacks, while women were instructed to wear dresses, blouses, or skirts. Even the shoe guidelines were gendered. It was a stark reminder of how deeply rooted and outdated some gender norms still are.

I brought it up during the training when we reached the topic of dress codes. I read the email aloud, and everyone laughed at how antiquated it seemed. But when I asked how many of them had reviewed their own company's dress code in the last year or two, no one raised their hand. Just imagine how a nonbinary person would feel starting work at a business with a dress code like this!

We discussed the evolution of dress codes; remember when pantyhose were required attire? Many organizations still have policies that are just as outdated, often going unnoticed because no one thinks to review them. By drawing attention to this, I encouraged the group to take a closer look at their own policies to ensure they reflect the inclusive and equitable values they strive for today. I got an email the following week from someone who attended this talk and reviewed her company's dress code. Sure enough, it had been so long since the last review that it still discouraged open-toed shoes in the office and set hair length limits for men and women! It was a valuable reminder that even well-meaning companies can unintentionally create environments that don't feel as welcoming as they should.

Anti-Discrimination, Anti-Harassment, and Anti-Bullying Policies

A safe and inclusive workplace starts with solid anti-discrimination, anti-harassment, and anti-bullying policies. These policies should clearly state the company's dedication to maintaining an environment free from any form of discrimination or harassment. By adopting a zero-tolerance stance, employers show they prioritize every employee's well-being and dignity.

Handling bias and microaggressions proactively is essential in creating a respectful workplace and can help prevent escalation into more serious discrimination or harassment complaints. By addressing these subtle, often unconscious behaviors early, organizations can foster an environment where respect is prioritized, reducing the likelihood of formal complaints and creating a more positive workplace for everyone.

Here are some actionable steps to help recognize and address these issues and create an environment where employees feel comfortable reporting them:

- **Bias, Emotional Intelligence, and Empathy Training:** Provide regular training sessions to help employees understand bias, microaggressions, and the importance of emotional intelligence. These sessions should include examples of common microaggressions, differences between conscious and unconscious bias, and strategies for identifying and addressing their own biases.

- **Encourage Open Dialogue:** Foster an environment where employees feel comfortable discussing their experiences with bias or microaggressions. Hosting regular forums, creating anonymous reporting systems, and ensuring both

HR and leadership maintain an open-door policy for these discussions can make a significant difference.

- **Implement Clear Reporting Mechanisms:** Encourage open dialogue through informal feedback mechanisms such as anonymous suggestion boxes for reporting micro-aggressions, while maintaining separate formal channels for discrimination or harassment complaints.

- **Take Immediate and Appropriate Action:** When incidents are reported, respond swiftly by conducting thorough investigations and implementing corrective actions (such as additional training or meditation between parties). Ensure transparency throughout the process to build trust among employees.

- **Monitor and Adjust Policies:** Regularly review and adjust company policies based on employee feedback, emerging trends, or incidents to ensure the company stays up to date on best practices for addressing bias and microaggressions.

Handling Discrimination and Harassment Complaints

Establish and enforce a transparent and efficient process to address the unfortunate cases of discrimination or harassment. Here's a step-by-step guide to ensure that employees feel confident their complaints will be taken seriously, thoroughly investigated, and appropriately resolved.

- **Develop Clear Reporting Channels:** Ensure employees know exactly how and where to report incidents of discrimination or harassment.
  - o **Provide Multiple Reporting Methods:** Offer a variety of reporting options, such as in-person meetings, email submissions, online forms, or anonymous hotlines to ensure everyone feels comfortable reporting.

- ○ **Make Channels Easily Accessible:** Include clear instructions on how to access reporting tools, such as links in the company's intranet, posters in common areas, or handouts distributed during training sessions.

- ○ **Regularly Remind Employees:** Use internal communication methods like newsletters, team meetings, or company-wide emails to regularly remind employees of their rights and available reporting options.

- **Initiate a Transparent Investigation Process:** Once a complaint is reported, an investigation should be launched immediately. Ensure transparency throughout the process:

  - ○ **Communicate Investigation Steps:** Share a clear outline of the investigation process with both the complainant and the accused, detailing what to expect at each stage.

  - ○ **Set a Clear Timeline:** Provide a timeline for the investigation, such as "We aim to complete this investigation within ten business days," to manage expectations.

  - ○ **Ensure Impartiality:** If necessary, involve a neutral third-party investigator to eliminate potential bias, especially when internal teams may have conflicting interests.

- **Provide Support to All Parties:** Throughout the process, it's essential that both the complainant and the accused feel respected and supported.

  - ○ **Offer Confidential Counseling or Employee Assistance Programs (EAP):** Provide affected individuals with access to professional support, such as counseling or peer support groups, throughout the investigation.

  - ○ **Create a Safe Interview Environment:** Conduct interviews in neutral, comfortable settings to put all parties at ease and ensure they feel safe discussing sensitive information.

o **Regular Check-Ins:** Maintain open communication with all parties involved, offering reassurance and addressing any concerns during the process.

- **Implement Corrective Actions:** Once the investigation is complete, appropriate corrective actions should be taken based on the findings. This could include:

o **Disciplinary Actions:** Depending on the severity of the incident, actions might range from verbal warnings to suspension or termination.

o **Additional Training:** Implement specialized training for the individuals or departments involved, whether it's bias training, conflict resolution workshops, or programs to review terminology and pronoun usage to prevent future occurrences.

o **Mediation:** Facilitate a mediation session between parties to rebuild trust and ensure a positive work environment moving forward, if both parties are comfortable.

- **Communicate Outcomes and Maintain Confidentiality:** After the investigation concludes, it's important to communicate the outcomes while maintaining confidentiality.

o **Share Corrective Actions Taken:** Inform the complainant whether corrective actions were implemented, without necessarily disclosing specific details.

o **Reinforce Company Values:** Reiterate the organization's commitment to a safe, inclusive, and harassment-free environment for all employees.

o **Protect Confidentiality:** Ensure that sensitive details of the complaint and investigation remain confidential to protect both the complainant and the accused.

- **Provide Continuous Education and Prevention:** To prevent future incidents of discrimination and harassment, implement ongoing training and awareness programs.

  o **Regular Policy Revisions:** Revisit harassment and discrimination policies during traini987ng sessions to ensure em-ployees stay informed of their rights and responsibilities.

  o **Early Recognition:** Educate employees on how to recognize early signs of bias or harassment and encourage reporting before issues escalate.

  o **Creating a Respectful Workplace Culture:** Foster a culture of inclusivity and respect through regular team-building activities, inclusivity workshops, and leadership-driven initiatives that prioritize a positive and respectful environment.

Case Study: Virgin Atlantic Takes Flight: Redefining Airline Dress Codes

In 2022, Virgin Atlantic revamped its uniform policy, allowing flight attendants, pilots, and ground staff to choose attire that aligns with their gender identity and personal style. The new designer uniforms let staff choose between pants and skirts, regardless of gender. This change came just four months after Virgin announced that they lifted the ban on visible tattoos for public-facing employees. Job applications have doubled since Virgin made these progressive changes.[159]

The policy isn't without its challenges. To meet the cultural norms and legal requirements of different destinations, Virgin Atlantic adapts its uniform rules based on thorough risk assessments. Crews are advised to wear uniforms that correspond to the gender on their passport for flights to Saudi Arabia and were advised similarly when transporting the England soccer team to the FIFA World Cup in Qatar in 2022.[160]

Virgin Atlantic's policy is part of a broader commitment to gender inclusion, which includes time off for transition-related medical treatments, inclusive changing rooms, and the option for employees to include pronouns on name badges. Additionally, the airline is rolling out mandatory inclusivity training for tourism partners to address LGBTQ+ barriers worldwide.[161]

Virgin wasn't the first airline to roll out a gender-neutral uniform policy. Alaska Airlines introduced gender-neutral uniforms prior to Virgin's policy change, but Alaska Airlines' change was driven by legal pressure rather than an internal initiative. A nonbinary flight attendant filed a complaint in 2020 that was resolved two years later with several outcomes, including uniform changes, fines, and employee training on federal and state protections for gender identity and expression.[162]

Other airlines have also made gender-inclusive uniform changes. JetBlue allows employees to choose the uniform, hair, and/or makeup regardless of traditional gender stereotypes. Canadian airline WestJet offers uniform options to all employees, renaming its collections from "women" and "men" to the more neutral "Lakes" and "Rocky Mountain" collections. Some airlines, like British Airways, are keeping gendered uniforms but allowing employees of all genders to wear makeup, don jewelry, and carry handbags.[163]

Virgin Atlantic's proactive and high-profile approach sets it apart. Alaska Airlines, while arriving at a similar outcome, serves as a key example of how external pressures can force important policy changes, even if inclusivity wasn't the initial goal.

Addressing Resistance from Employees

In the previous chapter, we discussed how resistance from leadership and external stakeholders can challenge gender inclusion efforts. But what happens when resistance comes from within the organization, from employees themselves? While resistance from both external stakeholders and internal employees can disrupt inclusion initiatives, the nature of established relationships between HR and employees allows for a more personalized approach to understanding and addressing employee motivations. Employee resistance to gender inclusion can stem from psychological, cultural, or social factors, and understanding these concerns is essential to effectively dispel them and support the organization's values.

The three-step model for managing resistance outlined in the Leadership section serves as a foundation here as well. This section expands on that model by providing HR with specific, relational strategies for engaging with employees directly and fostering a culture that proactively reduces resistance. Refer to "Addressing Resistance from Leaders and External Stakeholders" (Chapter 5) for more on the leadership model.

Whether you're just beginning your gender inclusion efforts or are already implementing inclusive practices, this section provides strategies to meet your needs. Proactive organizational strategies lay the groundwork for a welcoming culture, potentially preventing resistance before it arises. Individual strategies, on the other hand, offer direct tools to navigate specific cases of resistance when they occur.

Resistance in social contexts has been studied for decades, from Social Identity Theory in the 1970s[164] to Identity Process Theory in the 1980s,[165] to more recent studies on identity management.[166] These frameworks provide a foundation for understanding the root causes of resistance to gender inclusion and offer strategic ways to address it.

Psychological Resistance

Psychological resistance arises when employees feel that gender inclusion challenges their personal identity or long-held beliefs about gender. For example, an employee may resist using "they/them" pronouns because it disrupts their binary understanding of gender. Some employees may feel hesitant to engage in discussions about nonbinary pronouns, not necessarily out of objection, but because it conflicts with their deep-seated understanding of themself. This resistance can manifest subtly, perhaps through non-participation in inclusivity initiatives.

For some employees, their identity may be closely tied to traditional gender norms, which can create an initial psychological barrier to accepting gender-inclusive language. Over time, as employees feel more supported and safer exploring gender inclusion, they may shift their perspective and feel more comfortable adopting inclusive practices. Here are some strategies to dispel psychological resistance:

Proactive Organizational Strategies

- **Create an Affirmation Culture:** Encourage a work environment that values individual contributions, framing inclusion as an enhancement to a supportive work culture.

- **Provide Self-Reflection Exercises:** Incorporate exercises into training that encourage employees to explore their personal values, helping to build openness to new ideas.

- **Discussion Groups and Feedback Sessions:** Use informal discussion groups or feedback sessions where employees can explore their views in a non-judgmental space. These sessions help show that inclusion supports, rather than disrupts, their values.

Individual Strategies

- **Open, Non-Judgmental Conversations:** Meet privately with the employee to discuss any specific discomforts or concerns around gender-inclusive practices. Create a safe, respectful space to explore their reservations. Follow the three-step approach in "Addressing Resistance from Leaders and External Stakeholders" (Chapter 5).

- **Personalized Reflection Resources:** Offer individualized resources, such as articles or reflection exercises, that gently challenge binary beliefs while respecting personal values.

- **Ongoing Check-Ins:** Schedule regular one-on-one check-ins to revisit their thoughts on inclusive practices, offering continued support and space to process any shifts in their understanding over time.

Moral or Cultural Resistance

This type of resistance occurs when inclusion policies conflict with an employee's personal values, religious beliefs, or moral outlook. For example, an employee may refuse to work with or provide services to a transgender or nonbinary person because it conflicts with their religious beliefs. Employees may resist participation in gender-inclusive initiatives if they feel these initiatives challenge their core values.

Employees who see themselves as part of a specific religious or cultural identity may feel these values are at odds with inclusion policies. However, as inclusivity is reframed as a form of respect and fairness, these employees may find it possible to engage without feeling that their core values are compromised. Here are some strategies to dispel moral or cultural resistance:

Proactive Organizational Strategies

- **Reframe Inclusivity as Respect:** Position inclusion as a universal practice of respect and fairness, appealing to shared values across different belief systems.

- **Humanize Through Stories:** Bring in speakers or share stories to illustrate that inclusion is about mutual respect, not a conflict with personal beliefs.

Individual Strategies

- **Respectful Dialogue:** Engage in a private conversation where you respectfully acknowledge the employee's beliefs and explain how gender inclusion aligns with the organization's values of respect and equity.

- **Offer Alternative Learning Resources:** Provide options such as written resources or video trainings for employees uncomfortable with live sessions, giving them room to engage at their own pace.

- **Values-Aligned Framing:** Reinforce that participation in inclusion efforts is part of honoring a respectful workplace culture, even if it may differ from personal beliefs.

Pragmatic Resistance

Pragmatic resistance is rooted in practical concerns, where employees may fear saying the wrong thing or feel overwhelmed by the changes required. An employee might be apprehensive about adopting gender-neutral language due to concerns about potentially embarrassing missteps or negative reactions if they get it wrong. A common example of pragmatic resistance is an employee refusing to refer to someone with "they/them" pronouns because they believe it is grammatically incorrect.

Over time, as employees witness leaders and peers openly learning from mistakes, they may feel more comfortable trying inclusive language themselves, knowing it's okay to learn. Here are some strategies to dispel pragmatic resistance:

Proactive Organizational Strategies

- **Provide Practical Resources:** Offer training, tools, and resources designed to ease employees into inclusive practices without overwhelming them.

- ○ **Role-Playing Scenarios:** Use interactive exercises to help employees gain confidence in inclusive language, alleviating fears around mistakes.

- ○ **Productivity-Focused Training:** Emphasize how inclusive practices, such as clear communication around names and pronouns, can streamline interactions, ultimately enhancing productivity.

- **Model Inclusive Practices in Everyday Tasks:** HR (and leaders) should integrate inclusive language and practices in daily interactions, demonstrating that these can seamlessly fit into routines.

- ○ **Meeting Introductions:** Start team meetings by modeling inclusive language to show how it can flow naturally.

- ○ **Quick Correction Practices:** Show that quick self-corrections are effective and non-disruptive, reducing employees' fear of mistakes.

Individual Strategies

- **Address Concerns Around Change and Productivity:** Meet with employees who express concerns about how inclusive practices might impact their productivity. Discuss how these changes can be implemented in ways that minimally disrupt their workflow and may even enhance team collaboration. For example:

- ○ **Customize Practice Plans:** Create a personalized plan that allows the employee to practice inclusive language within their daily tasks, reinforcing that it's a manageable adjustment rather than a sweeping change.

- ○ **Identify Productivity Benefits:** Work with the employee to identify specific ways inclusive practices, like using the correct pronouns, can save time by fostering clearer communication and reducing misunderstandings.

- **Reassure Through Incremental Implementation:** For employees who feel overwhelmed by change, gradually introduce inclusive practices rather than implementing them all at once. This incremental approach can help reduce fears around disruption and ease them into new habits.

  o **Introduce One Practice at a Time:** Start by focusing on one inclusive practice, such as pronouns, before adding others, showing that adjustments can be manageable.

  o **Follow Up for Feedback:** Schedule regular check-ins to address any productivity or workflow concerns, reinforcing that these changes are meant to support, not hinder, their work.

Group-Based Resistance

Group-based resistance occurs when employees feel that gender inclusion threatens their group's dominance or status within the workplace. Cisgender employees, who typically represent the dominant group, may perceive inclusion efforts as a shift in established norms that challenges their understanding of workplace culture. This resistance is tied to ingroup versus outgroup dynamics, much like the loyalty people feel toward their sports teams. Employees may feel a deep loyalty to their ingroup and see gender inclusion as a threat to the status quo. For example, employees might resist gender-neutral restrooms, perceiving them as an unnecessary change that benefits only a minority group.

As the organization emphasizes shared values and the collective benefits of inclusion, employees may gradually expand their perception of the ingroup to encompass a more inclusive workplace identity.

Proactive Organizational Strategies

- **Emphasize Shared Benefits:** Use data or real-world examples to show how inclusion benefits everyone, reinforcing the notion that inclusion strengthens the team.

- **Foster a Collective Identity:** Reinforce a sense of shared purpose and unity within the team, stressing that inclusion fosters overall success and strengthens the organization's collective identity.

Individual Strategies

- **Private Discussion on Team Goals:** Meet with the employee to explore their concerns privately, reframing inclusion as beneficial to the group and aligned with shared goals. In a private discussion, acknowledge the employee's concerns around group norms, and explore how inclusion aligns with and even strengthens the group's shared goals and identity.

- **Highlight Positive Social Shifts:** Show that changes toward inclusivity are part of a broader social trend, helping employees feel that they're participating in positive change, not sacrificing established norms.

- **Set Small, Inclusive Goals:** Encourage the employee to start with small, inclusive practices, showing that incremental changes can lead to an improved sense of team unity without a perceived loss of tradition.

Regardless of your efforts or approach, some employees may ultimately choose not to align with the organization's inclusive values. In such cases, HR must weigh whether continued engagement with resistant employees supports or detracts from the company's core mission. While the goal is always to educate and encourage inclusivity, HR must also ensure that workplace culture aligns with the organization's values. If ongoing resistance disrupts the work environment or conflicts with inclusion efforts, leadership may need to determine the best course of action to maintain a respectful and equitable workplace.

Supporting Gender Transitions at Work

The period of transitioning is particularly sensitive; individuals may be ostracized or pressured by peers to suppress their identities during this time, increasing their susceptibility to depression, anxiety, and even suicidal thinking.[167] Human Resources can cultivate an inclusive and respectful workplace culture by supporting employees through their gender transition. This process demands sensitivity and a deep respect for each individual's experience, ensuring that transitioning employees feel valued, understood, and empowered.

A foundational step is to encourage open, honest communication between employees intending to transition and HR or management. These conversations should be approached with the utmost confidentiality and empathy, laying a foundation of trust and understanding. Such dialogue paves the way for effective planning and support, tailored to each employee's unique journey.

The journey of transitioning at work requires a concerted effort across the organization, fostering an environment rooted in respect, empathy, and inclusion. HR should devise and implement individualized transition plans that respect the employee's choices and timeline, offering practical support in various workplace aspects, from policy adjustments to healthcare benefits.

Each employee's gender transition journey is unique, involving deeply personal considerations and choices. The role of HR is to listen attentively to transitioning employees, working collaboratively with them to understand their specific needs and preferences for communication, disclosure, and support. It is crucial to respect their privacy and avoid inadvertently outing them before they are ready or without their permission.

To effectively support transitioning employees, HR should collaboratively develop a tailored transition plan that respects the employee's autonomy and choices. This plan should include the following aspects:

- **Establish a Point Person:** Ideally, leaders and direct supervisors are equipped to support an employee with their transition, but this may not always be the case. In situations where a direct supervisor might not provide the best support, establish a designated point person. This individual should ideally be in a leadership position or have sufficient authority and training to effectively advocate for the transitioning employee throughout the process. This individual may:
  - o Provide consistent and empathetic support
  - o Facilitate communication between the transitioning employee and other departments or team members, as needed
  - o Ensure that all aspects of the transition plan are implemented smoothly and respectfully
  - o Address any concerns or challenges that may arise during the transition process
- **Timeline and Steps:** Create a clear outline of the stages and timelines involved in the transition process. Recognize that the employee leading their transition determines the pace and nature of this journey. This step involves a detailed discussion with the transitioning employee to ensure their comfort and readiness at each stage.
- **Support Networks and Mental Well-Being Resources:** Transitioning is not only a physical journey but also a

deeply emotional and psychological one, requiring robust support from businesses.

o **Support Networks:** Encourage transitioning employees to connect with support groups, whether they are peer mentorship groups or professional counseling services. These networks offer shared experiences and invaluable emotional support. HR managers should actively provide information about treatment options, organizational support groups, and other available resources. They can also develop strategies to help employees manage work/life challenges during the transition.

o **Mental and Emotional Well-Being Resources:** The mental and emotional aspects of gender transition can be challenging. Ensure transitioning employees are aware of and have access to mental health resources tailored to their needs. This includes counseling services specializing in gender identity, stress management resources, and strategies for coping with emotional challenges.

• **Employee Assistance Programs:** A well-structured Employee Assistance Program (EAP), if available, can be invaluable. Ensure your EAP includes services that cater specifically to transgender employees' needs. This might encompass counseling services, legal assistance with name and gender marker changes, and guidance on navigating healthcare related to gender affirmation. Providing these resources ensures comprehensive support for transitioning employees' overall well-being.

• **Pronouns and Chosen Name:** Affirming an employee's identity in their professional environment means consistently respecting their pronouns and chosen name. Simply updating records is not enough.

○ **Uniform Use Across Communications:** Ensure that their pronouns and chosen name are applied consistently across all interactions, including emails, meetings, user logins, and official documents. Consistency validates their identity.

○ **Efficient Update Process:** Implement a streamlined process for updating the employee's name and pronouns across systems, such as email signatures, security badges, and internal directories, with a focus on privacy and respect.

○ **Employee-Led Timing:** Allow the employee to set the pace for introducing their new name and pronouns to the team, based on their comfort level.

● **Documentation and Records:** Supporting an employee's transition includes updating all relevant documentation to reflect their affirmed gender identity.

○ **Timely Document Changes:** Promptly adjust internal records, such as employment contracts, ID badges, and HR databases, with the employee's new name and gender marker. For legal documents, provide guidance on the process, recognizing that some states may impose restrictions on gender marker changes.

○ **Guidance for Legal Documentation:** Provide assistance with official changes, including resources, internal or external, for updating legal identification documents when necessary. Follow up with any record changes that are dependent on legal updates, such as payroll records.

○ **Inclusive Policy Language:** Review HR documents, such as the employee handbook, to ensure gender-neutral language (as discussed in the "Workplace Policies and Practices" section of this chapter). This reinforces inclusivity for all employees, not just those transitioning.

- **Dress Code:** Navigating dress code policies is a significant part of transitioning at work. HR should handle this with flexibility and sensitivity to ease the transition process for the employee. This can also serve as an opportunity to move the organization toward a more inclusive and flexible approach to employee attire.

  o **Temporary Dress Code Adjustments:** During an employee's transition, be flexible with dress code requirements. This might mean temporarily relaxing certain dress code rules to support the employee's changing presentation, helping them feel comfortable and authentic.

  o **Uniform Access:** For roles requiring uniforms, ensure the gender-specific uniform the employee needs is readily available. Allow them to transition at their own pace and comfort level by providing access to alternative uniforms without mandating a change.

  o **Inclusive Dress Code Policies:** This is also a great time to review and update the organization's dress code policies (as discussed in the "Workplace Policies and Practices" section of this chapter). Ensure these policies are inclusive and free from gendered language or expectations. Updating dress codes not only supports the transitioning employee but also promotes a broader culture of inclusivity within the organization.

- **Access to Gender-Affirming Healthcare and Coverage Consistency:** Supporting employees through gender transition means ensuring they have access to gender-affirming healthcare. Helping with the costs of medical procedures and providing access to gender-identity-specific healthcare benefits can significantly reduce the stress and anxiety associated with coming out at work.[168] Reach out to your third-party administrator, benefits broker, or consultant for guidance.

- o **Inclusive Healthcare Policies:** HR should strive to offer benefits that cover gender-affirming medical procedures, hormone replacement therapies, and mental health support.

- o **Consistency in Coverage:** Aim for consistent healthcare coverage. For instance, if hormone replacement therapy is offered for menopausal symptoms, similar coverage should be available for transgender women. This approach aligns with principles of fairness and equality and helps mitigate potential legal risks, demonstrating a commitment to equitable treatment for all employees.

- o **Tailored Benefit Options:** Healthcare benefits depend on whether the business is self-insured, fully insured, or a hybrid model for coverage. While self-insured businesses have more flexibility in tailoring their healthcare benefits, fully insured businesses do not. Review your policies to ensure inclusivity within the constraints of your insurance plans and state regulations. If specific gender-affirming treatments are not feasible, HR can explore alternatives like additional wellness programs, mental health resources, or potential partnerships with nonprofit agencies that may offer assistance.

- o **Employee Guidance and Support:** Provide clear information about healthcare coverage related to gender transition. Help employees navigate insurance queries, understand what treatments are covered, and assist in accessing necessary medical care.

- **Security Clearances and Badges:** When an employee is transitioning, updating security clearances and badges ensures that their daily work experience is seamless and respectful. HR should proactively manage these updates, aligning them with the employee's transition timeline.

  o **Timely Update of Security Details:** Coordinate with the relevant departments to update security clearances and badges in a timely manner. This should coincide with the employee's chosen timeline for transitioning, ensuring there is no period where their identity and security access are misaligned.

  o **Seamless Access Control:** Ensure all systems recognizing the employee, from door access controls to digital sign-ins, are updated to reflect their current identity. This prevents any potential security hiccups and contributes to a smooth daily routine for the transitioning employee.

  o **Discreet and Respectful Handling:** Handle these updates with discretion and respect for the employee's privacy. Sensitive communication about these changes should be kept confidential, and discussions should be conducted in a manner that upholds the dignity of the transitioning individual.

  o **Training for Security Staff:** Brief and train security staff about the updates to ensure that they are aware of the changes and can interact respectfully and appropriately with the transitioning employee.

- **Inclusive Facility Access:** Inclusive facility access supports an employee's gender transition. Ensure that transitioning employees have access to facilities that align with their gender identity while addressing any concerns from other staff members with sensitivity and understanding.

- o **Respecting Restroom and Facility Preferences:** Allow transitioning employees to use facilities that correspond with their gender identity.

- o **Provision of Gender-Neutral Options:** Offer gender-neutral facilities as an additional option, but do not compel transitioning employees to use them if they prefer to use standard facilities aligned with their gender identity.

- o **Educating Staff on Facility Inclusivity:** Implement training or awareness sessions for all staff to foster understanding and respect for restroom inclusivity, creating a supportive and respectful environment for everyone.

- o **Addressing Concerns with Empathy and Assurance:** Handle any concerns from other employees about a transitioning colleague's access to certain facilities with empathy and reassurance. Emphasize respect for everyone's privacy and dignity in these discussions.

- o **Clear Communication of Policies:** Make sure all staff are aware of the organization's gender inclusion policies to ensure a cohesive understanding across the team.

- **Bystander Intervention:** When managing misgendering or deadnaming incidents, prioritize the transitioning employee's comfort by discussing their preferences for handling these situations. Some may prefer to address it themselves, while others might appreciate gentle corrections from colleagues. Be sure to communicate the transitioning employee's preferences regarding bystander intervention to colleagues so everyone knows what to do. Communicate the employee's preferences to their coworkers to ensure everyone is aligned. Always consider bystander safety, intervening only if it can be done safely and respectfully. This approach supports both the transitioning employee and their coworkers during sensitive situations. Refer to "Inclusive Talk: Verbal Communication Strategies" in "Strategies for Gender-Inclusive Communication" (Chapter 4) for more information.

- **Communication Strategy:** When planning a communication strategy for an employee's transition, address their preferences for sharing information with coworkers and clients, treating each group distinctly.

  o **Disclosure Preferences:** Preferences can vary greatly; some employees may opt for a gradual approach, introducing their transition in stages, while others might choose immediate and full disclosure.

  o **Internal Communication:** For coworkers, use internal communication channels like team meetings, emails, or personalized letters based on the employee's comfort level and the organization's culture. The transitioning employee should have a significant say in how the message is conveyed, ensuring their narrative is respected and accurately represented.

  o **External Communication:** In terms of client communication, the strategy might differ based on the nature of the relationships and the business context. Some employees may prefer direct communication with key clients they interact with regularly, while for others, a more general announcement or a subtle transition in email signatures and business cards might suffice.

In situations where an employee is transitioning, it's beneficial to provide specific training for their colleagues. This education aims to help team members understand the nuances and experiences of transgender individuals, fostering empathy and reducing potential biases.

Educational sessions or materials should cover topics like the use of appropriate vocabulary, understanding the challenges faced by transgender colleagues, and guidelines on respectful interactions. Create an environment where the transitioning employee feels genuinely supported and understood.

Remember, many colleagues may be unfamiliar with how to approach or support a transitioning coworker. Providing this training equips the whole team with a better understanding of the difficulties their colleague is facing as well as the knowledge and confidence about how they should/shouldn't handle the situation.

Case Study: Clark Musto's Transition at Johnson & Johnson

After over a decade in the pharmaceutical industry, Clark Musto relocated to the Bay Area, where he met his future wife and found a supportive community. At that time, Clark presented as a woman and identified as a lesbian. Despite working for a progressive company, the insurance benefits there were restrictive; they required at least a year of hormone replacement therapy to cover top surgery. While Clark felt affirmed in seeking the surgery, he did not feel ready for hormone therapy, leading him to defer his transition.[169]

Years later, Clark attended an LGBTQ+ recruiting event, Lesbians Who Tech, where he learned about Johnson & Johnson's inclusive benefits package, which covered gender-affirming surgery without a hormone therapy prerequisite. Encouraged by the company's commitment to diversity, he applied and was soon hired as a clinical research manager. As a new employee, he was initially hesitant to ask for support, but Johnson & Johnson's resource group, named Open&Out, quickly connected him with their San Francisco chapter lead, who reassured him, "Don't worry—you have the backing of the entire company."[170] She also offered to connect him with Johnson & Johnson's trans liaison, who was available to guide him through workplace transition support if he chose to proceed.

Clark soon realized that transitioning at work would be more involved than he had anticipated. The liaison explained that returning to work after surgery would raise questions, particularly since his appearance would noticeably change. He found that he wasn't only coming out as trans but also asking others to make adjustments alongside him: "to use he/him pronouns, and to get used to a new name, a new email, and a new bathroom."[171]

He then worked closely with the trans liaison and HR to develop a transition plan that included medical leave and a communication strategy for his return. During his leave, the company collaborated with PFLAG to hold an education session for his colleagues, ensuring they were prepared to support him respectfully.[172]

Upon returning to work, Clark was deeply moved by his colleagues' understanding and acceptance. Thanks to the education session, Clark's colleagues were already using his new name and pronouns, though occasional early slip-ups occurred.

> "I saw the presentation that was given while I was out, and there was a bullet point that really brought that sense of support home for me: 'Don't "out" transitioning or transitioned coworkers. Gossip and rumor-spreading in the workplace about an individual's gender identity/ expression will not be tolerated.' It meant a lot to me."[173]

Reflecting on his experience, Clark said, "I feel like I'm really being seen as me for the first time—not just as a guy, but me."[174] His experience underscored the importance of documented policies and a structured support system for transgender employees, highlighting Johnson & Johnson's commitment to a harassment-free, inclusive workplace.[175]

Recruiting and Retaining Talent

Building a gender-inclusive workforce begins with recruiting and retaining diverse talent. In this section, we'll explore strategies to create an inclusive recruitment and retention process.

Gender-Inclusive Job Posts

Gender inclusion begins with the first interaction potential employees have with your organization: the job posting. Crafting gender-inclusive job posts shows your commitment to diversity and encourages individuals from all backgrounds to apply. Here's how HR can enhance this stage:

- **Gender-Neutral Language in Job Descriptions:** Use gender-neutral language in job descriptions to avoid reinforcing stereotypes or excluding gender-diverse candidates. Replace gender-specific terms with inclusive language to create a welcoming environment for all applicants. Refer to "Principles of Gender-Neutral Communication" (Chapter 3) for more on gender-inclusive language.

- **Equal Opportunity Employment Statements:** Include statements in your job postings that highlight your commitment to equal opportunity employment, regardless of shifting policies. Phrases like "Diversity welcome," or "We encourage applicants of all genders, backgrounds, and identities to apply," signal your openness to diversity. While the current EEOC has deprioritized gender identity protections, explicitly mentioning "gender identity" in your equal opportunity statement shows that your organization recognizes and respects diverse gender identities and reinforces your organization's independent commitment to inclusion.

- **Equal Opportunity Employment Information:** Provide candidates with Equal Opportunity Employment information. This could include an easily accessible link to your organization's diversity and inclusion policy, highlighting your commitment to creating an equitable and inclusive workplace. When applicants see that your organization values diversity, it not only attracts a wider range of candidates but also sends a positive message to clients and customers, reflecting your dedication to diversity at every level.

- **Staying Updated on Federal Policies:** Employment protections and enforcement priorities shift with different administrations. While gender identity remains protected under Title VII and *Bostock v. Clayton County*, the current EEOC is refusing to enforce these protections. If the EEOC returns to full compliance with the law, organizations should ensure their policies reflect the latest federal enforcement practices. However, if federal law itself is changed to remove these protections, companies will need to make critical decisions about how to uphold their inclusion commitments.

- **Inclusive Application Processes:** Creating an inclusive application process is the next step in fostering a gender-inclusive workplace. HR can implement various strategies to ensure that the application phase is welcoming and accessible to candidates of all gender identities.

- **Avoid Gender-Specific Form Fields in Applications:** Make your application process more inclusive by avoiding gender-specific form fields in applications. Refer to the "Writing with Respect: Written Communication Strategies" section of "Strategies for Gender-Inclusive

Communication" (Chapter 4) for detailed guidance. Gender-neutral form fields reduce the risk of alienating gender-diverse applicants. By removing unnecessary gender identifiers, you create a more inclusive and comfortable application experience.

- **Reconsider Mandatory Fields that May Discourage Gender-Diverse Applicants:** Look at your application's mandatory fields to make sure they don't put off gender-diverse applicants. Instead of forcing candidates to choose from only Mr. or Ms., include gender-neutral options like Mx. or Other. This simple change shows your commitment to inclusivity and can make a big difference in how applicants perceive your organization.

- **Blind Resume Review to Mitigate Unconscious Bias:** Unconscious bias can affect the hiring process, especially during resume reviews. To counter this, implement blind resume reviews by hiding personally identifiable information such as names and pronouns, allowing reviewers to focus solely on qualifications and experience, ensuring fairer evaluations based on merit.

- **Grow the Application Pool:** Expanding the reach of job postings to diverse and inclusive platforms encourages gender inclusion during recruitment. To attract a wide range of talented candidates, consider posting job openings on platforms beyond the mainstream. Here are a few resources to help diversify your applicant pool:

  - **National LGBTQ+ Bar Association:** The National LGBTQ+ Bar Association is a national association of LGBTQ+ legal professionals and their allies. Utilize their career center to post job openings and connect with LGBTQ+ lawyers who are dedicated to fostering inclusive workplaces.

- o **LGBT Career Link (Out & Equal):** Out & Equal Workplace Advocates is the world's largest nonprofit organization specifically committed to creating safe and equitable workplaces for lesbian, gay, bisexual, and transgender individuals. They offer a free service, LGBT Career Link, for job seekers. Post your job opportunities here to reach a broader audience of LGBTQ+ talent.

- o **Local Organizations:** Find local resources in your area that can help broaden your applicant pool. For example, TransWork is a valuable initiative that connects transgender and nonbinary job seekers and entrepreneurs with supportive employers and business partners. It operates as a program of the Independence Business Alliance and focuses on increasing access to opportunities for transgender individuals in the Greater Philadelphia, Pennsylvania region.

Inclusive Interviewing Techniques

To select the best candidates, conduct job interviews in a manner that prevents discrimination and meets legal guidelines, especially concerning gender and family status. HR can lead the way in ensuring interviews are inclusive and respectful.

- **Address Gender and Family Status Issues:** During interviews, approach questions related to gender or family status carefully. Many questions in these areas can be not only discriminatory but also illegal in numerous jurisdictions. Train interviewers to avoid such inquiries. Interview questions should focus on candidates' qualifications, experience, and skills relevant to the position.

- **Train Interview Panels on Gender-Inclusive Practices:** Provide training to interview panels that emphasizes the importance of avoiding gender bias, stereotypes, and discriminatory questions. One aspect to consider is the growing expectation among younger job candidates for recognition of gender identity. For instance, 88% of Generation Z candidates agree that recruiters or potential employers should inquire about their pronouns, however, only 18% of Gen Z respondents have ever been offered or asked for pronouns during the recruiting process.[176] This disparity highlights a significant gap in current recruitment practices and underscores the importance of incorporating pronouns into the interview process. Please refer to "Inclusive Talk: Verbal Communication Strategies" in "Strategies for Gender-Inclusive Communication" (Chapter 4) for a more in-depth review.

- **Incorporate Diversity and Inclusion Questions in the Interview:** To foster an inclusive workplace, consider incorporating diversity and inclusion questions into the interview process. Ask candidates about their experiences working in diverse teams, handling inclusivity challenges, or promoting diversity in their previous roles. These questions not only help identify candidates who align with your organization's values but also emphasize your commitment to diversity. Additionally, train interviewers to recognize nonverbal cues from candidates, such as eye-rolling or dismissive body language, that may indicate resistance to gender inclusion. This helps ensure that candidates selected are supportive of the organization's inclusive culture and values.

- **Ensure Panel Diversity:** To maintain a fair and inclusive interview process, ensure that interview panels themselves are diverse. Diverse interview panels are better equipped to evaluate candidates from various backgrounds and perspectives. This diversity can help identify the best fit for your organization without bias.

Onboarding for Inclusion

To help new employees integrate smoothly into your organization's culture, onboarding should go beyond logistics to ensure an inclusive, welcoming environment. HR professionals can implement practices that specifically address gender inclusion and foster support.

- **Introduce Inclusive Benefits in Orientation:** Share details on parental leave policies and other inclusive benefits that reflect the organization's commitment to diversity. Address any specific supports for LGBTQ+ families and make it clear that benefits are regularly reviewed to ensure they meet the needs of all employees. HR should also advocate for equitable parental leave benefits, ensuring employees are fully aware of their rights and entitlements. Additionally, fostering a culture of support for employees with family responsibilities, regardless of gender or sexual orientation, reinforces the company's values of inclusivity and understanding.

- **Inclusive Mentorship Programs:** Assigning inclusive mentors or buddies can enhance the onboarding experience. Studies show that new hires with mentors report higher satisfaction and support throughout their onboarding journey, contributing to a more welcoming and connected workplace. [177]

Gender Inclusion in Performance Reviews

Performance reviews support an employee's growth and development within an organization. However, they can inadvertently perpetuate gender biases if not approached mindfully. HR professionals can take proactive steps to promote gender inclusion in the performance review process, fostering a fair and equitable workplace.

- **Ensure Objective and Accomplishment-Based Evaluations:** To foster gender inclusion in performance reviews, focus on measurable skills and accomplishments rather than subjective or gendered traits. HR should promote clear, transparent criteria for both evaluations and promotions, ensuring that all employees understand the requirements for advancement and recognition.

- **Provide Holistic and Bias-Free Reviews:** Encourage the use of peer reviews and 360-degree feedback systems to provide a well-rounded perspective on performance. At the same time, provide reviewers with training and guidelines to help them recognize and mitigate unconscious biases. These combined efforts reduce the chances of biased evaluations and promote a more inclusive culture.

- **Mitigate Bias in Feedback and Promotions:** Address potential gender biases in promotion evaluations. Offer ongoing training to managers and reviewers to prevent biases from affecting advancement decisions. By focusing on clear, objective criteria and ensuring a structured, bias-free feedback process, organizations can create a more inclusive pathway for career growth.

- **Create a Feedback Loop:** Actively engage with employees to create a feedback loop, encouraging them to report instances of bias or discrimination during performance reviews. Creating a safe space for dialogue and feedback empowers employees to voice their concerns and ensures that gender bias is swiftly addressed.

Retaining Gender-Diverse Talent

Retention of gender-diverse talent contributes to creating an inclusive workplace. HR professionals can implement strategies to ensure that employees of all genders feel valued, supported, and motivated to stay with the organization.

- **Leverage Employee Resource Groups (ERGs):** Employee Resource Groups (ERGs) are vital in retaining gender-diverse talent by providing community, support, and belonging. ERGs allow individuals to connect, share experiences, and advocate for change.
  - **Smaller Businesses:** When ERGs aren't feasible, consider forming inclusion committees to organize community-building events (e.g., fundraising for causes like the Trevor Project). Additionally, offer Diversity Dialogues or Lunch 'n Learns, where employees can suggest topics to foster open discussions on gender inclusion and other diversity issues. This gives employees a voice and helps create a more inclusive culture.
  - **Larger Organizations:** Support and promote ERGs by providing resources and recognition. These groups play a significant role in fostering a sense of belonging, which directly contributes to employee satisfaction and retention.
- **Ensure Fair and Transparent Pay Structures:** A transparent and equitable pay structure is crucial to retaining talent.
  - **Address Gender Pay Gaps:** Regularly review and analyze compensation data to identify and address any gender pay gaps. Perceived equity in pay leads to higher employee commitment and retention.

     o **Training to Eliminate Bias:** Provide training to managers on fair compensation practices, ensuring performance evaluations and promotions are free from bias that could contribute to unequal pay.

- **Provide Benefits That Consider the Needs of Diverse Genders:** Design benefit packages that cater to the diverse needs of employees, ensuring inclusivity in health benefits, parental leave policies, and other forms of support.

     o **Consistency in Coverage:** Healthcare plans should cover treatments and services that are relevant to the diverse gender identities of employees. Parental leave policies should accommodate diverse family structures, including same-sex couples and adoptive parents, and be flexible enough to meet the needs of all employees, regardless of gender identity.

     o **Tailored Benefit Options:** Offering healthcare benefits that support diverse gender identities is crucial for retaining talent. While self-insured businesses often have more flexibility in tailoring healthcare benefits, fully insured businesses face restrictions. Regularly review policies to maximize inclusivity within the limits of insurance plans and state regulations. Where specific gender-affirming treatments may not be feasible, HR can consider alternatives, such as enhanced wellness programs, mental health support, or partnerships with nonprofit agencies to meet employee needs.

Employee Turnover and Exit Interviews

Employee turnover is a natural part of any organization, but it must be managed effectively, especially concerning gender diversity. HR professionals can take specific steps to understand why employees leave and how to use this information to create a more inclusive workplace.

- **Gender-Sensitive Exit Interviews:** Exit interviews are valuable opportunities for HR to gain insights into the reasons behind employee departures. Conduct gender-sensitive exit interviews to gain deeper insights into the unique challenges faced by gender-diverse employees. Create a safe and open environment during these interviews, asking gender-related questions such as:
  - o Did you ever feel that your gender identity or expression affected your opportunities or treatment within the organization?
  - o Were there instances of gender bias or discrimination that you encountered during your time here?
  - o Did you feel supported in your gender identity and expression throughout your employment?
- **Analyze Turnover Data with a Gender Lens:** Regularly examine turnover data through a gender-inclusive perspective to uncover potential patterns of exclusion. This analysis helps identify whether certain gender-diverse employee groups are departing from the organization at higher rates than others. The process involves collecting data on gender identity during onboarding, segmenting turnover data by gender, and conducting root cause analysis, comparative analysis, and action planning.

Summary Checklist for Human Resources

HR as Champions of Inclusivity

- ☐ Model inclusive behavior: active listening, continuous education, and use of inclusive language.
- ☐ Foster open communication and create safe spaces for employees to provide feedback.
- ☐ Collaborate with leadership and departments to integrate inclusivity into the company culture.
- ☐ Develop training programs tailored to the unique needs of each department, addressing specific challenges and opportunities in their roles.
- ☐ Ensure training is accessible to all employees, from executives to entry-level positions, adapting formats to accommodate different needs (e.g., shift workers, remote employees, and private sessions for executives).
- ☐ Stay informed on legal developments by monitoring federal and state policies, consulting employment law experts, and ensuring company policies align with civil rights laws rather than shifting political agendas.

Workplace Policies and Practices

- ☐ Regularly review and update HR policies to ensure gender inclusion.
- ☐ Use gender-neutral language in the employee handbooks and all policy documents.
- ☐ Implement gender-neutral dress codes and job titles.

Addressing Resistance from Employees

- ☐ Address any instances of individual resistance with tailored approaches based on the specific type (psychological, moral/cultural, pragmatic, or group-based).

☐ Emphasize the shared benefits of inclusion to reinforce that inclusivity strengthens team cohesion and benefits all employees.

☐ Foster a collective identity that aligns with inclusive values and promotes a sense of belonging for everyone.

☐ Create an affirmation culture where individual contributions are valued, and inclusion is viewed as integral to a positive workplace.

☐ Model inclusive language and practices consistently in daily interactions, setting a standard for all employees.

Supporting Gender Transitions at Work

☐ Develop individualized transition plans respecting employee autonomy.

☐ Provide access to mental health resources and support networks.

☐ Update records to reflect affirmed gender identity and chosen names.

☐ Ensure access to gender-affirming healthcare and consistent coverage.

☐ Update security clearances and badges in alignment with the transition timeline.

☐ Respect restroom and facility preferences and educate staff on inclusivity.

Recruiting and Retaining Talent

☐ Use gender-neutral language in job descriptions, postings, and hiring materials.

☐ Implement blind resume reviews to mitigate unconscious bias.

☐ Ensure diverse hiring panels and inclusive interviewing techniques.

- ☐ Include equal opportunity employment information in job postings.
- ☐ Offer benefits that consider the needs of diverse genders.
- ☐ Conduct gender-sensitive exit interviews.

Training and Continuous Learning

- ☐ Implement comprehensive DEI training programs.
- ☐ Provide ongoing training on gender identity and inclusivity.
- ☐ Create spaces for private or anonymous questions.
- ☐ Stay informed about best practices and legal requirements through professional development.

CHAPTER 07

LEGAL: ADVOCATING FOR INCLUSION

When I began working with law firms in Philadelphia, Pennsylvania in the mid-1990s, the environment was anything but diverse. The culture was strict, with a clear expectation best described by the saying "If you don't come in on Saturday, don't bother coming in on Sunday." Law firms back then felt like something out of a legal drama: plush Turkish rugs, dark wood-paneled walls, and somber portraits of old men staring down at you, reminders of the old guard. Tattoos and piercings were out of the question, and work-life balance wasn't on anyone's radar. For almost two decades, I held off getting an eyebrow piercing, knowing that new firms wouldn't let me in the door.

Beyond appearances, the language used in law firms was just as formal, reflecting centuries of legal tradition. Legal English, or "legalese" as it is now known, was argued to be necessarily precise because "what is written may later be the subject of interpretation by laypeople, other lawyers, and judges."[178] Words like *hereinunder* and *forthwith* (or, as we know them, *below* and *immediately*) were commonplace in legal documents.

Yet, while the legal documents demanded exacting language, this precision somehow did not extend to gender. For centuries, the pronoun "he" was used as a universal term, considered inclusive of all people, or at least as inclusive as men in the eighteenth century believed it to be. It wasn't until the 1960s that this began to shift, and legal writing started replacing the universal "he" with "he or she."[179]

Fast forward to today, and law firms, like many other institutions, are changing. Tattoos and piercings are now more common, work-life balance is no longer a myth, and there's a concerted effort to simplify legal language to make it accessible. And while the singular "they" used universally remains contentious in some courts, the New York Advisory Committee on Judicial Ethics issued an opinion in 2021 stating that a judge may not require the use of "he" or "she" when someone informs the court that their designated pronoun is "they."[180] This is a meaningful step forward.

This chapter focuses on the legal departments within organizations and their role in advocating for gender inclusion. However, it's important to note that many businesses outsource their legal work or rely on external counsel. The cultural influence of law firms on in-house legal teams remains significant. Given that many in-house counsel began their careers at law firms, the practices and perspectives cultivated in firms continue to shape the legal field as a whole.

Legal Compliance and Handling Discrimination

A company's legal department plays a critical role in maintaining compliance, protecting employee rights, and mitigating legal risks. As federal and state policies shift, legal teams must ensure that workplace protections remain aligned with established case law rather than political trends. This means taking a proactive stance—upholding anti-discrimination commitments, resisting unnecessary policy rollbacks, and preparing for potential legal challenges.

Beyond shaping company-wide compliance strategies, legal teams are also responsible for handling individual employee discrimination cases with fairness, sensitivity, and a clear understanding of legal obligations. Whether navigating broad regulatory changes or conducting internal investigations, the legal department must work closely with HR to create policies that are both legally sound and ethically grounded.

Legal Compliance in an Era of Rollbacks

The 2025 federal rollbacks on DEI and workplace protections have left businesses in uncharted legal territory. While Title VII remains in effect and federal case law continues to protect gender identity, enforcement has been severely weakened, and state-level restrictions are increasing. Legal teams must take a deliberate, informed approach—prioritizing existing civil rights laws over newly issued policies that contradict them and ensuring their companies do not preemptively comply with unlawful mandates.

Rather than automatically aligning company policies with every new state or federal directive, legal teams should assess changes critically and consider their long-term implications. Businesses that prematurely roll back protections may not only face future legal consequences but also risk damaging employee retention, workplace culture, and brand reputation. Key considerations for legal departments include:

- **Title VII Still Applies:** Despite federal agencies deprioritizing enforcement, courts have upheld that gender identity discrimination is unlawful under Title VII. Companies should not assume that new federal policies override these protections.

- **Monitor Lawsuits and Legal Challenges:** Multiple lawsuits are already challenging anti-trans policies. If courts block or overturn these rollbacks, companies that preemptively complied may have to reverse course.

- **Assess Risks of Premature Compliance:** Some businesses are rolling back DEI initiatives due to pressure from federal agencies threatening to withhold funding or contracts. However, early compliance is not legally required and may expose companies to future liability.

- **Develop Clear Internal Protocols:** Legal teams should work with HR to ensure that policies align with existing case law rather than shifting political agendas. Review all employee handbooks, nondiscrimination policies, and compliance training materials to confirm they remain inclusive.

- **Prepare for Potential Legal Challenges:** If a company faces legal threats (e.g., lawsuits, funding loss) for maintaining inclusion policies, legal teams should explore all avenues for legal recourse. Businesses do not have to comply immediately with unlawful mandates and may have grounds to challenge them in court.

Legal Oversight in Discrimination and Harassment Cases

Even as the federal government weakens enforcement of workplace protections, companies remain legally and ethically responsible for handling internal discrimination and harassment claims. The legal department plays a critical role in ensuring that every claim is taken seriously, investigated thoroughly, and resolved in compliance with both civil rights laws and company policies.

To uphold these responsibilities, legal teams must collaborate closely with Human Resources to translate external legal requirements into clear, actionable internal policies. Employee handbooks, non-disclosure agreements, and other employment-related documents should be reviewed to ensure they are both legally compliant and free from gender-based discrimination. This collaborative approach ensures that workplace protections are not just theoretical but also actively integrated into company policies and practices. Refer to "Workplace Policies and Practices" in Chapter 6 for more information.

The legal department ensures the organization meets statutory obligations while handling cases sensitively. Steps in the process include:

- **Internal Investigation:** Be involved from the start to guide a thorough, unbiased, and confidential investigation. Establish procedures for evidence collection, interviews, and case documentation.

- **Compliance with Laws:** Even with federal enforcement weakened, legal teams must ensure full compliance with existing anti-discrimination laws, including mandatory reporting where required. This is particularly important for companies operating in multiple states, as legal protections vary.

- **Disciplinary Actions:** Legal should guide HR in determining appropriate consequences for confirmed discrimination or harassment. This may range from mandatory DEI training and formal warnings to termination or even legal action in severe cases.

Collaboration Among HR, Legal, and External Consultants: Work closely with HR to create a compliant and humane approach to handling discrimination or harassment cases, considering the emotional impact on all parties. Develop a multidisciplinary strategy for addressing cases effectively. For example, HR may manage the employee-facing side of the case, ensuring support and clear communication, while legal ensures procedural fairness, compliance, and risk management. Companies should also consider bringing in external consultants or legal specialists to strengthen investigative processes and prevent future issues. I am often brought into businesses by employment lawyers to provide training or guidance on best practices, ensuring the company not only resolves the issue but also addresses underlying causes and promotes long-term inclusivity.

Crafting Gender-Neutral Documents

The legal department plays a crucial role in ensuring gender neutrality in various documents, such as employee contracts, corporate policies, and legal forms. As you will recall from "Writing with Respect: Written Communication Strategies" in Chapter 4, gender-neutral writing is about being *gender accurate*. If you know the pronoun of the person or people you're writing about, always use their correct pronouns. Neutrality is only necessary when you're writing about someone whose pronouns are unknown or when pertaining to anyone.

Here's a brief overview of key practices specific to legal documents:

- **Replace Traditional Masculine Pronouns:** One straightforward method involves substituting masculine pronouns with neutral terms. For instance, replacing "his or her position" with "the position."

- **Use Neutral Phrases:** Incorporate neutral language, such as "person" or "individual," to refer to a document's subject.

- **Define and Repeat:** Define specific terms and repeat them in the document, avoiding the need for pronouns.

- **Complete Sentence Restructuring:** In some instances, it might be necessary to restructure sentences entirely to eliminate pronouns.

While accepted in other types of documents, some neutral methods in legal writing are less accepted:

- **Listing all pronouns:** "He/she/they" is considered awkward in formal legal writing and should be avoided.

- **"They" as a singular pronoun:** While many recognize "they" as an inclusive singular pronoun, some judges consider its usage grammatically nonstandard or inappropriate for formal legal writing (and who are we to argue with a judge?).

- **Explanation clauses:** Use of a clause such as, "Unless the context otherwise requires, a reference to one gender shall include reference to the other genders," is no different from the incorrect use of "he" to signify everyone.[181]

It's important to check the guidelines for your specific state or jurisdiction, as acceptance of these methods may differ.

Vendor and Third-Party Agreements

Gender-inclusive efforts should extend beyond internal operations to encompass the organization's external relationships, including those with vendors, suppliers, and other third parties. The legal department is key in aligning these agreements with the company's inclusivity policies. Key components of this process include:

- **Review and Align Agreements:** Ensure all vendor agreements are in line with the company's inclusivity standards.

- ○ **Pre-Contract Review:** Examine terms and conditions to identify any clauses that conflict with the company's inclusivity objectives.

- ○ **Negotiation and Modification:** If issues are found, negotiate to modify or remove problematic clauses, or consider alternative vendors.

- **Incorporate Inclusivity Clauses:** Include necessary clauses to maintain gender-inclusive practices.

- ○ **Non-Discrimination Clauses:** Include clauses that mandate non-discrimination and the use of gender-neutral language.

- ○ **Compliance Requirements:** Specify expectations for gender-inclusive practices and potential penalties for non-compliance.

- **Collaborative Approach:** Ensure a team-based effort between departments to enforce inclusivity. Work with procurement, HR, and leadership to ensure a holistic approach to vendor relationships.

By scrutinizing and negotiating external agreements, the legal department significantly extends the company's gender-inclusivity policies, fostering a more inclusive business ecosystem. For example, during a pre-contract review with a potential vendor, the legal department might discover that the vendor's non-discrimination clause lacks specific protections for gender identity or expression. In such a case, the legal team would work with the vendor to revise the clause, ensuring it aligns with the company's inclusivity policies. If the vendor resists updating their terms, refer to "Addressing Resistance from Leaders and External Stakeholders" in the "Leadership" chapter (Chapter 5) for strategies to navigate these challenges.

Law Firms and Gender Inclusivity

Inclusivity in Case Management Systems

Many law firms and some larger legal departments within organizations will deploy case management systems to oversee all aspects of their caseload, including but not limited to relevant parties and contacts, settlement negotiations, billing, documents, and emails. While every product is different, these case management systems all typically offer the ability to generate documents from templates that populate text, including the ability to import contact information into the document. For example, a template can generate a letter with a client's honorific, name, and pronouns, such as, "We represent *Ms.* Jones in *her* case against. . ."

These templates are coded in Microsoft Word or Corel Word-Perfect (yes, that's right, WordPerfect) to generate honorifics and pronouns based on a gender field in the contact card. Gender-inclusive documents can be achieved by coding the templates with logic that inserts the appropriate honorific or pronoun based on gender. This way, documents can automatically have "she," "he," or "they" conjugated appropriately throughout the document. There are many different customization options:

- **Fully customizable:** Some systems offer the ability to create your own fields. In this case, you could create specific fields for pronouns and honorifics, ensuring you always use the correct data.

- **Partially customizable:** Some products offer customizable fields for gender on the contact cards, allowing you to select from options like "Man," "Woman," and "Nonbinary." The vendor, your IT team, or external consultants can help determine what can be customized and how to implement it.

- **Restricted customization:** Other products only offer two options, "Male" and "Female," but there are workarounds:
  - Use the system's "Other" field (often available when generating contact cards for companies) to represent nonbinary individuals.
  - Fields that are not used for other purposes can sometimes be reappropriated for gender or pronouns.

These internal systems are not visible to clients, but they allow you to generate inclusive documents that acknowledge all identities.

If you're evaluating case management systems, be sure to investigate each product's gender-inclusive features. Some products I've worked with include TrialWorks, Aderant Total Office, PracticeMaster, and FileVine, but there are many others. While software selection involves multiple criteria, gender inclusivity should be part of your review process. Look for features such as a third-gender option on contact cards or customizable gender fields. Today, it's uncommon to find systems lacking any gender-diverse capabilities, and a product with no options likely signals outdated functionality in more than just inclusivity.

Firms may use a different billing system, even if the case management system includes a billing or financial module. If your systems are separate, it is equally important that these systems support gender inclusivity. Ensure billing systems use the correct honorifics, pronouns, and client preferences so that every interaction, including invoices and correspondence, is inclusive and respectful.

Pronouns in Attorney and Staff Bios

Law firms list every attorney on their firm's website. Some firms (dare I say, the more inclusive ones) also list their support staff. Bios provide basic information about the people who will be working on your case: education and employment history, expertise, contact info, and more. Pronouns are valuable information for many potential clients. If I'm undecided between two attorneys, I'll surely pick the one who listed their pronouns over the one who did not, because that attorney is signaling to me that they will be respectful of my nonbinary identity.

Likewise, a firm with no pronouns listed across any bios sends the opposite message. It suggests to me that inclusion isn't a priority for the firm. It's possible, though highly unlikely, that no one in the firm would have chosen to list their pronouns.

Law firms steeped in traditional practices may worry that including pronouns could turn away clients who expect a more formal or conservative environment. However, this assumption risks overlooking the growing number of clients who are parents, grandparents, or relatives of transgender or nonbinary individuals and care deeply about how inclusively their legal team operates.

For a more detailed discussion of the benefits and challenges of including pronouns in professional bios, refer to "Inclusive Talk: Verbal Communication Strategies" in Chapter 4.

Client Engagement in Sensitive Practice Areas

In many practice areas, such as family law, elder law, probate law, and trust and estates law, attorneys and support staff must be particularly mindful of the interpersonal dynamics among family members. It is essential to recognize microaggressions and not validate behaviors that undermine a client's identity. For instance, consider a situation where a father uses his adult child's legal name, but the mother uses they/them pronouns and a different name for the child. This likely indicates that their child is nonbinary, and the father is deadnaming them. As a legal professional, you must be adept enough to identify these cues and avoid participating in deadnaming or misgendering.

Recognizing and handling such situations with care is critical to fostering a supportive and inclusive environment for all clients.

Other practice areas, such as immigration law, healthcare law, and education law, must balance the complexities of identity, policy, and institutional practices. Training on the specific nuances of each practice area equips legal teams to handle the respective dynamics thoughtfully, not only supporting clients but also preventing harm through sensitive, informed interactions.

Mergers and Acquisitions

Mergers and acquisitions (M&A) are complex transactions that offer a unique opportunity to align or enhance a company's gender inclusion policies. As part of the due diligence process, the legal department should evaluate the gender inclusion practices of any company that is a potential target for merger or acquisition.

- **Initial Assessment:** Evaluate the target company's policies and practices related to gender inclusion.
    - **Internal Policies and Practices:** Review the target company's policies, employment practices, and any history of gender-based discrimination or harassment.
    - **HR Collaboration:** Work with HR to compare policies and identify gaps or concerns.
- **Public Image and Market Position:** Ensure the target company's public image and market positioning align with your inclusion values. For guidance on handling resistance within the target company, refer to "Addressing Resistance from Leaders and External Stakeholders" in the "Leadership" chapter (Chapter 5).

- o **Brand Alignment:** Assess the target company's reputation and public image to ensure alignment with your company's values on gender inclusion.
- o **Customer Base:** Evaluate the target company's customer base and market positioning to identify any potential conflicts.
- **Contractual Clauses:** Integrate inclusion standards directly into the M&A agreement. Should the target company's leaders express resistance to inclusion clauses, see "Addressing Resistance from Leaders and External Stakeholders" in the "Leadership" chapter (Chapter 5) for strategies to address this challenge.
  - o **Inclusion Clauses:** Include specific clauses in the M&A agreement that require the target company to meet your standards for gender inclusion. These can be conditions for completing the transaction or milestones to be achieved post-acquisition.
- **Proactive Solutions:** Implement strategies to ensure the newly merged entity adheres to gender inclusion policies.
  - o **Training and Policy Revisions:** Recommend solutions such as training programs, policy updates, or structural changes to align the newly merged entity with the company's gender-inclusive vision.

Incorporating gender inclusion into the M&A due diligence process helps avoid reputational risks and fosters a cohesive, inclusive culture post-acquisition.

Continuing Legal Education

Continuing Legal Education (CLE) ensures that the legal team stays updated on ever-changing laws and best practices. Given the growing importance of Diversity, Equity, and Inclusion

(DEI) in today's business world, the legal department should prioritize CLEs that focus on these topics, including gender inclusion.

Many states now require or strongly encourage CLE credits in ethics to cover DEI matters. These courses delve into the ethical obligations of lawyers to foster environments free from discrimination and bias, including gender bias. They offer guidance on implementing gender-inclusive practices within legal frameworks, addressing potential conflicts, and understanding the evolving landscape of gender-related laws and norms.

Insights obtained from CLEs should be incorporated into document drafting, client and colleague interactions, and the creation and interpretation of company policies. The legal department should not only attend such CLE courses but also lead in sharing these insights with other departments, ensuring a company-wide understanding of gender-inclusive best practices.

In addition to attending external courses, the legal department should collaborate with HR to facilitate in-house training sessions tailored to address the company's specific needs and challenges. This cross-departmental interaction ensures that legal insights on gender inclusivity are aligned with the practical needs of other departments, contributing to a holistic approach to gender inclusion within the organization.

Summary Checklist for Legal

Ensuring Legal Compliance and Handling Discrimination

☐ Stay informed on state, federal, and international laws, prioritizing established case law over shifting political directives.

☐ Monitor lawsuits challenging DEI rollbacks to anticipate potential legal changes.

☐ Prepare legal strategies to challenge unlawful mandates or defend against funding threats.

☐ Scrutinize all employment-related documents—handbooks,
policies, NDAs—for legal compliance and gender inclusion.

☐ Ensure company policies remain inclusive and do not preemptively comply with unlawful mandates.

☐ Collaborate with HR and external consultants to uphold workplace protections and maintain an inclusive environment.

☐ Guide a thorough, unbiased, and confidential internal investigation for discrimination or harassment claims.

☐ Ensure compliance with legal reporting requirements, particularly in states with varying protections.

☐ Oversee disciplinary actions to align with company policy and legal obligations.

Crafting Gender-Neutral Documents

☐ Ensure generic and template legal forms and documents use gender-neutral language.

☐ Maintain gender accuracy when creating documents for known entities.

☐ Ensure precision and clarity when using "they" as a singular pronoun in court documents.

☐ Consider alternative gender-neutral methods for judicial documents.

Vendor and Third-Party Agreements

☐ Review terms and conditions of agreements for alignment with inclusion objectives.

☐ Negotiate to modify or remove problematic clauses.

☐ Include non-discrimination clauses and compliance requirements in agreements.

☐ Collaborate with procurement, HR, and leadership on vendor relationships.

Mergers and Acquisitions

☐ Review the target company's policies, employment practices, and history of discrimination.

☐ Assess the target company's reputation and public image for alignment with values on gender inclusion.

☐ Include inclusion clauses in M&A agreements.

☐ Recommend training programs and policy updates post-acquisition.

Continuing Legal Education

☐ Prioritize CLE courses focused on Diversity, Equity, and Inclusion (DEI).

☐ Incorporate gender-inclusive practices into everyday legal practice.

☐ Lead in sharing DEI insights with other departments.

☐ Collaborate with HR to facilitate in-house training sessions.

CHAPTER 08

IT: ENSURING INCLUSIVE SYSTEMS AND NETWORKS

It was the early 2000s, and I found myself mediating between an irate finance manager and a grumbling IT team, all because of a username. Denise had just gotten married and requested to have her email changed from "djones" to "dsmith." It should have been simple, right? Spoiler alert: it wasn't, and it wasn't the only time this happened.

The IT team updated her email, but everywhere Denise looked, her old name, Jones, was still lurking in the document scanner, the internal directories, even her email screen. Every time she saw it, her frustration grew. To Denise, this wasn't a technical issue; it was about respect. But the IT team didn't see it that way. "What's the big deal?" they thought. Maybe that's the patriarchy talking, telling us that when women ask for something to be fully fixed, they're just "being difficult."

Now, imagine if Denise were a trans person, seeing her deadname pop up everywhere. That's more than frustrating; it's deeply personal and terribly painful.

Today's technology makes it much easier to handle these kinds of updates, and something as simple as a name change should never feel like a drawn-out battle. Yet, the process still requires care and attention to ensure inclusion at every step.

This is especially critical for outsourced IT providers and CIOs. Beyond fixing problems, they're advising businesses on how to align their technology with modern values. If your IT department or provider can't model the inclusivity your business promotes, how can they be trusted to build the systems that will support it?

Tech Language and Identity Representation

IT teams play a crucial role in shaping the digital tools employees use daily, yet language inclusivity is often overlooked in system configurations. One simple but impactful step toward more inclusive language is enabling the Inclusivity Checker in Microsoft Word's grammar settings. This feature flags gendered or non-inclusive language, prompting users to adjust their phrasing to be more inclusive regarding gender bias, neutral pronouns, and gender-specific language (among other areas). And before you ask, Google paused its inclusivity settings in 2022, and WordPerfect doesn't offer such a feature.

By setting this feature as a default across the organization, IT departments can help users who may not even be aware of it to communicate more inclusively. Many IT professionals and end users aren't familiar with all the nuanced features in software like Microsoft Word, which often runs on outdated defaults. Enabling inclusivity settings fosters a more inclusive workplace, even in subtle ways like grammar checks, and aligns with the organization's commitment to equity and respectful communication.

Creating a gender-inclusive IT environment starts with both small technical adjustments and the everyday language we use. Tools like Microsoft Word's Inclusivity Checker are a great first step, but IT departments can go further by evaluating and updating the broader terminology used across systems and processes.

Words shape our perceptions, and by choosing inclusive terms, IT departments help set a welcoming tone for everyone. Here are some ways to update tech terminology:

- **Cybersecurity:** Swap out terms like "whitelisting" and "blacklisting" for "allow list" and "blocklist" to eliminate racial undertones. Replace "manually" or "manual" with "by hand" or "user-controlled" to avoid gendered language. Instead of "disabled" and "enabled," use "inactive" and "active" for clearer, more inclusive descriptors.

- **Networking Contexts:** Terms like "master" and "slave" can be problematic. Opt for "primary" and "secondary," "controller" and "device," or "leader" and "follower" to convey roles without oppressive language.

- **Project Management:** Replace "man hours" with "person hours" or "work hours" for a non-gendered approach. Similarly, use "workforce" or "staff" instead of "manpower" to reflect inclusivity.

- **Applications Involving Personal Milestones:** Labels like "spouse 1" and "spouse 2" or "partner 1" and "partner 2" are more inclusive than "bride" and "groom." This makes applications inclusive for all couples, regardless of their gender identity.

Inclusivity in server naming conventions is another often overlooked detail. While naming servers after constellations, planets, or versions (e.g., "2K12" or "2K15") might seem neutral, it's important to avoid names that perpetuate gender norms or stereotypes. For instance, using "King" and "Queen" or "Mars" and "Venus" to denote primary and secondary servers can reinforce traditional gender roles. Instead, you can inject some personality while staying gender-neutral by naming servers after Star Trek starships (like *Enterprise* or *Voyager*) or mythical places like "Atlantis" and "Asgard." It's a win-win: you get personality *and* inclusion.

Inclusion is also about ensuring that employees' names and pronouns are consistently and accurately displayed across all digital platforms. IT departments can leverage existing tools like identity and access management systems (IAM) or email signature software to manage user profiles. Some systems allow for custom fields or the repurposing of existing ones to include pronouns, even when universal pronoun fields aren't built in yet. Handling these details with care—including updating name changes due to marriage, divorce, or gender transition—affirms individual identities and creates a welcoming atmosphere for everyone.

By consciously updating both our technical vocabulary and the way we handle personal information, these changes, while seemingly small, can have a big impact on fostering a more inclusive and welcoming workplace for everyone.

Inclusive Onboarding and Offboarding

Welcoming new employees and saying goodbye to departing ones are perfect opportunities for IT departments to show the organization's commitment to gender inclusion. While HR handles broader aspects, IT implements the technical solutions that affirm each individual's gender identity throughout their time at the company.

- **Initial Account Setup:** During onboarding, IT can work with HR to ensure new hires can specify their pronouns and chosen name from the start. These details should be consistently reflected across all digital platforms, including email, intranet, and internal software.

- **Personalized Training Modules:** If your organization uses an online training platform, configure it to address employees by their pronouns and chosen name in training modules and any automated certificates of completion.

- **Digital Badges and Employee Profiles:** Design digital badges or profiles to incorporate not just the employee's name and title, but also their pronouns, if the employee chooses to disclose them.

- **Respectful Account Deactivation:** During offboarding, ensure the departing employee's digital accounts and profiles are deactivated respectfully, using the employee's pronouns and chosen name in any farewell messages or acknowledgments.

- **Data Retention and Privacy:** Handle the deactivation and storage of accounts with privacy in mind, particularly around gender identity. Ensure that any contributions the employee made (e.g., posts or comments) continue to display the correct pronouns and chosen name, even after their departure.

- **Exit Feedback Process:** Collaborate with HR to include an exit survey that is mindful of gender identity issues. This feedback is valuable for refining and improving inclusion initiatives going forward.

By paying attention to these details, IT departments not only respect individual identity but also send a powerful message that the company values each person, from their first day to their last.

APIs and Third-Party Integrations

In our increasingly interconnected digital world, IT departments often use APIs (Application Programming Interfaces) and third-party integrations to boost functionalities and streamline tasks. It's crucial to scrutinize these external elements for their commitment to gender inclusion. Before adopting any third-party service or tool, IT should evaluate them for non-inclusive language or settings. Should a vendor resist adjusting their offerings to align with your organization's inclusion standards, refer to "Addressing Resistance from Leaders and External Stakeholders" in the "Leadership" chapter (Chapter 5) for guidance.

Being proactive in this vetting process ensures that all systems, whether internal or external, align with the organization's standards and goals for gender inclusion. For a specific example, see "Human Resources: Fostering an Inclusive Culture" (Chapter 6) on HR selecting inclusive HRIS and payroll systems.

For instance, a customer relationship management (CRM) tool might default to form fields with titles like "Mr." or "Mrs." This can be exclusionary for those who don't identify within the gender binary. Before integrating such a CRM into the company's existing infrastructure, the IT department should ensure the platform allows for customizable titles or, at the very least, an "Other" option. Failing to vet these systems can inadvertently signal that the company does not fully support gender diversity and inclusion, which is increasingly important to every employee who may walk through the door, especially for younger generations like Gen Z, who, as discussed earlier, actively seek workplaces that align with their values of inclusion and respect.

A lack of integration between systems can also lead to significant problems. A transgender or nonbinary student, using their preferred name throughout the application process, expects this name to be used consistently throughout their time at the university. Initially, the acceptance letter and promotional materials use the preferred name, and so do the finance and billing departments. However, issues arise when the student housing department sends documents or marketing swag using the student's deadname, indicating a failure in the system's integration and communication between departments. This undermines students' trust in the institution's inclusivity.

To avoid such discrepancies, IT departments must ensure that all systems, from email platforms to HR databases, are integrated effectively to maintain a consistent and inclusive user experience. Proactively vetting and managing third-party integrations is key to ensuring that they reflect the company's values around diversity and respect. Moreover, these tools should be adaptable and capable of keeping up with the company's evolving inclusivity practices.

Mitigating Bias in Biometric and Other Systems

As technology continues to evolve, biometric systems, facial recognition, and other scanning technologies are increasingly used in everyday security measures, from employee access to financial transactions. Unfortunately, these technologies, and others like them, are not always designed with gender diversity in mind, which can create challenges for transgender and nonbinary individuals. Many biometric systems rely on binary gender assumptions, which leads to misidentification and exclusion for those who do not fit within traditional male or female categories.

For example, facial recognition software often fails to accurately identify transgender and nonbinary individuals due to its reliance on binary gender datasets. These systems are trained primarily on data that categorizes individuals as male or female based on physical traits like bone structure, facial hair, or makeup, which may not align with a person's gender identity. Additionally, many transgender individuals may not have had the opportunity or resources to update their legal identification, further complicating their interaction with such systems.

IT departments play a critical role in identifying and mitigating the biases inherent in various systems, including but not limited to biometric technologies. To support inclusion, IT teams should:

- **Research and Recommend Advanced Solutions:** Proactively research biometric and recognition systems that are designed with inclusion in mind. This includes selecting systems that offer more than just facial recognition, such as fingerprint or voice recognition. IT teams should prioritize solutions that offer flexibility and avoid reinforcing gender binaries.

- **Advise Departments on Limitations:** Inform relevant teams, such as HR or security, about the limitations of current systems regarding gender inclusion. Ensuring that all departments are aware of these shortcomings allows the organization to implement alternative solutions, such as manual identity verification or multiple recognition methods.

- **Test and Vet Systems for Inclusivity:** Before implementing any biometric system, IT teams should rigorously test the technology to assess how it handles nonbinary and transgender identities. This testing should include individuals from diverse gender backgrounds and other intersecting identities, such as race and ethnicity, to ensure the system does not inadvertently exclude or misgender users.

Incorporating Inclusivity into System Design

Beyond biometric considerations, there are additional ways to support inclusion across IT infrastructure:

- **Customizable Identity Fields:** Ensure that systems allow for gender-neutral options or custom identity fields, such as allowing users to select "Nonbinary," "Prefer not to say," or another identity marker. Where possible, create fields for pronouns and chosen names.

- **Ongoing Education and Feedback:** Engage in continuous education about emerging technologies that address gender inclusion. Feedback loops with users who are transgender or nonbinary should be integrated into system evaluation and updates, ensuring the technology evolves alongside the company's inclusion goals.

Creating Inclusive Virtual Spaces

As remote work becomes increasingly prevalent, virtual spaces like online meetings, intranets, and digital workspaces serve as the new water cooler for employees. IT departments should establish guidelines to make these spaces inclusive. For instance, during virtual meetings, ensuring that everyone's pronouns (if they choose) and chosen names are visible can be a simple yet impactful measure. Additionally, if the company utilizes digital avatars or employee representations, offering customizable and nonbinary options allows everyone the freedom to express their gender identity authentically.

In addition to gender inclusion, privacy and accessibility should be top priorities. IT should ensure that virtual platforms respect the privacy of all employees, especially for those who may be concerned about being outed or misgendered. Accessibility features, such as screen reader compatibility, closed captioning, and high-contrast display options, help create a fully inclusive digital experience. By supporting these essential aspects, IT departments can ensure that every employee feels respected and valued, regardless of their physical location.

Cybersecurity and Privacy for LGBTQ+ Staff

IT support involves more than fixing technical issues; it's about ensuring the digital well-being of all employees. For LGBTQ+ employees, this means extra measures to protect against online harassment, potential outing, and unauthorized disclosure of personal information.

Here are some key actions IT departments can take to enhance cybersecurity and privacy:

- **Anti-Harassment Measures:** Implement software solutions, such as AI-based tools, to detect and filter hate speech, cyberbullying, or harassment targeting LGBTQ+ employees. These tools should flag discriminatory language or symbols that might otherwise go unnoticed. Ensure they are integrated into email systems, internal messaging platforms, and collaboration tools.

  - **Validate and Audit Automated Tools**: Regularly audit these tools to ensure effectiveness and combine automated filtering with human review for comprehensive protection. For example, a middle school found that its filtering software failed to catch inappropriate language from students using slang, fragmented phrases, and gaming references to issue threats. This oversight allowed the bullying of a nonbinary teen to go unnoticed on the school's online platform, emphasizing the importance of combining technology with human review to protect against harassment.

- **Secure Data Storage:** Store personal data securely, including gender identity and sexual orientation. Use encryption and restricted access controls to minimize unauthorized data leaks and ensure that sensitive information is protected.

- **Privacy Policies:** Collaborate with HR to develop and maintain privacy policies that clearly outline the levels of confidentiality surrounding employees' personal information. Provide training to all staff on handling sensitive information respectfully and in compliance with legal standards.

- **Monitoring and Reporting Systems:** Establish a robust reporting system for digital harassment or privacy breaches, allowing for anonymous submissions to encourage employees to report incidents without fear of retribution. Communicate clearly to employees how and where to report incidents to foster a safe reporting environment.

- **Safe Online Spaces:** Create dedicated online spaces where LGBTQ+ employees can communicate safely. Internal forums, Slack or Teams channels, and intranet chat groups with controlled access can provide a secure platform for discussing topics of interest or concern. These spaces should be private and restricted to ensure that only designated participants can join, promoting a confidential and safe environment.

Auditing Language for Compliance

Regular audits of software, documentation, and code are essential to ensure that the language used aligns with the organization's inclusivity guidelines. IT departments should schedule periodic audits to scrutinize not only front-end user interfaces but also back-end systems, such as databases, internal documentation, error messages, system alerts, and API responses. When non-inclusive language is identified, plans should be implemented to revise it promptly.

For example, an error message that reads, "Username does not match our records. Please ask the account owner or his or her administrator for help," could be updated to, "Username does not match our records. Please ask the account owner or their administrator for assistance."

Similarly, an API response might currently require, "User must choose between 'Male' or 'Female' in the gender field." An inclusive language audit could suggest updating this to: "User may enter 'Male,' 'Female,' 'Nonbinary,' 'Prefer not to say,' or another specified gender identity in the gender field." This audit could also identify instances where a gender field might be better substituted with a pronoun field.

Summary Checklist for IT

Tech Language and Identity Representation

- ☐ Replace cybersecurity, networking, and project management terms to be gender neutral.
- ☐ Choose gender-neutral server naming conventions.
- ☐ Ensure employees' names, pronouns, and titles are accurately displayed across all digital platforms.
- ☐ Manage name changes across all systems to avoid deadnaming.

Inclusive Onboarding and Offboarding

- ☐ Include pronouns and chosen name in initial account setup.
- ☐ Configure training modules to address new hires by their pronouns and chosen name.
- ☐ Design digital badges to incorporate pronouns if disclosed and desired.
- ☐ Deactivate accounts using the departing employee's pronouns and chosen name.
- ☐ Ensure privacy in data retention and display pronouns and chosen name in historical posts and comments.
- ☐ Create an exit survey that is mindful of gender identity issues.

APIs and Third-Party Integrations

- ☐ Evaluate third-party services for non-inclusive language or settings.
- ☐ Ensure platforms allow for customizable options in form fields.
- ☐ Ensure all departments use updated information consistently to avoid deadnaming.
- ☐ Research and select biometric (or other) systems that allow for flexibility beyond binary gender recognition.
- ☐ Advise departments (e.g., HR, Security) on the limitations and inclusive practices of biometric (or other) systems.

☐ Test biometric (or other) systems for inclusivity across gender identities, focusing on misidentification risks for transgender and nonbinary users.

☐ Create custom fields or repurpose existing ones in identity and asset management systems for pronouns if fields do not exist.

☐ Develop feedback loops with transgender and nonbinary users to continually evaluate system inclusivity.

Creating Inclusive Virtual Spaces

☐ Ensure pronouns (optional) and chosen names are visible in virtual meetings.

☐ Provide nonbinary options for digital avatars.

☐ Establish guidelines for inclusivity in online meeting platforms and intranets.

Cybersecurity and Privacy for LGBTQ+ Staff

☐ Implement tools to detect and filter hate speech and cyberbullying (with human review).

☐ Store personal data securely with encryption and restricted access.

☐ Develop privacy policies outlining confidentiality levels for personal information.

☐ Establish anonymous reporting systems for digital harassment or privacy breaches.

☐ Create dedicated online spaces with controlled access for LGBTQ+ employees.

Auditing Language for Compliance

☐ Schedule regular audits of software, documentation, and code for inclusivity.

☐ Update non-inclusive language in error messages, system alerts, and API responses.

☐ Ensure inclusive language in all system documentation and interfaces.

CHAPTER 09

MARKETING AND BRANDING: CRAFTING INCLUSIVE NARRATIVES

In the 1950s, an ad for a new kind of bottle cap by Alcoa Aluminum of America featured a woman with a delightfully surprised expression, her hand poised daintily near the bottle as the copy began, "All it takes is a dainty grasp, an easy, two-finger twist." The tagline read: "Easily—without a knife blade, a bottle opener, or even a husband!" Ads like these reinforced the idea that women were weak and dependent, reflecting the rigid gender roles and societal expectations of the time.

Fast forward to 1997, when Holiday Inn aired a Super Bowl ad to promote their billion-dollar hotel upgrades. The ad featured a trans woman who attends her high school reunion, confidently walking across the room as men gape at her. As they stare, a voiceover lists the costs of her surgeries—"New nose, $6,000. New lips, $3,000," and so on—drawing a comparison to hotel renovations and implying that her identity as a woman is artificial, a deceptive mask created by surgery. One man excitedly flirts with her until he realizes she is trans, at which point his expression shifts to shock. The voiceover concludes, "It's amazing the changes you can make for a few thousand dollars. Imagine what Holiday Inns will look like when we spend a billion," reinforcing the harmful notion that trans women aren't "real" women. After receiving complaints, Holiday Inn pulled the ad, which had already done damage by exploiting a trans woman's identity as a punchline.[182]

In contrast, Absolut Vodka's 2016 ad titled "Darla" embraced a narrative of allyship and acceptance. The ad tells the story of a cisgender man reconnecting with a friend who had transitioned. "She was the same person, the same heart. She hadn't changed. I had," the man reflects, underscoring that her identity as a trans woman was valid and that it was his perspective that needed to evolve.[183] Absolut made a conscious choice to hire a trans actress for this role, providing a job to a trans woman in an industry that often casts cis actors in trans roles (much like Holiday Inn did). Though the ad is told through the lens of a cisgender man and doesn't feature the trans woman's own voice, it was still a far cry from the mockery seen in the Holiday Inn ad.

Absolut didn't stop at messaging. Their "Out & Open" campaign actively supports LGBTQ+ bars that serve as crucial community hubs. The campaign amplifies the real-life stories of gender-diverse LGBTQ+ individuals to ensure that their voices are heard. By raising funds to preserve these spaces, Absolut demonstrates that true allyship involves real-world impact and sustained support for marginalized communities.[184]

Marketing has often reflected certain aspects of the world we live in, though not always the most inclusive or forward-thinking ones. As society evolves, marketing can now expand understanding, challenge outdated stereotypes, and represent diverse identities authentically. Brands that embrace inclusion are creating genuine connections with their audiences and contributing to a more equitable future.

While retail serves as a central example in this chapter, the principles discussed here are applicable across any business or industry that engages in marketing and branding.

Gender-Neutral Marketing and Branding Strategies

Understanding your audience is fundamental to success. This understanding enables you to create products, services, and marketing campaigns that resonate meaningfully with them. When it comes to implementing gender neutrality in marketing and branding, comprehending the diverse identities and preferences of your audience is of utmost importance. Some methods for conducting inclusive audience research and gathering insights include:

- **Surveys and Questionnaires:** Conduct surveys and questionnaires that include questions about gender identity and preferences. Ensure that these surveys are designed to allow respondents to express their gender identity beyond binary categories.

- **Social Listening:** Use social media monitoring tools to listen to conversations about your brand and industry. Analyze discussions on gender and inclusion to understand what matters most to your audience.

- **Audience Segmentation:** Segment your audience based on various criteria, including gender identity, but also consider other factors such as age, location, and interests. This segmentation helps in tailoring your marketing efforts.

Gender-Neutral Messaging and Branding

Creating gender-neutral messaging and branding appeals to a wider and more diverse audience.

- **Inclusive Language:** Avoid gender-specific terms and pronouns when possible. Use gender-neutral language that accommodates all gender identities. For example, instead of addressing customers as Mr. or Ms., consider using gender-neutral alternatives like Mx. In environments that allow for more casual conversational style, I suggest dropping honorifics entirely.

- **Imagery and Visual Design:** To resonate with a broad audience, ensure that advertisements and other promotional materials portray a wide range of gender identities. Feature individuals of different gender presentations, ethnic backgrounds, and abilities. By avoiding imagery that reinforces traditional gender roles or stereotypes, brands can create a more inclusive and authentic visual narrative. This approach not only signals a commitment to diversity but also strengthens the emotional connection between the brand and its audience—an important factor, as research from Gallup shows that 70% of brand preference decisions are driven by emotional factors rather than rational ones.[185]

- **Color Schemes:** Select color schemes that do not rely on stereotypical associations like pink for females and blue for males. Opt for colors that are neutral and not linked to specific genders. This shift in color choices can make a brand's products and messaging more appealing and relatable to a diverse audience.

Product and Service Development

The commitment to gender-neutral marketing should extend into all aspects of product and service development, including design choices and materials. This includes offering gender-neutral product options and creating materials that respect and acknowledge diverse identities. Here are some key reasons brands are prioritizing gender-neutral approaches:

- **Designing for Inclusivity:** Consider offering the option to include pronouns on business cards, email signatures, customized letterhead, and other materials that represent the brand. This small design choice can make a big impact, signaling to customers and employees that your business respects and acknowledges gender diversity.

- **Broadening Market Reach:** Offering gender-neutral product options not only demonstrates a commitment to inclusion and diversity but also significantly expands a brand's market reach. By providing products that cater to diverse identities, your brand becomes more accessible, which fosters a sense of belonging and increases customer engagement. For example, fashion brands like Zara and Gucci have introduced gender-neutral clothing lines, appealing to a broader audience beyond traditional gender categories. Similarly, Calvin Klein's iconic CK Everyone fragrance has been popular for decades because it transcends the boundaries of traditionally masculine or feminine scents, offering broad appeal to those who prefer something versatile. This trend is especially relevant for Generation Z, with more than half of them choosing to shop outside of traditional men's or women's sections, reflecting a growing preference for brands that don't confine them to traditional gender norms.[186]

- **Meeting Customer Demand:** Consumers are increasingly seeking products and brands that align with their values, including gender inclusion. One notable example of a company listening to their customers was Target. In 2015, an Ohio woman tweeted a picture of a sign in Target's toy section that separated "building sets" from "girls' building sets." The image went viral, sparking a widespread debate about the appropriateness of gender-specific toys.[187] Just two months later, Target announced that it was eliminating gender-based signage throughout their stores and removing the separation of boys' and girls' toys from their shelves. This change met the growing consumer demand for more inclusive products and experiences, reinforcing Target's reputation at the time as a responsive, inclusive brand.

- **Enhancing Brand Reputation:** Embracing gender-neutral product development can significantly enhance a brand's reputation. Brands seen as forward-thinking and inclusive garner positive attention and support from both customers and the broader community. For instance, Mattel, the maker of Barbie, launched the Creatable World line in 2019. These dolls come with a variety of hair, clothing, and accessory options allowing kids to mix and match without being confined to traditional gender norms.[188] This innovation not only expanded Mattel's customer base but also reinforced its reputation as a brand that listens to and evolves with cultural shifts.

Designing Inclusive Marketing Campaigns

Gender-neutral marketing campaigns foster inclusion and resonate with consumers across the gender spectrum. Here are some elements to consider when designing such campaigns:

- **Authentic Representation:** Authenticity is paramount. Campaigns should accurately reflect the diversity of gender identities, ensuring individuals from different backgrounds and experiences feel seen and heard. My favorite example is the Gillette commercial featuring a dad teaching his trans son how to shave for the first time. The ad was widely praised for authentically representing a pivotal moment in many young men's lives, while also reflecting and including the experiences of trans men.

- **Inclusive Messaging:** Craft messages that avoid gender assumptions. Use inclusive language and pronouns (e.g., they/them) to create a welcoming atmosphere. Lego revamped its online store to allow shoppers to browse by themes, ages, and interests without categorizing toys as "for boys" or "for girls." Their messaging reinforces the idea that their products are for all children, helping to create a more inclusive shopping experience for everyone. Refer to "Strategies for Gender-Inclusive Communication" (Chapter 4) for additional strategies.

- **Diverse Visuals:** Visual elements play a significant role in marketing campaigns. Ensure that imagery and multimedia represent a wide range of gender identities and expressions. Apple's ongoing updates to its emoji library offer gender-neutral and nonbinary characters alongside traditional male and female options, ensuring that everyone can feel represented. By expanding visual representation through something as simple as emojis, Apple demonstrates how even small changes in diverse visuals can create a more inclusive experience for users.

- **Intersectionality:** Recognize that gender identity intersects with other aspects of identity, such as race, ethnicity, and sexual orientation. Campaigns should acknowledge these intersections and avoid reinforcing stereotypes. Dove's "Real Beauty" campaign has consistently featured people of different races, body types, and ages, ensuring that anyone can see themselves represented in their ads.

- **Inclusive Product Placement:** Showcase products and services without relying on traditional gender roles. Challenge gender stereotypes in your advertising. Axe has gone from glorifying extreme male stereotypes to actively dismantling them. Their "Find Your Magic" campaign aims to break free from toxic masculinity and encourages men to embrace their individuality.

- **Engage with Diverse Voices:** Collaborate with individuals and influencers from diverse gender backgrounds to bring authenticity to your campaigns. Fenty Beauty by Rihanna partnered with influencers across the gender spectrum to promote its inclusive beauty products, catering to a wide range of skin tones, gender expressions, and body types.

- **Feedback and Testing:** Seek feedback from focus groups and conduct testing to ensure that your campaigns are genuinely inclusive and well-received. Dove launched its "Campaign for Real Beauty" in 2004 after conducting a major global study, *The Real Truth About Beauty: A Global Report*, which revealed that only 2% of women worldwide would describe themselves as beautiful. This feedback informed Dove's campaign, which focused on redefining beauty standards and ensuring that women of all backgrounds felt represented.[189] Since then, Dove has continued its research, with a 2024 follow-up study revealing ongoing shifts in beauty perceptions, helping the brand further evolve its campaigns to remain relevant and inclusive.[190]

Case Study: Potato Head's Rebrand: Playing with Inclusivity

Toys have long reflected prevailing gender norms. Traditionally, boys' toys emphasized action and adventure, while girls' toys leaned toward nurturing and domesticity. This clear-cut divide began in the 1940s when manufacturers recognized the potential for gendered marketing. Before that, toys were not so rigidly marketed to different genders. The post-World War II consumer culture in America, with greater disposable income, saw toy companies capitalizing on this by marketing products specifically for boys or girls.[191]

In recent times, the toy industry has seen a significant shift. In 2019, Mattel unveiled a line of gender-neutral dolls, breaking free from traditional gender markers in toy design. Hasbro joined this wave of change in 2021 by dropping the Mr. from its iconic Mr. Potato Head toy.

The original Mr. Potato Head, introduced in the 1950s, didn't include a potato. Instead, it consisted of accessories like eyes, noses, and mouths, leaving children to find their own potato in the kitchen—a creative and DIY approach to playtime. Over the years, Mr. Potato Head evolved, embracing different characters and themes, but it always carried the Mr. title, signaling a specific gender identity.

Hasbro's decision to rebrand Mr. Potato Head was a significant departure from tradition. By dropping the Mr. from the name, children were free to determine the gender of their potato companion, fostering creativity and inclusivity in play.

Embracing gender neutrality, Hasbro's move was met with both praise and criticism. Advocates applauded the company for embracing diversity and providing children with more inclusive play options. Critics, however, raised concerns about the erasure of traditional gender identities in toys. Despite mixed reactions, Hasbro's decision ignited conversations about the importance of allowing children to explore gender and identity in a safe and imaginative way.

Hasbro's reimagining of Potato Head demonstrates how a classic toy can adapt to changing societal norms while fostering creativity and empowering children to define their play experiences on their terms.

Overcoming Challenges and Backlash

When you commit to gender-neutral marketing and branding, you're saying something simple yet powerful: transgender and nonbinary people exist, and everyone deserves to see themselves reflected in the products and services they choose. Gender-inclusive branding is an extension of your organization's values. Sometimes, those values will be put to the test in the form of criticism from clients or customers.

This section offers strategies to navigate backlash with resilience while maintaining your commitment to inclusion as a core value. If the resistance arises from external stakeholders, such as vendors or business partners, please refer to "Addressing Resistance from Leaders and External Stakeholders" in the "Leadership" chapter (Chapter 5) for additional guidance.

- **Hold Firm to Inclusive Values**
  - **Stay Consistent:** Avoid altering your message or pulling back on inclusion efforts in response to backlash. Consistency strengthens trust with supporters and avoids alienating those who value your inclusive stance. For example, YouTube sensation Ms. Rachel, creator of the children's channel "Songs for Littles," faced backlash in early 2023 for featuring a musician using they/them pronouns. She faced it again in June 2024 for wishing viewers a happy Pride. By "standing strong in love," as she put it, Ms. Rachel weathered the storm; in less than six months, her channel grew by two million subscribers.[192]
  - **Selective Engagement:** Assess the nature and volume of backlash before responding. For minor or isolated criticism, let your message stand. If backlash escalates or includes harmful misrepresentations, respond calmly and briefly, reaffirming the brand's commitment to inclusivity without over-engaging detractors. When the Macy's Thanksgiving Day Parade faced a petition and boycott threat in 2023 over two nonbinary performers, Macy's chose not to engage directly. They proceeded

with the planned event, stating, "We look forward to celebrating this iconic Thanksgiving tradition again next week." This simple affirmation allowed Macy's to hold its position without getting drawn into defensive explanations: affirming without addressing.[193]

- **Demonstrate Inclusion as a Core Value**

  o **Consistent Commitment:** Embed inclusion consistently across the organization through sustained policies, partnerships, and initiatives. By making inclusion a visible, ongoing commitment, the organization fosters a strong, authentic reputation that can help mitigate the need for reactive responses in moments of backlash.

  o **Avoid the Appearance of Pinkwashing:** Ensure that inclusion efforts are not limited to seasonal initiatives but are integrated into the organization's practices year-round. This approach reassures supporters that the commitment is authentic and not reactionary.

- **Build an External Network of Allies**

  o **Engage Supportive Partners and Advocates:** Foster relationships with loyal customers, influencers, and partner organizations who genuinely share and support the brand's inclusive values. Your network can organically provide advocacy and show broader community support during moments of backlash, authentically reinforcing the brand's position. For instance, Costa Coffee, the largest coffee chain in the UK, faced boycott threats after a mural on one of their mobile coffee vans went viral. The mural depicted a transgender person with top surgery scars enjoying a coffee. In response, LGBTQ+ advocates publicly praised Costa Coffee for "being on the right side of history," showing solidarity with the brand's commitment to inclusion.[194]

Even when brands face backlash, the conversations they generate can be a net positive. Public debate often brings renewed attention to the brand and can foster meaningful discussions about inclusivity, reinforcing the brand's role in shaping societal change. Rather than spelling doom, these conversations can highlight the brand's commitment to evolving with its audience.

Case Study: Nike's Bold Stand: Turning Backlash into Brand Strength

Nike, a globally recognized athletic apparel giant, has long been at the forefront of promoting inclusivity and diversity through its marketing campaigns. Committed to making sports accessible to everyone and fostering LGBTQ+ belonging and visibility, Nike's marketing initiatives serve as exemplary showcases of success in advocating for diversity, even in the face of backlash.

Celebrating Trans Athletes

In 2016, Nike unveiled the "Unlimited Courage" campaign, celebrating the extraordinary journey of Chris Mosier, the first openly trans athlete to earn a spot on a US National Team for the men's sprint duathlon. Mosier's story of determination and triumph in the face of adversity captured the essence of the Nike Unlimited campaign. At the age of four, Mosier became aware of the misalignment between his gender identity and biological sex. Competing in female athletics, he felt he was not representing his true self. Mosier's tenacity drove him to pursue his dreams and, in his words, "Everything that I've done . . . has been with a 'Just Do It' mindset."

The *Unlimited Courage* film, which debuted during prime time at the Rio Olympics, built on the success of earlier films in the Nike Unlimited series, which had already attracted over 260 million global views. Mosier's story underscored the importance of representation and inclusion in sports.[195]

In another campaign titled "Play New," Nike featured Mara Gómez, the first transgender woman in Argentina's professional soccer league. Like "Unlimited Courage," this campaign further exemplified Nike's ongoing commitment to inclusion and its challenge to traditional gender norms in sports.[196]

Responding to Backlash

In 2023, Nike faced backlash for featuring influencer Dylan Mulvaney, a transgender woman, in its marketing campaigns promoting female clothing. The backlash led to calls for a boycott of the company, but Nike stood firm in its commitment to inclusivity. In a pinned comment on its verified Instagram account, the company encouraged customers to "Be kind, be inclusive . . . Encourage each other." Olympic swimmer Sharron Davies expressed frustration at Nike's decision, but Nike responded by removing comments that did not align with the spirit of diversity and inclusivity.[197] This response underscored Nike's dedication to its principles of allyship and providing a safe environment for all.

Despite the backlash, Nike's stance garnered significant support from progressive and LGBTQ+ groups. The decision to stand by Dylan Mulvaney was praised across social media by influencers and customers, with some even using #NikeSupport to amplify their gratitude. Their "Be True" Pride collection, released soon after this incident, further solidified their stance with the message, "Sports without the LGBTQIA+ community is incomplete."[198]

Nike's commitment to gender inclusion continues to draw criticism. At the end of 2024, XX-XY Athletics, an anti-trans competitor founded on exclusionary principles, targeted Nike for its support of transgender and nonbinary athletes.[199] And Nike's response to this ongoing backlash? It's perfect. They just do . . . nothing.

Gender Representation in Digital Content

In today's digital age, ensuring gender representation in digital spaces is an integral part of embracing gender neutrality in marketing and branding.

Visual Representation

Images, multimedia, and visual content can either reinforce traditional gender stereotypes or challenge them. To foster an inclusive digital environment, imagery must reflect a diverse range of gender identities and expressions.

When crafting digital content, consider the following:

- **Diversity Matters:** Ensure that your visual content showcases individuals with a wide spectrum of gender identities, including but not limited to transgender, nonbinary, and genderqueer individuals. Representation should extend across age, race, ethnicity, and abilities as well.

- **Avoiding Stereotypes:** Be vigilant about avoiding harmful gender stereotypes in your visuals. Challenge norms by portraying individuals in roles and activities that defy traditional gender expectations. For example, show women excelling in STEM fields and men engaging in nurturing roles.

Sourcing inclusive visual content may require a shift in perspective, as traditional stock imagery has often centered around narrow, conventional representations of gender, age, race, and ability. Embrace a more inclusive approach. Here are some suggestions:

- **Diverse Stock Image Libraries:** Be diligent in searching traditional stock image platforms, such as Shutterstock and Getty Images, to find images that authentically represent a broad range of gender identities. While these platforms offer some diversity-focused collections, inclusive imagery may require careful curation to avoid stereotyped or themed visuals.

- **User-Generated Content:** Encourage your audience to contribute user-generated content that showcases diverse gender experiences. Leverage hashtags and campaigns to collect and curate authentic visuals.

- **In-House Photography and Artwork:** If feasible, invest in creating your own visual content that aligns with your brand's commitment to inclusion. Collaborate with photographers and artists who share your vision.

Inclusive Design Elements

Website design choices can either alienate or welcome visitors of all gender identities. Consider the following principles:

- **Neutral Color Schemes:** Embrace neutral color schemes that do not reinforce gender stereotypes. Avoid over-reliance on "gendered" colors like pink and blue. Go for colors that convey a sense of neutrality, such as earth tones, greens, and yellows.

- **Inclusive Forms and Surveys:** When designing forms and surveys, provide options for gender that go beyond the binary. Include categories like "Nonbinary," "Prefer Not to Say," or simply offer an open-text field where individuals can self-identify. For a deeper dive into the strategies and best practices of gender-inclusive language in forms design, refer to "Strategies for Gender-Inclusive Communication" (Chapter 4).

- **Accessible Design:** Ensure your website is designed with accessibility in mind. Features like alt text for images and easy navigation benefit all users, recognizing that individuals with diverse gender identities are part of a broader mosaic of intersecting identities and needs. By prioritizing accessibility, you create a digital space that welcomes and accommodates a wide range of users, fostering inclusion and ensuring a positive experience for everyone.

Fostering Inclusive Online Interactions

In the digital age, online interactions are the front lines of your brand's engagement with your audience. Ensure that these interactions are inclusive and gender-neutral. This section delves into strategies for fostering gender-inclusive online communication and handling gender-related interactions respectfully.

Social Media and Online Communication

In today's hyperconnected world, social media platforms are powerful tools for reaching diverse audiences. To communicate inclusively on these platforms, consider the following tips:

- **Use Inclusive Language:** Craft your social media content using inclusive language that respects diverse gender identities. Avoid binary language and assumptions about your audience's gender. For instance, use gender-neutral terms like "everyone," "people," or "individuals." Refer to "Principles of Gender-Neutral Communication" (Chapter 3) for more information on universal terminology.

- **Respect Pronouns:** Respect and use individuals' pronouns in your posts, both of your own employees and of individuals to whom you respond on social media. Offer the option of including pronouns in your social media profiles as appropriate to signal your commitment to inclusion.

- **Challenge Stereotypes in Imagery:** Be conscious of the imagery and narratives you share. Choose visuals and narratives that challenge stereotypes and celebrate a wide range of gender identities and expressions.

Engaging with a diverse online audience requires a nuanced approach. Here are strategies for fostering respectful engagement:

- **Listen and Learn:** Pay attention to feedback on gender representation and be responsive to your audience's perspectives.
- **Amplify Diverse Voices:** Share and promote content from individuals across gender identities to give visibility to a range of experiences within your community.
- **Share Educational Content:** Regularly provide educational posts that foster understanding and empathy, explaining the importance of gender inclusion and its impact on community well-being.

Responding to Gender-Related Interactions Online

When addressing your followers and users on social media, use neutral terms that don't make assumptions about gender. Consider the following:

- **Avoid Gendered Greetings:** Instead of using gendered greetings like "sir" or "ma'am," use neutral alternatives like "Hello" or "Hi there."
- **Use Gender-Neutral Titles, If at All:** Address individuals using gender-neutral titles like "Mx." instead of "Mr." or "Ms." when their gender is unknown. Alternatively, avoid using them altogether.

Engaging with comments and messages on social media requires a thoughtful approach. Here's how to respond inclusively:

- **Respect Pronouns:** If commenters or users share their pronouns, use them in your responses. This signals respect for their gender identities. Remember that pronouns might not be visible on the comment itself. Take the extra step before responding to review a commenter's profile to see if they listed their pronouns. Misgendering someone in a comment is detrimental to both their individual experience and your brand's reputation as it can lead to feelings of exclusion and alienation.

- **Addressing Negative Comments:** When responding to negative or insensitive comments regarding gender inclusion, maintain a respectful tone. Correct misinformation calmly and provide educational resources if appropriate. Refer to the section on "Overcoming Challenges and Backlash" in this chapter for more detailed information.

- **Moderation:** Implement moderation guidelines to maintain a safe and inclusive online space. Remove comments that are hateful, discriminatory, or harmful to the community.

Summary Checklist for Marketing and Branding

Gender-Neutral Marketing and Branding Strategies

- ☐ Conduct surveys and questionnaires to gather insights on gender identity and preferences.
- ☐ Utilize social media listening tools to monitor conversations about your brand and inclusivity.
- ☐ Include gender identity in audience segmentation, among other valuable criteria.
- ☐ Use gender-neutral language in all messaging and branding.
- ☐ Ensure advertisements and promotional materials portray a diverse range of gender identities.
- ☐ Choose color schemes that do not reinforce gender stereotypes.

Product and Service Development

- ☐ Offer gender-neutral product options.
- ☐ Ensure products cater to diverse identities.
- ☐ Reflect gender inclusion in product development.

Designing Inclusive Marketing Campaigns

- ☐ Ensure authentic representation of diverse gender identities in campaigns.
- ☐ Use inclusive language and pronouns.
- ☐ Include diverse visuals in marketing materials.
- ☐ Acknowledge intersections of gender identity with other aspects of identity.
- ☐ Avoid reinforcing gender stereotypes in product placement.
- ☐ Collaborate with individuals and influencers from diverse gender backgrounds.

Overcoming Challenges and Backlash

- ☐ Maintain consistency in messaging and avoid altering inclusion efforts.
- ☐ Address backlash selectively.
- ☐ Ensure inclusion is authentic and not limited to seasonal initiatives.
- ☐ Engage with a network of supporters, partners, and advocates who align with your values.

Gender Representation in Digital Content

- ☐ Use diverse imagery reflecting a wide spectrum of gender identities.
- ☐ Source inclusive visual content.
- ☐ Ensure website design and copy is gender inclusive.
- ☐ Provide options for gender beyond the binary in forms and surveys.
- ☐ Prioritize accessibility in website design.

Fostering Inclusive Online Interactions

- ☐ Use inclusive language in social media posts.
- ☐ Respect and use individuals' pronouns in online interactions.
- ☐ Challenge gender stereotypes in shared content.
- ☐ Amplify diverse voices within your community.
- ☐ Respond to comments and messages with inclusive language.
- ☐ Implement moderation guidelines to maintain a safe and inclusive online space.

CHAPTER 10

SALES: NURTURING INCLUSIVE CLIENT RELATIONSHIPS

In 1992, author and relationship counselor John Gray published *Men Are from Mars, Women Are from Venus*, which reached #1 on the *New York Times* best-selling relationship book list and became an iconic symbol of the 1990s. For decades, the prevailing mindset was that binary gender differences dominated communication styles. This mindset spread into sales philosophy, suggesting that the potential to increase sales was based on understanding how men and women communicate and using characteristics typical of each gender when needed.[200]

However, scientific research, such as is supported by the Gender Similarities Hypothesis, challenged this traditional view, revealing that males and females are, in fact, similar on most psychological variables, with differences varying in magnitude based on age and context.[201] This shift in our understanding of gender differences has broader implications for how we approach sales and communication.

Historically, sales may have been perceived as a realm where aggressive tactics and homogeneity prevailed. However, times have changed and so have the expectations of both customers and employees. Today's customers come from diverse backgrounds, and they expect their interactions with sales professionals to reflect their values and experiences. Sales teams and organizations that ignore this shift risk missing out on top-tier talent and potentially alienating a sizable portion of their customer base.

Empowering Sales Teams Through Inclusion

Creating an inclusive market means approaching sales with curiosity and respect for each client's unique identity. In other words, don't see a "lead"; see the person. This shift allows sales teams to connect meaningfully and meet clients where they are, recognizing the diversity of experiences and needs across the board.

Leadership plays a vital role in fostering inclusion within sales teams, but not all leadership teams are informed about gender inclusion. Refer to "Leadership: Setting the Tone for Inclusion" (Chapter 5) to understand the importance of leadership when setting the tone for gender inclusion.

- **C-Suite Advocacy for Inclusive Sales:** Secure the backing of C-suite executives to transform sales approaches to be more gender inclusive. Should a leader be resistant to inclusivity in sales, refer to "Addressing Resistance from Leaders and External Stakeholders" in the "Leadership" chapter (Chapter 5) for a three-step approach to overcoming this obstacle.

- **Making the Business Case:** Present the value of inclusion in sales to senior management. Demonstrate the impact of inclusion on enhancing sales performance and elevating the brand reputation. Refer to "Why Gender Inclusion at Work Matters" (Chapter 1) for more information.

Sales is all about building relationships, understanding customer needs, and providing tailored solutions. In this context, inclusion helps shape successful sales strategies. Here's why it matters:

- **Enhanced Customer Connection:** In a globally diverse era, customers gravitate toward businesses that understand and reflect their values. A diverse sales team can communicate more effectively with various clients. Understanding specific cultural norms can unlock new markets or strengthen existing relationships.

- **Diversity as a Bridge to Customers:** Sales representatives bridge the gap between a company and its diverse customer base. When customers interact with sales professionals who share similar backgrounds, experiences, or languages, it creates a sense of familiarity and trust. Understanding cultural nuances allows salespeople to tailor their approach to align with customers' expectations.

- **Reflecting the Market:** In today's global marketplace, customers hail from a myriad of backgrounds. A sales team that mirrors this diversity is better positioned to understand and anticipate the needs of different customer segments. This understanding is beneficial when developing targeted marketing strategies, product offerings, and sales tactics that appeal to a diverse customer base.

- **Personalization and Empathy:** Diversity within a sales team fosters empathy, enabling salespeople to personalize interactions and offer solutions that resonate with customers' needs. When customers feel understood and valued, they are more likely to remain loyal to the brand.

Training helps sales teams embrace gender inclusion effectively. Focused programs and resources equip your team with the skills to understand and engage with diverse gender identities, enhancing their ability to connect with a broader client base.[202]

- **Ongoing Education:** Stay current on matters of diversity and inclusivity. Regular training keeps sales teams informed and adept at gender inclusion. Equip them with skills to understand and engage with diverse gender identities so they can connect with a broader client base.

- **Practical Training Programs:** Provide sales professionals with resources and training programs informed by industry experts. These programs should focus on practical, real-world applications of gender inclusion in sales.

By fostering leadership support and enhancing skills through training, sales teams can effectively embrace and implement gender-inclusive strategies, leading to stronger client relationships and improved sales performance.

Building Inclusive Sales Pipelines

Inclusive prospecting is a strategic necessity as well as a moral imperative. Embracing a diverse clientele, particularly within the LGBTQ+ community, opens doors to new segments and opportunities. The positive impact of inclusivity on sales success is well-documented, giving companies a distinct edge in growth and customer loyalty:

- **Leveraging Diverse Sales Teams for Success:** A 2022 MedReps study found that diverse sales teams are better positioned to understand and address a wide range of customer needs, fostering stronger connections that drive sales growth and improve customer satisfaction.[203]

- **Mitigating the Risks of Non-Inclusive Practices:** Non-inclusive prospecting can lead to missed opportunities and damage a company's reputation. For instance, failing to use gender-neutral language or making assumptions about client identity can alienate potential customers. These practices can erode trust and create unnecessary barriers, risking not only client relationships but also brand perception.

- **Enhanced Client Relationships Through Inclusion:** Companies that approach sales with respect for LGBTQ+ diversity build stronger client relationships, foster trust, and elevate brand loyalty.

Inclusive prospecting requires strategies that recognize and embrace the diverse identities and needs within the LGBTQ+ community and beyond. Here are some strategies for inclusive prospecting:

- **Expanding Client Diversity:** Ensure your prospecting strategies are inclusive by actively engaging with under-represented groups, tapping into LGBTQ+ networks, and broadening your client base. For more ideas, refer to the "Networking for Inclusive Sales" section later in this chapter.

- **Inclusive Lead Processes:** Develop inclusive lead-generation and nurturing processes, avoiding assumptions about clients' identities. Use gender-neutral language in written and verbal communication and avoid visual cues that might mislead on gender. Refer to Part Two of this book for an in-depth review of effective communication strategies to build into lead processes.

- **Inclusive Sales Team:** Build a sales team that reflects the diversity of your clients. A diverse sales team can relate to a wider range of clients, fostering trust and connection from the initial point of contact.

- **Informed Sales Education:** Some sales team members may be unfamiliar with gender diversity or may rely on outdated, gendered sales strategies. Educating teams on gender identity and expression enables them to connect meaningfully with diverse clients, reducing the risk of lost sales and negative brand perception.

- **Intersectional Awareness:** Recognize that clients may have multiple intersecting identities and experiences. A multilingual team can further support inclusivity, bridging language gaps and building deeper relationships.

Networking for Inclusive Sales

Networking is a powerful sales methodology that leverages personal and professional connections to find qualified leads through referrals. It plays a multifaceted role in lead generation, relationship building, and overall business growth. Sales professionals should understand the role of networking and its potential to foster inclusion.

As highlighted in a study by Forrester Consulting, networking is a linchpin of sales success. The study found that sales teams with extensive networks and the ability to engage effectively with diverse audiences are better positioned to meet the needs of a diverse customer base.[204]

Inclusivity within networking offers both moral and strategic benefits. Diverse networks open doors to new clientele and foster business growth. Engaging with individuals from diverse backgrounds gives sales professionals a competitive edge in today's marketplace. Salespeople who demonstrate cultural competence and inclusivity are more likely to build strong client relationships, enhance their professional reputation, and drive business success. Here are some strategies for building an inclusive network:

- **Join LGBTQ+-Friendly Networks:** Engage with local and national LGBTQ+ networking organizations, such as your local or state LGBTQ+ chamber of commerce, or national organizations like the National Gay and Lesbian Chamber of Commerce (NGLCC). For example, my local chapter, the Independence Business Alliance (IBA) in Philadelphia, Pennsylvania, provides a platform to connect with other allies and individuals from the LGBTQ+ community.

- **Foster Diverse Connections:** Actively seek to connect with individuals from a variety of backgrounds to expand the diversity of your network. Building diverse connections helps sales professionals understand the needs and preferences of different customer groups, fostering stronger relationships and enhancing client satisfaction.

- **Cultivate Inclusive Relationships:** Build relationships based on mutual respect and understanding. Ensure that people feel valued and heard, regardless of gender identity or background. Fostering an inclusive culture where diverse voices are respected enhances both networking and sales outcomes.

Being an ally in networking also involves using inclusive language and recognizing and addressing bias:

- **Using Inclusive Language:** Using inclusive language and the correct pronouns is essential for fostering an inclusive environment in networking settings. This acknowledgment builds trust and rapport with clients. Sales professionals should have practical tips on navigating gender identity and pronoun usage to ensure respectful and inclusive interactions. Refer to Part Two of this book for detailed information.

- **Recognizing and Addressing Bias:** Sales professionals may encounter non-inclusive behavior or bias during networking events. Recognizing and addressing these behaviors in real time is crucial to promoting inclusion in all interactions. For strategies on handling bias, refer to the "Leadership" chapter on "Addressing Resistance from Leaders and External Stakeholders" (Chapter 5).

Building an inclusive network not only benefits individual sales professionals but also presents opportunities for positive community impact:

- **Community Engagement:** Inclusive networks provide opportunities for meaningful community impact. Sales professionals can contribute by participating in events that promote diversity and inclusion. For example, the William Way LGBTQ Community Center in Philadelphia, Pennsylvania, hosts several events that welcome sponsorship and participation: The Indigo Ball is a black-tie gala uniting businesses, activists, artists, and allies; the Way Forward Breakfast is a fundraising event for high-level givers; and, of course, there is the Philly Pride Run. Sales teams can sponsor these events or encourage company-wide participation, such as organizing a team for the Pride Run or bringing colleagues to community-building events like the Indigo Ball.

- **Amplifying Diverse Voices:** Actively amplifying the voices and experiences of underrepresented groups within networks demonstrates a commitment to inclusion. This can be done by sponsoring speaking engagements, panels, or workshops that focus on diversity and inclusion, particularly in collaboration with LGBTQ+ organizations. For example, partnering with local community centers or advocacy groups to host panels featuring diverse speakers, such as trans or nonbinary professionals, can help amplify those voices while building stronger ties with the community.

Summary Checklist for Sales

Empowering Sales Teams Through Inclusion

- ☐ Secure C-suite advocacy for gender-inclusive sales approaches.
- ☐ Present the business case for inclusion to senior management, if necessary.
- ☐ Understand the shift from binary gender communication styles to a more nuanced approach.
- ☐ Recognize the ethical and strategic advantages of embracing diversity in sales.
- ☐ Provide ongoing education on diversity and inclusion for sales teams.
- ☐ Implement practical training programs focused on real-world applications of gender inclusion in sales.

Addressing Challenges to Improve Customer Relations

- ☐ Identify and understand resistance within the sales team.
- ☐ Provide comprehensive training to understand gender inclusion and pronoun usage.
- ☐ Encourage clear and open communication within sales teams.
- ☐ Solicit feedback from sales teams and clients to continuously improve practices.
- ☐ Track and measure the effectiveness of gender-inclusive strategies.

Building Inclusive Sales Pipelines

- ☐ Develop strategies to recognize and cater to diverse identities within the LGBTQ+ community.

☐ Integrate inclusion into lead generation and nurturing processes.

☐ Build a diverse sales team that reflects the clients you serve.

☐ Educate sales teams on gender identity and expression.

☐ Recognize and address intersectional identities and experiences.

Networking for Inclusive Sales

☐ Understand the strategic role of networking in fostering inclusivity.

☐ Join LGBTQ+-friendly networking organizations.

☐ Actively seek out and connect with individuals from diverse backgrounds.

☐ Use inclusive language and correct pronouns in networking settings.

☐ Engage with communities to promote diversity and inclusion.

☐ Amplify the voices and experiences of underrepresented groups within networks.

CHAPTER 11

CUSTOMER SUPPORT AND SERVICE: DELIVERING INCLUSIVE SUPPORT

In Chapter 2, while explaining microaggressions, I shared a story about a restaurant where, despite their best intentions, the staff repeatedly misgendered my friend and me, addressing us as "ladies" throughout our meal. While the term may have been used out of politeness, hearing it again and again was a constant reminder that I was being seen in a way that didn't reflect who I truly am. What started as seemingly courteous behavior quickly became a series of interactions that left me feeling unseen and uncomfortable.

Toward the end of our meal, the manager approached us to ask, "How is everything tonight, ladies?" I sank into my seat, feeling the weight of being misgendered yet again. My friend saw my discomfort and asked me if I wanted to say something. This is how repeated misgendering wears you down: I am a gender inclusion advocate, and yet in that moment, I felt "done." Instead, my friend spoke up, explaining that using "ladies" can feel more harmful than polite when you don't know someone's gender. The manager apologized, insisting they were just being courteous.

Now for the final moment that capped off the night. After the manager apologized and assured us it was all meant in the name of courtesy, we watched him walk over to our server to speak with her. When she returned to our table, her demeanor had noticeably shifted. No longer friendly, she avoided eye contact and curtly asked if we were ready for the check. It seemed our feedback had made her uncomfortable and perhaps even defensive, which added a new layer of discomfort to the situation.

Sadly, this wasn't a one-time experience; every visit followed the same pattern. I offered to train their staff on inclusive customer service techniques, but they declined, holding firm to their idea of politeness. They'd made it about them, not their customers. This is why we must rethink how we approach customer service.

Inclusive customer support ensures that every interaction, from the language used to the overall tone, reflects respect and empathy for all customers, regardless of their gender identity. Part Two of this book provides comprehensive insights and strategies for delivering exceptional, gender-inclusive customer support. This chapter will build on those foundations, diving into specific practices and techniques unique to customer support environments.

Revamping Customer Service Training

Many traditional customer support training programs involve scripts that enforce binary gender stereotypes. Here are a few tips to get you started:

- **Avoid Unknown Courtesy Titles (Honorifics):** If you have a relationship with a customer and you know their honorific, feel free to use it. When addressing a new customer, however, "Good morning, how can I help you today?" is extremely polite when spoken in a kind tone and is more inclusive than, "How can I help you, [sir or ma'am]?"

- **Emphasize Inclusive Language:** If you do not already know the customers (and their pronouns), use gender-neutral greetings instead of "Ladies" or "Gentlemen."

  o **Pairs:** Using the restaurant example, instead of "Are you ladies ready to order?" something like "Are you both ready to order?" avoids gender assumptions.

  o **Groups:** Greeting a group with "How are you all doing this evening?" avoids gendered terms and ensures that every member of the group feels included.

- **Identify Correct Pronouns:** If a customer has provided their pronouns in prior interactions or documentation, make every effort to use them. Ensure your customer support process allows representatives to easily access a returning customer's correct pronouns. This may involve working with IT to ensure that access to any systems with a pronoun field is visible to the customer service team.

- **Avoid Gender Assumptions:** A simple "How may I assist you today?" is better than making assumptions based on appearance or voice, which can lead to misgendering. Avoid all gender assumptions in both in-person and phone support interactions.

- **Active Listening and Validation:** Listen actively, not just to the content of a customer's request, but also for cues like pronouns that may be used by the customer or an accompanying friend. Using our restaurant example, when the server asked if we knew what we wanted to order, my friend could have said, "I know, but I'm not sure they do," which cues the server to know that I use "they" pronouns.

- **Address Misgendering and Pronoun Correction:** If you misgender a customer, apologize briefly but sincerely and move on without making the interaction about your mistake.

  o **If the customer corrects you:** Accept the correction with appreciation. A simple "Thank you, I'm sorry," followed by repeating your sentence with the correct information, helps reinforce their identity respectfully while keeping the conversation on track.

  o **If the customer seems particularly frustrated or annoyed:** Show understanding rather than dismissing their feelings as hypersensitive. Keep in mind that they may have been misgendered multiple times today, even if it wasn't by you. Your respectful and calm response can help improve their day and shift the tone of the interaction.

Training sessions that include roleplay scenarios related to gender identity can better prepare customer service staff for real-world interactions. The more empathetic the service, the more likely customers of all gender identities will feel welcomed and respected.

Intersectional Customer Support

Customer support representatives must understand that customers' identities are multifaceted. They may also identify with various racial, ethnic, cultural, and ability-based groups. To provide truly inclusive support, consider the following:

- **Intersectionality Awareness:** Train your staff to understand the concept of intersectionality, which acknowledges that individuals may face overlapping forms of discrimination or privilege based on multiple aspects of their identity. This understanding can inform more empathetic and tailored customer interactions.

- **Cultural Competency:** Foster cultural competency among your team by providing training on different cultures, traditions, and customs. This ensures that customers from diverse backgrounds receive respectful and considerate service.

- **Accessibility:** Ensure your physical and digital spaces are accessible to customers with disabilities. This includes providing accessible facilities, materials, and website features, as well as training staff on how to assist customers with disabilities effectively.

- **Language Inclusivity:** If your customer base includes non-native English speakers, offer multilingual support when possible. Ensure your website and materials are available in multiple languages, and train staff to communicate effectively with customers who speak different languages.

- **Inclusive Marketing for Inclusive Representation:** Work with your marketing team to ensure that campaigns and materials represent diverse identities and backgrounds. This helps prevent customer service representatives from having to explain or justify potentially offensive content. For more on handling potential backlash from customers, see "Overcoming Challenges and Backlash" in the "Marketing" chapter (Chapter 9).

Leveraging Customer Feedback

Feedback is a valuable tool for enhancing your customer support's gender inclusivity. By actively seeking and listening to feedback, you can identify areas for improvement and adjust as needed. Strategies for encouraging customer feedback include:

- **Feedback Collection:** Establish a system for collecting and categorizing feedback related to gender inclusion to identify recurring themes or issues.

- **Accessibility:** Make it easy for customers to provide feedback on your gender inclusion practices through online forms, suggestion boxes in your physical location, QR codes, or dedicated email addresses.

- **Proactive Engagement:** Encourage customers to share their experiences and suggestions on gender inclusion. Let them know that their feedback shapes your business's approach.

- **Anonymous Surveys:** Conduct anonymous surveys to gather candid feedback from customers who may be hesitant to share their thoughts openly.

- **Online Presence:** Engage with customers on social media and review sites, responding to feedback as it arises.

- **Satisfaction Surveys:** Periodically send customer satisfaction surveys that include questions about gender inclusion practices, covering aspects such as:

  o **Inclusive Greetings and Language:** Ask for feedback on gender-neutral language and inclusive greetings.

  o **Forms and Data Collection:** Gather input on the inclusivity of options provided on forms and surveys.

  o **Addressing Mistakes:** Inquire about experiences and preferences if misgendering occurs to help refine handling procedures.

  o **Responding to Gender-Related Questions:** Gather feedback on how staff addresses gender-related questions.

o **Inclusive Product and Service Options:** Collect feedback on inclusive product offerings and collaborate with marketing (see Chapter 9) to align services with diverse needs.

Once feedback has been gathered, it's essential to analyze the information and implement necessary changes. Here are steps to guide this process:

- **Regular Review:** Regularly review and analyze customer feedback to pinpoint areas that require improvement. Look for patterns and trends to guide your actions.

- **Collaborative Strategies:** Work with your customer support team to develop strategies for addressing specific issues raised in feedback.

- **Creating Safe Spaces:** Use customer feedback to identify areas that may require changes to create a more welcoming and safer environment for all customers.

- **Implementing Changes:** Implement changes based on the feedback received. This may involve updating policies, conducting additional staff training, or making adjustments to the physical space.

- **Transparent Communication:** Share information about gender-inclusive changes made in response to customer feedback. Transparency in your commitment fosters customer trust.

- **Conflict Resolution:** Work with marketing and HR to handle any backlash. For customer concerns, see "Overcoming Challenges and Backlash" (Chapter 9). For employee resistance, see "Addressing Resistance from Employees" (Chapter 6).

Summary Checklist for Customer Support and Service

Revamping Customer Service Training

- ☐ Update customer support scripts to enforce gender neutrality.
- ☐ Use gender-neutral greetings and remove courtesy titles such as "sir" and "ma'am."
- ☐ Identify and use customers' correct pronouns when provided.
- ☐ Avoid gender assumptions based on appearance or voice.
- ☐ Address misgendering with brief and sincere apologies.
- ☐ Implement roleplay scenarios related to gender identity in training sessions.

Intersectional Customer Support

- ☐ Train staff to understand the concept of intersectionality.
- ☐ Foster cultural competence through training on various cultures, traditions, and customs.
- ☐ Ensure accessibility in physical and digital spaces.
- ☐ Offer multilingual support and train staff to communicate effectively with non-native English speakers.
- ☐ Review marketing materials to ensure they represent diverse identities and backgrounds.

Leveraging Customer Feedback

- ☐ Encourage proactive engagement for feedback on gender inclusion practices.
- ☐ Utilize social media platforms for engaging with customers and responding to feedback.
- ☐ Send periodic customer satisfaction surveys that include questions about inclusion.
- ☐ Gather feedback on inclusive product and service options and share it with the marketing and branding department.

☐ Regularly review and analyze feedback to identify recurring themes or issues.

☐ Develop collaborative strategies with the marketing and HR teams to address specific issues.

☐ Communicate transparently about changes made in response to feedback.

☐ Use feedback to identify areas for creating safer and more welcoming environments.

CHAPTER 12

SUPPLY CHAIN AND PROCUREMENT: FOSTERING INCLUSIVE PARTNERSHIPS

Supplier diversity has become an essential part of modern procurement strategies, allowing businesses to build stronger, more resilient supply chains by engaging with underrepresented suppliers. These programs encourage companies to partner with minority-owned, women-owned, LGBTQ+-owned, veteran-owned, and disability-owned businesses. By doing so, they create opportunities that drive innovation, improve efficiency, and contribute to a more inclusive economy.

Through my experience of having a certified LGBTQ+-owned business, I've seen how supplier diversity initiatives open doors and create real opportunities for underrepresented groups. When organizations prioritize diverse suppliers, they foster innovation while contributing to a more equitable marketplace.

Organizations that set targets for supplier diversity spend not only help historically marginalized groups gain access to valuable business opportunities, but they also reap the rewards of diverse perspectives and solutions. The evolution of supplier diversity programs has broadened their scope, reflecting an ongoing commitment to inclusion across a variety of sectors.

This chapter explores the growing importance of supplier diversity in supply chains and procurement, and how businesses can implement these programs to foster innovation, economic empowerment, and long-term resilience.

Why Supplier Diversity Matters

Supplier diversity programs do not merely benefit underrepresented businesses; they are a strategic advantage for the organizations that implement them. Embracing a supplier diversity initiative creates a competitive edge, fosters innovation, and enhances corporate reputation.

- **Commitment and Investment:** Leading companies recognize the long-term value of supplier diversity, committing over $50 billion in partnerships with Minority- and Women-Owned Business Enterprises (MWBEs) over the next decade.[205] This investment demonstrates that diverse suppliers are not only sources of innovation but can drive economic impact, improving the resilience of the business and fostering growth.[206]

- **Economic Impact of MWBEs:** MWBEs significantly contribute to the economy, particularly in sectors that have historically lacked diversity. Companies that partner with MWBEs often experience year-over-year cost savings, which can exceed those offered by conventional suppliers. By partnering with MWBEs, corporations promote wealth creation and improved outcomes, especially in executive and management positions for underrepresented communities. This contributes directly to business performance and long-term sustainability.[207]

- **Innovation and Fresh Perspectives:** Partnering with minority-, women-, LGBTQ+-, disabled-, and veteran-owned businesses infuses new ideas and per-spectives into the supply chain. These businesses often bring innovative solutions to problems, especially in niche markets where their unique backgrounds help them see opportunities or inefficiencies that larger suppliers might overlook. This dynamic exchange of ideas drives growth and operational improvements for both the diverse sup-plier and the contracting company.[208]

- **Cost Efficiency and Flexibility:** Diverse suppliers, espe-cially small and mid-sized enterprises, often provide com-petitive pricing and tailored service offerings that larger suppliers may not match. They are able to adjust pricing structures, product offerings, or delivery schedules to meet specific client needs, creating cost-effective and cus-tomized solutions that enhance value.

- **Strengthening Corporate Resilience:** Building a more resilient supply chain is crucial for any organization, espe-cially in a post-pandemic world. Local and smaller diverse suppliers offer reliability and reduce dependency on single, large suppliers who might be vulnerable to disruptions. As Coca-Cola's Terrez Thompson noted, diverse suppliers have demonstrated agility that larger suppliers may lack, particu-larly during periods of economic or supply chain instability, such as the COVID-19 pandemic. By integrating these sup-pliers, organizations enhance their ability to pivot quickly and respond to market changes or unforeseen challenges.[209]

- **Enhanced Brand Reputation:** Modern consumers are more values-driven than ever before, with 65% of Amer-icans reporting that their social values influence their purchasing decisions.[210] Highlighting partnerships with diverse suppliers aligns companies with these values, boosting brand loyalty and attracting conscious consumers.

- **Driving Economic Empowerment:** Investing in diverse suppliers not only benefits the businesses directly involved but also contributes to the broader economy by supporting historically marginalized communities. This economic empowerment fosters a more equitable marketplace, which in turn stimulates growth across industries. Companies like Marriott International and IBM have demonstrated that their supplier diversity programs contribute to long-term sustainability and profitability.[211]

Industry Trends in Supplier Diversity

The landscape of supplier diversity continues to evolve, marked by growing corporate commitment, innovation, and global expansion. The "2022 State of Supplier Diversity Report" by Supplier.io highlights these transformations:[212]

- **Corporate Commitment and Longevity:** Over 34% of supplier diversity programs have been in place for more than a decade, up from just 4% in 2017. This longevity reflects how deeply embedded supplier diversity has become in corporate strategies. Newer programs continue to emerge, with 21% of respondents indicating their initiatives were less than a year old in 2022.

- **Global Expansion:** Increasingly, supplier diversity programs are taking a global approach, with 13.2% of respondents reporting international initiatives in 2022, up from 8% the previous year. This global expansion involves extending supplier diversity efforts to include diverse businesses in international markets, such as women-owned or minority-owned enterprises across borders. Companies collaborate with organizations like WEConnect International and the Global Supplier Diversity Alliance (GSDA) to identify certified diverse suppliers outside their home countries. This allows them to create more inclusive, resilient supply chains that reflect global diversity and mitigate risks through regional adaptation to local certification practices and cultural differences. Expanding supplier networks internationally also strengthens cross-border partnerships, enhancing both business innovation and global inclusivity.

- **Alignment with Corporate Culture:** 81% of companies reported that their supplier diversity program now aligns with broader organizational values, emphasizing the shift from compliance-driven initiatives to a culture-driven approach.

- **Inclusion of Diversity Metrics:** According to the report, 39% of companies surveyed include diversity metrics in management's performance objectives. While leadership engagement remains high, there is room for improvement in terms of accountability, making it a topic of further consideration.

- **Staffing and Budget Challenges:** Nearly 60% of respondents expressed that securing adequate staffing and budget remains "somewhat to extremely challenging" within their organizations, both for domestic and global supplier diversity programs. This challenge highlights the ongoing need for advocacy and greater resource allocation to maintain and grow these initiatives, ensuring that companies can effectively implement supplier diversity across all markets.

Federal Supplier Diversity: Longstanding Success, New Challenges

Federal supplier diversity programs have their roots in the 1950s, evolving over decades to support small and diverse suppliers through set-aside contracts. These programs have consistently delivered strong results. Research shows that small and diverse suppliers who win contracts through set-aside programs outperform their counterparts, with fewer cost overruns and shorter delays than those who secure contracts through open competition. This is because set-aside programs increase competition, attracting 31% more bidders while ensuring that only vetted, high-quality suppliers participate. These policies reduce project failures and maximize taxpayer value, making them a proven tool for government efficiency.[213]

Despite this, the 2025 administration has targeted supplier diversity initiatives, claiming that set-aside contracts for small and diverse businesses amount to "public waste" and harm government performance.[214] This false narrative ignores decades of data showing that supplier diversity programs enhance efficiency and competition rather than hinder it. While federal agencies may be pressured to abandon supplier diversity efforts, businesses still have the power to maintain and expand their own inclusive procurement strategies—driving innovation, strengthening supply chains, and increasing brand loyalty.

Implementing Supplier Diversity

To effectively implement supplier diversity, organizations must begin by developing a comprehensive program. This involves assessing the current supplier landscape, setting measurable goals, securing leadership buy-in, and educating internal stakeholders.

- **Assess Current Supplier Landscape:** Begin by evaluating your current supplier base. Identify where there may be a lack of diversity and where opportunities for diverse suppliers exist. A procurement audit can help determine how much spend is currently allocated to diverse suppliers and where improvements can be made.

- **Set Measurable Goals:** Establish clear and measurable goals for supplier diversity. This can include specific targets for procurement spend with diverse suppliers, the number of diverse suppliers engaged, or metrics related to the development of supplier diversity initiatives. Ensure these goals are aligned with your organization's broader Diversity, Equity, and Inclusion (DEI) strategy.

- **Secure Leadership Buy-In:** Senior leadership must be on board to make supplier diversity a priority. Demonstrate how supplier diversity supports the company's strategic goals, enhances innovation, and improves competitive advantage. Leadership commitment is critical for securing the resources needed to grow the program. For more information on fostering leadership engagement and inclusivity, refer to "Leadership: Setting the Tone for Inclusion" (Chapter 5). You might even want to give leadership a copy of this book!

- **Engage External Partners and Advocacy Groups:** Collaborate with diverse supplier advocacy groups, such as the National LGBT Chamber of Commerce (NGLCC), National Minority Supplier Development Council (NMSDC), and others, to identify, certify, and engage diverse suppliers. While there is no comprehensive list, major groups in the US and internationally are listed in "Practicing Inclusive Procurement" later in this chapter.

- **Address Resistance:** Resistance to supplier diversity initiatives can stem from conscious or unconscious bias or misunderstandings about the value of diversity. Implement strategies to educate procurement teams, business leaders, and decision-makers on overcoming these forms of resistance. Refer to "Addressing Resistance from

Leaders and External Stakeholders" in the "Leadership" chapter (Chapter 5) for specific strategies.

- **Implement a Supplier Diversity Database:** Establish a database or supplier portal that allows diverse suppliers to register and be considered for opportunities, ensuring they are included in procurement processes and tracked for future engagements. Before implementing new software, it's important to consult with HR, legal, and IT to see if any existing systems within the organization offer modules that can be purchased or adapted to meet procurement needs. If not, work with these teams to identify and define requirements for selecting the best solution. There are many products out there, ranging from smaller, niche tools like Procurify or SupplierGATEWAY to larger enterprise platforms like SAP Ariba or Oracle Procurement Cloud.

- **Measure Progress and Report Results:** Continuously track the progress of your supplier diversity efforts. Regularly report on metrics such as spend with diverse suppliers and the number of diverse suppliers engaged. Publicizing this progress can drive accountability and demonstrate the company's commitment to diversity.

Whether starting from scratch or seeking to expand existing efforts, the following strategies will help organizations enhance their supplier diversity initiatives. While supplier diversity programs have historically centered on industries like manufacturing and retail, there is now a growing need to expand these programs into fast-growing sectors such as law, finance, and professional services. This section explores the specific actions organizations can take to ensure inclusion reaches all areas of the supply chain, including those that have traditionally been underrepresented.

- **Embrace Expanding Sectors:** Supplier diversity efforts are increasingly relevant in fast-growing sectors, particularly within the professional services economy. Expanding supplier diversity in professional services by including minority-owned financial consultancies, women-owned law firms, or LGBTQ+-owned technology consultancies can help close this gap. For instance, my own consulting company, Aikotek, is certified as an LGBTQ+-owned business and regularly bids on consulting work with businesses and government agencies. Including certified diverse suppliers in the bidding process fosters innovation and inclusivity across the supply chain.

- **Partnering with Minority- and Women-Owned Businesses (MWBEs):** Prioritize partnerships with MWBEs. Minority-owned businesses, women-owned enterprises, and other diverse suppliers can bring fresh perspectives, innovation, and competitive advantages to businesses in less diverse sectors, creating a more inclusive and resilient supply chain.

- **Recognizing Societal and Investor Influence:** Societal issues and investor priorities increasingly shape business growth. Millennials, representing a significant portion of the workforce, prefer companies that excel in corporate social responsibility, including diversity and inclusion. Investors seek companies with robust DEI strategies, making diversity initiatives highly relevant aspects of a company's financial attractiveness.[215]

- **Internal Education and Awareness Programs:** Conduct regular training and awareness sessions for procurement teams, business leaders, and decision-makers on the importance and benefits of supplier diversity. These sessions should cover how to identify and engage diverse suppliers, address unconscious bias, and integrate suppliers diversity into strategic goals.

- **Supplier Diversity Champions:** Appoint supplier diversity champions in key departments (procurement, IT, finance) who will advocate for the inclusion of diverse suppliers, track performance, and ensure that diversity goals are met. These champions will act as internal advocates for expanding and supporting the supplier diversity program.

- **Supplier Diversity Goals and Accountability:** Set measurable supplier diversity targets, such as a percentage of total procurement spend allocated to diverse suppliers. Regularly track progress and hold teams accountable. Public reporting on progress can further drive accountability and show transparency.

- **Supplier Development and Mentorship Programs:** Implement development and mentorship programs that provide training, resources, and access to capital for diverse suppliers. These programs help diverse businesses scale and become long-term partners in the supply chain.

- **Collaboration Across Industries:** Join cross-industry coalitions to share best practices, resources, and supplier diversity networks. Collaboration can broaden access to diverse suppliers and improve the overall impact of diversity initiatives.

Practicing Inclusive Procurement

Inclusive procurement practices are the cornerstone of fostering diversity, equity, and gender inclusion within an organization's supplier base. By implementing these practices, businesses can create a level playing field, ensuring that all suppliers have equal opportunities to compete for contracts, regardless of gender or other diverse attributes.

Major Diverse Supplier Advocacy Groups

Diverse supplier advocacy groups support and promote the interests of underrepresented suppliers. Below are some of the major advocacy groups in the US and internationally:

US-Based Advocacy Groups

- **The National LGBT Chamber of Commerce (NGLCC):** Public policy advocates for the LGBTQ+ community and the exclusive certifying body for LGBTQ+-owned businesses.

- **Women's Business Enterprise National Counsil (WBENC):** The leading national organization advancing and certifying women-owned businesses, with a growing global presence.

- **Disability:IN:** The leading nonprofit resource for business disability inclusion worldwide, expanding opportunities for people with disabilities across the globe.

- **National Minority Supplier Development Council (NMSDC):** Advances business opportunities for excluded communities of color, including Asian-Indian, Asian-Pacific, Black, Hispanic, and Native American entrepreneurs, with an international reach through partnerships.

- **National Veteran-Owned Business Association (NaVOBA):** The exclusive certifier of veteran-owned and service-disabled veteran-owned businesses.

- **Financial Services Roundtable for Supplier Diversity (FSRSD):** Committed to advancing diverse supplier inclusion within the financial services industry.

- **US Pan Asian American Chamber of Commerce (USPAACC):** The largest nonprofit organization representing Pan Asian Americans and related groups in business, sciences, the arts, sports, education, public, and community services.

International Advocacy Groups

- **Canada:**
  - **Canadian Aboriginal and Minority Supplier Council (CAMSC):** Promotes the economic advancement of Aboriginal and minority-owned businesses in Canada.
  - **The Inclusive Workplace and Supply Council of Canada (IWSCC):** Supports businesses owned by veterans and/or people with disabilities through certification and corporate partnerships.
- **India:**
  - **Dalit Indian Chamber of Commerce & Industry (DICCI):** Inspires and supports Dalit entrepreneurs in business and industry, fostering wealth creation and economic contribution.
- **United Kingdom:**
  - **Minority Supplier Development UK (MSDUK):** Supports ethnic minority-owned businesses in the United Kingdom by connecting them with corporate partners.
- **South Africa:**
  - **South African Supplier Diversity Council (SASDC):** Focuses on integrating Black-owned businesses into South Africa's corporate supply chains.
- **Australia:**
  - **Supply Nation:** Connects Indigenous Australian businesses with corporate and government procurement teams.
- **Worldwide Advocacy Groups:**

o **Global Supplier Diversity Alliance (GSDA):** Supports businesses looking to develop and expand supplier diversity globally. Provides research, tools, and resources to help companies create inclusive supply chains.

o **WEConnect International:** A global network connecting women-owned businesses with buyers. WEConnect operates in multiple regions, including Europe, Asia, and Latin America.

Collaborating with Advocacy Groups to Promote Inclusivity

Collaborating with these organizations enhances an organization's efforts to promote inclusivity.

- **Partnerships and Collaborations:** Partner with diverse supplier advocacy groups, such as those listed above, to access a broader network of diverse suppliers. These organizations can help companies identify, certify, and engage with underrepresented suppliers across various industries.

- **Collaborating with Procurement Agencies:** Companies can further streamline their procurement processes by partnering with specialized procurement agencies like SDI International, which focus on managing inclusive procurement. Agencies like SDI help ensure that diverse suppliers, including LGBTQ+-owned businesses, are included in the supply chain. By working with such agencies, businesses can enhance their supplier diversity efforts while maintaining efficient procurement operations.

- **Capacity Building:** Support advocacy groups in their capacity-building initiatives for diverse suppliers. This can include training, mentoring, and providing access to resources that help underrepresented businesses grow and succeed.

- **Advocacy and Policy Influence:** Collaborate with advocacy groups to advocate for policies and regulations that promote supplier diversity and inclusion at both organizational and governmental levels.

- **Sharing Best Practices:** Exchange best practices and experiences with advocacy groups to continuously improve inclusive procurement efforts and stay aligned with evolving industry standards.

Fostering an Inclusive Procurement Environment

Inclusivity involves creating an environment where diverse suppliers feel welcome and encouraged to participate, from Requests for Proposals (RFPs) to evaluations.

- **Inclusive RFP Language:** Use inclusive language in RFPs that encourages participation from suppliers of all backgrounds and sizes.

- **Diverse Supplier Outreach:** Actively seek and engage with diverse suppliers, including women-owned, minority-owned, veteran-owned, and LGBTQ+-owned businesses.

- **Diverse Evaluation Panels:** Ensure diversity within evaluation panels to bring diverse perspectives to the decision-making process.

- **Fair Evaluation Practices:** Promote transparency and consistency in evaluation processes, ensuring they are based on objective criteria and free from biases.

Implementing Gender-Neutral Procurement Practices

Gender-neutral procurement practices aim to eliminate gender-based biases and discrimination from the procurement process.

These practices ensure that supplier selection and contract award decisions are based solely on merit, quality, and competitiveness, rather than gender-related factors.

- **Gender-Blind Evaluation:** Conceal supplier gender and diversity attributes during initial assessments to prevent unconscious biases from influencing decisions.

- **Objective Evaluation Criteria:** Define clear and objective criteria that prioritize qualifications, experience, and performance, rather than subjective factors.

- **Supplier Development Programs:** Support programs to enhance supplier capabilities and competitiveness without regard to gender.

- **Monitoring and Reporting:** Regularly monitoring procurement processes for gender neutrality and transparency. Reporting on gender-related data to assess progress and identify areas for improvement.

Case Study: BAYADA Home Health Care: Inclusive Procurement

BAYADA Home Health Care demonstrates a strong commitment to Diversity, Equity, and Inclusion (DEI) through its procurement and supply chain practices. During the COVID-19 pandemic, BAYADA partnered with Safe 'N' Clear, a disability-owned company, to provide clear face masks for clients with hearing impairments, showcasing their focus on aligning procurement with client needs.[216]

BAYADA aims to reflect the diversity of its clients and employees by increasing the diversity of its suppliers. The company works with businesses owned by women, racial or ethnic minorities, people with disabilities, veterans, or individuals who identify as LGBTQIA+, without requiring formal certifications.

This inclusive approach supports underrepresented communities and contributes to both return on investment (ROI) and return on mission (ROM).[217]

One successful example is BAYADA's Diverse Supplier Development Program, which supports small businesses like Bitter Crops Scrub Wear, a Black- and woman-owned company. Through mentorship and promotion on BAYADA's webstore and social media, the program helped the business grow while reinforcing BAYADA's commitment to gender diversity in its supply chain.[218]

Additionally, BAYADA regularly measures DEI sentiment through Employee Experience Surveys. Over the past three years, the proportion of employees who feel comfortable bringing their authentic selves to work has risen by three points, reaching 94% in 2023. This positive sentiment underscores how the company's DEI efforts, including procurement practices, benefit both employees and clients.[219]

This case highlights how inclusive procurement strategies not only drive business success but also have a social impact, reinforcing the importance of gender and diversity in creating a more equitable supply chain.

Summary Checklist for Supply Chain and Procurement

Implementing Supplier Diversity

- ☐ Develop a Supplier Diversity Program, including leadership buy-in and measurable goals.
- ☐ Assess the current supplier landscape and identify opportunities for diverse suppliers.
- ☐ Engage with suppliers from underrepresented groups (minority-owned, women-owned, veteran-owned, LGBTQ+).
- ☐ Allocate procurement spend to diverse suppliers.
- ☐ Integrate supplier diversity efforts into finance, professional services, and technology sectors.
- ☐ Partner with minority- and women-owned businesses (MWBEs).
- ☐ Ensure alignment with corporate culture and inclusiveness.
- ☐ Commit to and invest in MWBE partnerships.
- ☐ Include diversity metrics in management's performance objectives.
- ☐ Address staffing and budget challenges for supplier diversity programs.

Practicing Inclusive Procurement

- ☐ Collaborate with diverse supplier advocacy groups.
- ☐ Engage with diverse suppliers.
- ☐ Ensure diversity in evaluation panels.
- ☐ Use inclusive language in RFPs.
- ☐ Implement gender-neutral procurement practices.
- ☐ Conduct gender-blind evaluations.
- ☐ Define objective evaluation criteria.
- ☐ Support supplier development programs.
- ☐ Monitor and report on gender neutrality in procurement processes.

CHAPTER 13

FACILITIES MANAGEMENT: BUILDING INCLUSIVE SPACES

Facilities management, the way we design and maintain the environments where we work, plays a key role in shaping truly inclusive cultures. The reason I placed this chapter toward the end of the book isn't because facilities are less important. It's because I wanted you to fully grasp the challenges that transgender and nonbinary people face so that, by now, you can appreciate the life-altering impact something as "simple" as a restroom can have.

And no, that's not hyperbole.

Several years ago, I spent a day shopping with a good friend, hitting store after store, laughing as we searched for the perfect sofa. After hours of shopping, I spotted the restrooms near the entrance of the next store and steered us that way.

But as we approached, I noticed her demeanor change. Her steps slowed; her body tensed. I didn't know why, but something about the group of teenage boys hanging near the restrooms seemed to rattle her.

It didn't get better once we got inside. We took stalls next to one another, and I tried to lighten the mood by asking her a question about her new home. Nothing. I asked again, and still no response. The silence felt so heavy, and then it hit me. She didn't want anyone to hear her voice.

My friend is a trans woman. In that moment, she wasn't just thinking about using the restroom; she was calculating the risks. The fear of harassment or violence weighed on her every move. Even in that stall, she was terrified of being overheard and clocked, or worse.

This is what transgender people face every day: fear of harassment, violence, even physical harm. Imagine starting a new job and seeing restrooms labeled "Men" and "Women," with no indication of whether you'll be safe walking into either one. Many transgender people will go the entire workday without using the restroom at all to avoid that trauma, putting their own health at serious risk.

Now, imagine if my friend had started that same job, or walked into that store, and saw a sign next to "Men" and "Women" that read, "We welcome you to use the restroom that aligns with your gender identity." What a difference that would make. How much safer would she feel? How much more included?

The layout, signage, and facilities in a workplace speak volumes about an organization's values. More than that, they directly impact whether someone feels they belong or are in danger and whether their safety and well-being are truly prioritized. Whether you're a small startup operating out of a shared space or a large corporation with multiple facilities, these considerations matter.

Facilities Management Responsibilities and Scalable Strategies

Facilities management encapsulates a broad spectrum of services and processes that ensure functionality, comfort, safety, and efficiency in the built environment. The scope of facilities management varies based on the size and nature of the business, with different strategies needed to promote gender inclusion at each level.

- **Small Businesses–Creative and Resourceful Solutions:** Small businesses, particularly those in shared or leased spaces, often face challenges like limited control over structural changes. Facilities management, in these cases, intertwines with daily operations, and gender inclusion requires creativity. Some strategies include:
  - **Creative Solutions in Constrained Spaces:** Implement gender-neutral signage for existing single-stall restrooms or negotiate with building management for inclusive modifications.
  - **Outsourcing Facilities Management:** Engage external facilities management providers with expertise in gender inclusion to ensure that shared spaces align with inclusive practices. If direct control is limited, consider working with consultants who can advocate for inclusive solutions with building owners.
  - **Community and Collaboration:** Pool resources with other tenants or engage in collective dialogues with property owners to advocate for inclusive facilities.
- **Mid-Sized Companies–Structured and Inclusive Planning:** As businesses grow, so does the complexity of facilities management. Mid-sized businesses typically manage their own facilities, providing more control over space design and utilization. Gender inclusion at this level involves:
  - **Inclusive Space Design:** Designate gender-neutral restrooms, use inclusive signage, and create flexible, inclusive spaces such as lactation rooms or contemplation areas.

- o **Employee Feedback and Continuous Improvement:** Establish mechanisms to gather employee input about facilities and using that feedback to guide improvements.

- o **Internal Facilities Management:** Develop an internal facilities team trained in inclusivity to implement changes across locations.

- **Large Corporations–Strategic and Systemic Inclusion:** For large corporations, facilities management becomes a strategic function that impacts business operations and culture. These organizations typically have greater capacity to implement long-term infrastructure changes, enabling gender inclusion at a more systemic level. Strategies include:

  - o **Long-Term Inclusive Infrastructure:** Design new, inclusive facilities or refurbishing existing ones to meet the needs of diverse employees.

  - o **Inclusion as Part of Corporate Culture:** Implement company-wide policies for gender-neutral facilities, supported by regular audits to ensure physical spaces align with the company's diversity and inclusion goals.

- **Best Practices Across All Business Sizes:**

  - o **Inclusive Policy Development:** Collaborate with HR and legal teams to develop and implement clear policies that articulate your commitment to inclusion in facilities management.

  - o **Regular Review and Adaptation:** Continuously review and adapt facilities management strategies based on evolving needs and feedback from employees and customers.

  - o **External Partnerships:** Engage with external experts, consultants, or community organizations for valuable insights and resources to foster inclusivity.

In every case, the goal of facilities management is to create an environment that not only meets the functional needs of the organization but also resonates with its values and commitment to inclusion. Understanding the scope of facilities management in relation to the size and capabilities of your business is the first step in aligning your facilities management practices with your gender inclusion objectives.

Signage: More than Just Labels

Signage actively contributes to promoting gender inclusion. It communicates values, affirms identities, and fosters a welcoming environment for everyone, regardless of gender identity.

The US Department of Labor's Occupational Safety and Health Administration (OSHA) recommends that all employees, including transgender employees, have prompt access to appropriate sanitary facilities. The core belief underlying these policies is that all employees should be permitted to use the facilities that correspond with their gender identity. The employee should determine the most appropriate and safest option for themself.[220]

In 2025, the US administration's broader efforts to erase transgender identities included the removal of all references to transgender employees from the Department of Labor's website. While these resources have been eliminated from federal platforms, the guidance remains valid and has been archived for reference by several organizations, including the Human Rights Commission and GovInfo. Workplace best practices—rooted in dignity, safety, and inclusion—do not change based on political shifts. Organizations committed to equity can and should continue to follow these principles, ensuring all employees have access to facilities that affirm their identity.

When designing inclusive signs, focus on simplicity and clarity. Here are some best practices:

- **Use of Symbols:** Opt for universally recognized symbols that transcend language barriers. For instance, a toilet symbol without a gender-specific figure can be used for restroom signs.

- **Language and Terminology:** Choose language that is inclusive and nonbinary. Terms like "All-Gender Restroom," "Gender-Neutral," or "Inclusive Restroom" can be effective.

- **Placement and Visibility:** Ensure that the signage is placed at eye level and is easily visible. Consider using braille and tactile signs for accessibility.

- **Consultation:** When possible, involve diverse groups, including LGBTQ+ representatives, in the design and placement of signs to ensure that they meet the needs of all.

Beyond the general principles of inclusive signage, specific attention must be given to the implementation of gender-neutral language. This involves ensuring that the language used in signs throughout the facility aligns with the inclusive language principles discussed in Part Two: "Effective Communication Strategies."

- **Reflecting Gender-Neutral Job Titles and Names**
  - **Office and Department Signs:** Use gender-neutral job titles as outlined in "Principles of Gender-Neutral Communication" (Chapter 3) for all departmental signage.
  - **Nameplates and Employee Designations:** Offer options for employees to display their pronouns and preferred name.

- **Inclusive Language on Building Signs**
  - **Entrance and Reception Area Signage:** Choose welcoming language that includes everyone.
  - **Directional and Informational Signs:** Ensure gender neutrality, particularly for restrooms and emergency exits.
- **Consistency Across Departments**
  - **Maintain Language Consistency:** Align all communications, digital and physical, with inclusive language principles discussed in Chapters 3 and 4. Collaborate closely with HR and communications teams to achieve this consistency.
  - **Stay Updated with Signage:** Regularly reviewing and updating your signage is important to ensure it reflects current language and practices around gender inclusion. For example, several years ago, signs might have used the phrase "preferred pronouns," but now they should simply say "pronouns."

Examples of Effective Gender-Inclusive Signage

Inclusive signage is a small but significant step toward creating a more inclusive and welcoming space for all individuals. Thoughtfully design and implement such signs to make a powerful statement about your commitment to inclusion and respect for all. Here are some examples:

- **City of West Hollywood, California:** All single-occupant restrooms have been mandated to display gender-neutral signage since 2014. The City Council unanimously approved a measure to require new construction and significant business renovations to include gender-neutral signage on multi-stall restrooms, effective 2023.[221]

- **University of Oregon:** The university began implementing inclusive restroom signage in 2016, which not only designated restrooms as gender neutral but also provided information on accessibility features.[222]
- **City of Denver, Colorado:** Denver amended their building code in 2016 to require that all businesses post gender-inclusive signage on single-occupant restrooms.[223]
- **City of Philadelphia:** In 2013, Philadelphia passed a bill requiring city-owned buildings to have gender-neutral restrooms, accompanied by inclusive signage, making it one of the first major cities to do so.[224]

Ensuring Restroom Inclusivity and Privacy

Before implementing gender-neutral restrooms, it's essential to be aware of local laws and regulations. While a state law may welcome all people to use the restroom that aligns with their gender identity, certain counties within that state might require "Men" and "Women" signs for single-stall restrooms and only allow an "All Gender" sign if there is a third restroom onsite. In this case, a business can include a sign at the men's and women's rooms that all are welcome to use the restroom that aligns with their gender identity to promote safety and inclusion. Consult with your legal department if you are unsure about the laws in your area.

Options for Different Business Sizes

- **Single-Stall Restrooms:** Ideal for small businesses with limited space. These restrooms can easily be converted to gender-neutral facilities with inclusive signage, as laws allow.
- **Gender-Neutral Restrooms:** Larger businesses might designate certain restrooms as gender-neutral, serving

individuals of any gender identity. It's important to ensure these restrooms are conveniently located, not placed in hard-to-reach areas.

- **Multiple-Stall Gender-Inclusive Restrooms:** For larger spaces, offering multiple-stall gender-inclusive restrooms provides greater accessibility. These restrooms can be designed with full-height partitions and full-length doors, essentially creating private, individual rooms to ensure privacy and comfort for all users.

Privacy in Restrooms

Ensuring privacy in restrooms is a critical element in creating gender-inclusive spaces. Many individuals, including those who are transgender or nonbinary, feel safer when restroom stalls offer privacy features that minimize the risk of unwanted attention.

- **Full-Length Stall Doors and Walls:** Installing full-length stall doors and walls provides maximum privacy, essentially creating private, individual rooms within a multi-occupant restroom. This design helps individuals feel more comfortable and secure, particularly in gender-inclusive restrooms.

- **Occupancy Indicator Locks:** These locks show whether a stall is occupied, reducing awkward encounters and enhancing privacy in multiple-occupant restrooms. Occupancy indicator locks also provide visual confirmation for users, helping them feel more secure.

- **Extended Urinal Dividers:** In restrooms where urinals are present, consider extending privacy dividers between urinals further out from the wall and higher up to reduce visibility and create more personal space.

- **Tactile and Visual Accessibility:** Ensure that privacy features in restrooms are accessible for all individuals, including those with disabilities. Features like braille signage and easy-to-use locks help maintain inclusivity and comfort for all users.

Tips for Businesses in Leased Spaces or with Limited Control over Restrooms

- **Dialogue with Landlords:** Engage in conversations with property owners about installing privacy features like full-length stall doors or converting restrooms to gender-neutral spaces.
- **Temporary Solutions:** Suggest temporary changes like converting restrooms during specific hours or events.
- **Signage and Communication:** Use clear signage to indicate restroom inclusivity and educate employees and clients on restroom availability.

Comprehensive Facility Considerations

While restrooms are a significant focus in the discussion of gender inclusion in facilities management, other areas like locker rooms and showers also require attention to ensure an inclusive environment.

- **Privacy Concerns:** Ensure privacy in locker rooms and showers by providing private changing cubicles and shower stalls with secure, full-length doors.
- **Designating Inclusive Spaces:** For businesses with the resources, creating gender-neutral locker rooms and showers is ideal. These spaces should include individual changing and showering areas, usable by anyone, regardless of gender identity.

- **Signage and Communication:** Use clear and respectful signage to indicate the inclusive nature of these facilities and offer guidance on respectful usage.

- **Reasonable Restroom Access Options:** Employers can offer various restroom setups, such as multiple-occupant, gender-specific restrooms with lockable stalls, single-occupant gender-neutral restrooms, or multiple-occupant, gender-neutral restrooms with private stalls.

Emergency Facilities and Considerations

In any emergency, whether it's an evacuation, shelter-in-place situation, or a building lockdown, facilities need to ensure that all individuals, including those who are transgender or non-binary, have access to spaces where they feel safe and secure. Emergency responses should be inclusive of all gender identities and consider the unique vulnerabilities that some individuals may face in high-stress situations.

- **Safe Spaces:** In emergency situations like shelter-in-place orders or lockdowns, individuals, particularly those who are transgender or nonbinary, may face increased vulnerability. Facilities should have clearly marked safe spaces that are accessible to all.

- **Evacuation Procedures:** Ensure that evacuation procedures are inclusive and consider the needs of individuals with disabilities and diverse gender identities. For example:
  o Avoid directing people to gender-segregated spaces like locker rooms during an emergency.
  o Designate safe zones that are accessible and welcoming to all employees, regardless of gender identity.

- o Provide training to designated emergency team leads on how to offer inclusive support during evacuations, especially for vulnerable groups.

- **Emergency Communication:** Use gender-neutral language in all emergency communication to avoid misgendering and ensure that instructions are clear for everyone. Refer to Part Two: "Effective Communication Strategies" (Chapters 3 and 4) for more detailed information on gender-neutral language.

- Additional Considerations

  - o **Training and Awareness:** Provide staff training to understand and respectfully address the challenges faced by transgender and nonbinary individuals.

  - o **Feedback and Continuous Improvement:** Regularly seek feedback from employees and customers about the inclusivity of facilities and be open to making improvements.

Facilities management for gender inclusion varies by business size but shares a common goal: creating a safe, welcoming, and respectful environment. By tailoring strategies, businesses can better support all transgender and nonbinary individuals who enter the building.

Summary Checklist for Facilities Management

Introduction to Inclusive Facilities Management

☐ Recognize the importance of inclusive physical environments in promoting gender inclusion.

☐ Align all facilities management practices with company-wide inclusion principles.

Facilities Management Responsibilities and Scalable Strategies

☐ Adapt facilities management practices based on business size and resources.

- Small Businesses: Implement creative solutions for constrained or leased spaces.
- Mid-Sized Companies: Establish structured facilities management, including employee feedback.
- Large Corporations: Develop long-term infrastructure for inclusivity across multiple locations.

☐ Collaborate with HR and legal to develop clear, inclusive policies for facilities management.

☐ Regularly review and update facilities management strategies.

☐ Engage external experts for additional insights and resources.

Signage: More than Just Labels

☐ Use gender-inclusive signage to communicate values and inclusivity.

☐ Follow best practices for signage:

- Use universally recognized symbols.
- Use inclusive, nonbinary language.
- Ensure signage is visible and accessible.

☐ Implement gender-neutral language in all facility signage, including office signs and building directories.

☐ Regularly review and update signage to stay current with inclusive practices.

Ensuring Restroom Inclusivity and Privacy

☐ Provide inclusive restroom facilities:

- Convert single-stall restrooms to gender-neutral as permitted by law.

- Designate gender-neutral multi-occupant restrooms.

- Ensure multiple-stall restrooms have full-height partitions and full-length doors for privacy.

☐ Install privacy enhancements like full-length stall doors and occupancy indicator locks.

☐ Follow local laws on restroom signage and accessibility.

☐ Engage landlords about inclusive restroom options in leased spaces.

☐ Educate employees about restroom inclusivity policies.

Comprehensive Facility Considerations

☐ Ensure inclusivity in locker rooms and showers by providing private changing cubicles and shower stalls.

☐ Designate gender-neutral locker rooms and showers.

☐ Use clear, respectful signage for these facilities.

☐ Plan for inclusive emergency facilities:

- Designate safe spaces for emergencies.

- Ensure evacuation procedures consider gender identities and disabilities.

- Use gender-neutral language in emergency communications.

☐ Train staff on inclusivity in emergency procedures, restrooms, and locker room usage.

☐ Continuously gather feedback from employees on inclusivity in facilities.

Emergency Facilities and Considerations

☐ Designate and clearly mark safe spaces for emergencies, accessible to all employees, regardless of gender identity.

☐ Ensure that evacuation procedures avoid directing people to gender-segregated areas like locker rooms during emergencies.

☐ Provide training to designated emergency team leads on how to support vulnerable groups, including transgender and nonbinary individuals, during evacuations.

☐ Use gender-neutral language in all emergency communication to ensure clarity and inclusivity.

☐ Regularly review and update emergency plans to reflect the needs of diverse employees.

CHAPTER 14

SECURITY AND SAFETY SERVICES: PROTECTING WITH INCLUSIVE AWARENESS

Security and safety teams are often the first line of interaction with the public, holding the power to make someone feel either safe or targeted. Security services in the workplace, from a single guard in a shared building to a large department protecting university or corporate campuses, play an essential role in protecting physical safety and fostering an inclusive environment.

Unfortunately, security personnel can also be at the center of some of the worst experiences faced by transgender individuals in workplaces, stores, or events. It's not just a handful of incidents; there are countless cases of transgender people being harassed by security guards, so many that you might not want to search for it online unless you're ready for a flood of upsetting stories. In an effort to protect, security teams sometimes end up enforcing harmful biases. Take the case of Bang Face Festival, an international electronic dance music event, where a security team escalated a situation with a transgender woman to violent levels, despite other women in the bathroom insisting there was no issue.[225] Or the case of Simona Castricum, a DJ and author of transgender inclusion policies, who was accosted by security in a nightclub after entering a gender-neutral bathroom.[226] In these situations, security officers were not safeguarding individuals; they were reinforcing dangerous biases.

These stories are not unique. In businesses large and small, security guards sometimes become enforcers of exclusion, questioning identities or even resorting to violence, as in the tragic case of Banko Brown, a Black transgender man who was shot by a Walgreens security guard after being accused of shoplifting.[227] Banko's identity as both Black and transgender speaks to the deeper, intersecting biases that many people face. The convergence of racism and transphobia in security interactions often leads to heightened suspicion, mistreatment, or even violence, as marginalized individuals become targets of multiple forms of discrimination at once.

The role of security in protecting diverse communities is complex, especially when it intersects with gender identity. Whether your security team is a single professional or a large, dedicated department, whether you're securing a retail store, a corporate event, or an entire campus, the principles of inclusivity remain the same. Security personnel must protect not only the environment but also the dignity and rights of all individuals they encounter. In this chapter, we will explore how businesses can ensure their security and safety teams are prepared to protect with inclusive awareness, regardless of gender identity.

Hiring, Training, and Education for Security Personnel

Security personnel must be trained to interact inclusively, protecting both the physical safety and the dignity of all individuals, regardless of gender identity. This section focuses on the essential components of hiring, ongoing training, and the policies that guide inclusive practices.

Hiring for Inclusivity

When recruiting security personnel, organizations should prioritize candidates who demonstrate an understanding of inclusivity or possess experience working with diverse communities. Refer to "Human Resources: Fostering an Inclusive Culture" (Chapter 6) for more information on recruiting and retaining talent.

- **Incorporating Gender Inclusion Into the Hiring Process:** During interviews, ask candidates about their experience working with diverse communities or handling situations that required a gender-inclusive approach. This can help identify candidates who are already aligned with the company's values on inclusion. Interviewers should be trained to recognize nonverbal cues from candidates, such as eye-rolling or dismissive body language, that may indicate a lack of support for gender inclusion.

- **Inclusive Onboarding:** Security personnel should not be placed on the job before completing comprehensive training on gender-inclusive practices. This ensures they are prepared to interact respectfully and inclusively with all individuals from day one.

- **Hiring Outsourced Security Services:** Organizations must be diligent when hiring outsourced security services. Inquire about the training practices of these services, particularly their guidelines for interacting with diverse communities. Ensure that their personnel are well-versed in respectful and inclusive practices to maintain a safe and welcoming environment for all, especially transgender and nonbinary individuals.

- **Visibility and Representation:** Strive for diversity within the security ranks, including the hiring of openly transgender and nonbinary personnel. This diversity fosters trust and ensures that concerns unique to these communities are better understood and addressed. A diverse security team is more likely to create an inclusive environment where all feel protected and respected.

Training on Inclusive Security Practices

The Department of Justice's Community Relations Service (CRS) offered a training program specifically designed to improve law enforcement officers' understanding of and interactions with transgender communities. This model can be adapted for workplace security teams to ensure respectful and inclusive engagement.[228]

The CRS had been working on such programs since at least 2016.[229] However, in 2025, the administration removed this and all other DOJ resources on transgender people from federal websites as part of its broader rollback of inclusion initiatives. It remains unclear whether these programs will be permanently discontinued or reinstated through legal challenges. Regardless, the training framework remains a valuable model for security teams seeking to implement respectful and equitable policies.

While the DOJ program has been removed from federal websites, other organizations also offer comprehensive training resources on interacting with transgender and gender-nonconforming individuals, such as the International Association of Chiefs of Police (IACP).[230] Programs such as these provide essential guidance on bias awareness, de-escalation techniques, confidentiality, and respectful communication. Security teams can adapt these principles to their workplace policies, reinforcing a commitment to safety and dignity for all.

Despite federal removals, which at the time of this writing remain subject to ongoing legal challenges, organizations committed to safety and inclusion can still apply these best practices, ensuring that security personnel are trained to interact with all individuals with professionalism and respect.

The original DOJ CRS framework provided two formats for this training:

- **In-person or Virtual Program:** A four-hour session led by experts from both law enforcement and transgender communities.

- **Web-Based Self-Paced Program:** A three-hour interactive course that offers flexibility for participants to complete at their own pace.

These programs contain the following content:

- **Awareness and Understanding:** Training begins by defining terms and language pertinent to transgender and nonbinary individuals to ensure that security staff can communicate accurately and respectfully in everyday interactions.

- **Gender Identity Sensitivity:** Security personnel must be aware of the challenges faced by transgender and nonbinary individuals, particularly in situations where they may feel vulnerable (e.g., bag checks, restroom monitoring, biometric scanning, or ID verification). The goal is to minimize discomfort and avoid misgendering or invasive questioning.

- **De-Escalation Techniques:** Security personnel should be trained in de-escalation tactics that are sensitive to gender identity. For more details on these techniques, refer to the

"De-Escalation Through Inclusive Communication" section later in this chapter.

- **Bias Awareness:** Recognize and mitigate any biases the security personnel hold about gender identity. This is crucial in avoiding discriminatory behavior, particularly when assessing potential security threats and interacting with the public. Refer to "Addressing Resistance from Employees" in the "HR" chapter (Chapter 6) for more information.

- **Confidentiality and Respect:** Training should emphasize the importance of maintaining confidentiality when it comes to gender identity, particularly when handling sensitive information, such as in reporting or incident management.

These trainings were designed to:

- **Improve Communication Skills:** Enhance officers' ability to speak appropriately with and about transgender individuals, thereby increasing both public and officer safety.

- **Develop Civil Rights Understanding:** Gain a deep understanding of the civil rights issues affecting transgender communities.

- **Address Misconceptions:** Identify and address misconceptions that hinder the prevention of and response to hate crimes against transgender individuals.

- **Learn Best Practices:** Learn to implement tools and best practices to enhance relationships with transgender communities.

Ongoing Training and Feedback Mechanisms

Continuous education ensures that security personnel remain updated on the latest best practices and are prepared to respond respectfully to all individuals. To achieve this, organizations should focus on both training and maintaining open lines of communication through feedback mechanisms. Continuous education helps in:

- **Staying Current:** Security personnel should engage in regular training to stay informed about evolutions in inclusive terminology and best practices. This may include online modules, workshops, or self-paced courses that reflect the latest standards.

- **Adapting to New Understandings:** Continuous education should encourage flexibility, allowing personnel to adapt to evolving concepts around gender identity and expression.

- **Building Trust:** Through ongoing learning and daily respectful interactions, security personnel build trust not only with transgender and nonbinary individuals but also with their allies within the workplace or venue.

- **Feedback Mechanisms:** Organizations should implement channels like surveys, suggestion boxes, or follow-up assessments where transgender and nonbinary individuals can share feedback on their interactions with security personnel. Regularly reviewing this feedback allows the organization to identify areas of improvement and refine training as needed.

Training must be based on clearly defined policies that align with HR and legal guidelines. Security policies on gender inclusion should be in harmony with the broader organizational framework.

- **Policy Alignment:** All security policies on gender inclusion should align with HR and legal guidelines. Refer to the section on "Workplace Policies and Practices" in "Human Resources: Fostering an Inclusive Culture" (Chapter 6) for detailed information on HR policies.

- **Review and Update Language:** Ensure that all security policies use gender-neutral language, avoiding gender-specific terms and replacing them with inclusive language that applies to all gender identities.

- **Consistent Enforcement:** Establish mechanisms to enforce these policies consistently across the department, including training for officers and staff on the importance and application of these policies.

- **Regular Policy Reviews:** Conduct regular reviews of policies to ensure they remain relevant and effective, making adjustments in response to changes in legal requirements or workforce needs.

Respectful Interaction with Diverse Gender Identities

Security personnel must be trained to communicate respectfully with all individuals, including those with diverse gender identities. This foundational knowledge supports everyday interactions and prevents unnecessary conflict. Refer to "Effective Communication Strategies" (Chapters 3 and 4) for detailed information on gender-neutral language.

- **Understand and Use Correct Pronouns:** Security personnel should ask for and use the correct pronouns, demonstrating acknowledgment and respect for individuals' identities.

- **Avoid Assumptions Based on Gender Expression:** Security staff must avoid assumptions about a person's gender based solely on their appearance or mannerisms.

- **Technology Sensitivity:** Some security technologies, such as body scanners, facial recognition systems, and biometric identification, may not yet fully accommodate individuals with diverse gender identities. Transgender and nonbinary individuals might face challenges or discomfort due to mismatches between their appearance and the data these systems rely on (e.g., legal IDs or body scans). Security personnel should be trained to manage these situations with sensitivity, ensuring that individuals are not singled out or mistreated due to technology limitations. When issues arise, security should handle them discreetly and respectfully, offering alternative options when possible.

- **Language Sensitivity:** In cases where a person's gender identity is unknown, security personnel should use gender-neutral language, such as "person" or "individual," instead of gendered terms. Security should also avoid gendered salutations and honorifics like "sir" or "ma'am" with the public or unfamiliar employees.

- **Emphasizing Respect and Empathy in Communication:** Security staff should listen actively and respond with empathy, demonstrating respect in every interaction.

De-Escalation Through Inclusive Communication

In high-pressure situations, how security personnel communicate can be the difference between resolving a conflict and escalating it. This section discusses de-escalation strategies built around inclusive communication.

- **Empathy and Respect in High-Pressure Situations:** Grounding every interaction in empathy and demonstrating respect for all individuals, especially in high-stakes moments, prevents conflicts from escalating.

- **Cultural Competency and Context:** Understanding the specific challenges faced by transgender and nonbinary individuals allows security personnel to adjust their responses, especially during tense interactions.

- **Tailoring Communication in Emergencies:** In emergencies, security staff must remain calm and clear, using gender-neutral language and culturally competent strategies to prevent escalation.

Inclusive Incident Management

Managing incidents inclusively ensures that security personnel protect not only physical safety but also the rights and dignity of everyone involved. This section outlines how to handle all incidents through a gender-inclusive lens.

- **Bias-Conscious Incident Response:** Every incident, from theft to workplace altercations, should be handled with an awareness of potential biases. Security personnel must approach every situation with an open mind and work to minimize preconceived notions about gender identity. Refer back to the "Training on Inclusive Security Practices" section in this chapter for guidance on how ongoing training can help security teams reduce bias and respond more inclusively.

- **De-Escalation Tactics:** These tactics come into play when situations risk escalating due to misunderstandings around gender identity. Security personnel must know how to calm tensions and maintain respect for the individuals involved. Refer to the prior section on "De-Escalation Through Inclusive Communication" within this chapter.

- **Providing Safe Spaces:** In the event of a security incident, it's essential to provide private, secure spaces for individuals to report the situation without fear of being outed or misgendered.

- **Confidential Collection and Use of Sensitive Information:** In incidents involving transgender and nonbinary individuals, security personnel must prioritize confidentiality. Data related to gender-based incidents should be collected anonymously and securely. When reporting incidents, always respect the wishes of the affected person, ensuring their anonymity and securing sensitive information appropriately.

- **Addressing Gender-Based Violence and Discrimination:** Security personnel must actively and consistently contribute to addressing and mitigating gender-based violence and discrimination. To handle these sensitive issues, it's essential to:

  o **Create a Safe Environment:** Ensure safety and security, including providing private, confidential spaces for reporting and facilitating access to internal and external support structures.

  o **Uphold Confidentiality and Consent:** Security personnel should only share information with explicit and informed consent from the affected person and ensure confidentiality in all communications.

  o **Respect and Non-Discrimination:** Treat all individuals with respect, ensuring that language and actions do not suggest blame or discrimination.

  o **Cultural Sensitivity:** Be aware of cultural nuances and local contexts while addressing gender-based incidents. However, uphold the company's core values even when cultural practices may justify gender-based incidents.

  o **Develop Effective Response Plans:** Public safety departments should develop comprehensive response plans, including regular training, incident response protocols, and coordination with other departments like HR or legal.

- **Collaboration with HR and Legal:** For incidents that involve gender-related conflict or potential legal ramifications, security should collaborate closely with HR and legal departments to ensure that incidents are resolved in accordance with organizational values and laws.

- **Cooperation with Local Authorities:** For larger organizations, in situations involving legal implications or where public safety is at risk, security personnel should coordinate with local governments and authorities on gender-based security issues. Ensuring that security actions align with local legal frameworks helps safeguard the rights of all individuals and reinforces the organization's inclusive values.

- **Scenario-Based Training:** Include scenario-based training to help security teams practice handling real-world situations with transgender and nonbinary individuals. These scenarios should cover common issues like mismatched identification or misgendering.

Case Study: TSA Security: A Gender Neutrality Journey

Nobody enjoys the inconvenience of airport security, but for transgender and nonbinary people, the experience can be unbearable for several reasons. Nearly half of respondents in a 2022 US Transgender Survey reported that none of their identification documents, such as a birth certificate, passport, or driver's license, reflected their chosen name.[231] For nonbinary people, the "X" gender marker on state identification, in states that allow it, often clashes with the binary "Male" or "Female" options used by airlines. Adding to the confusion, body scanners at airports still rely on technology that forces airport security agents to pick either "Male" or "Female" based on appearance, which often leads to uncomfortable situations for transgender travelers. These inconsistencies between documents, identity, and security procedures not only cause delays but can leave travelers feeling exposed and vulnerable.

As part of a larger Biden administration push to advance equality for transgender Americans, the Transportation Security Administration (TSA) implemented changes to improve the travel experience for transgender and nonbinary travelers.[232] The TSA website offered a dedicated page that outlines what travelers can expect, from airport screenings, tips for preparing before arriving at the airport, and guidance on how to handle issues that may arise during the screening process. Travelers were also encouraged to file complaints if they experience any mistreatment.[233] Some of the key changes listed on the "TSA Cares" website included:

- **Gender-Neutral Scanners:** TSA began implementing gender-neutral algorithms for Advanced Imaging Technology (AIT) scanners that eliminate binary male or female body scans.

- **Third Gender Marker:** TSA added an "X" marker option for TSA PreCheck and US passports and is working with airlines to incorporate this option into their reservation systems. TSA PreCheck travelers pass through metal detectors, not body scanners.

- **Pat-Down Procedure Adjustments:** Travelers can now request a pat-down officer who aligns with their gender identity, ensuring more respectful screenings.

- **Improved Identity Validation:** Security checkpoints no longer consider gender as part of identity verification.

The most notable improvement came in June 2023, when the updated AIT scanners reduced false alarms by 50%, decreasing the need for invasive pat-downs.[234] However, shortcomings remain, particularly with biometric technologies like facial recognition, which tend to misclassify marginalized groups, especially in terms of gender and race.[235]

Internally, TSA has introduced a Gender Identity Policy to ensure fair treatment of transgender employees, including Transportation Security Officers (TSOs). This policy supports transgender TSOs in performing sensitive tasks like pat-downs.[236]

While progress was being made, TSA's work was far from complete. Yet, the implementation of gender-neutral technologies and policies showed a commitment to a more inclusive future for airport travelers and employees.

That progress came to an immediate halt.

As of January 20, 2025, all references to these policies have been removed from the TSA website. The federal government eliminated public guidance on gender-neutral security screenings, transgender identity validation, and the "X" gender marker option. Reports also indicate that TSA has begun altering body scanners to remove gender-neutral screening options and has barred transgender TSA officers from conducting pat-downs.[237] These changes are occurring with no public explanation or acknowledgment, creating widespread uncertainty for transgender and nonbinary travelers.

These policies existed—and they worked. The updated scanners cut false alarms by 50%, decreasing unnecessary pat-downs and improving efficiency for all travelers. They didn't just protect transgender people; they made airport security better for everyone.

The removal of these policies isn't an isolated incident—it's part of a coordinated effort to erase transgender identities from all federal guidance. The DOJ removed its training for law enforcement. The Department of Labor deleted workplace protections. And now, the TSA has erased security procedures that were already in place and actively helping travelers. They even removed the LGBTQI+ Travel information and replaced it with data only pertaining to LGB Travelers.

This case study was once an example of progress. Now, it's an example of how quickly inclusion can be erased—and how we must resist compliance with that erasure.

As the federal government turns its back on transgender and nonbinary people, private industries must step up. Corporations, airlines, and even private security firms can and must implement their own inclusive policies to ensure that transgender travelers are treated with respect, dignity, and fairness.

Summary Checklist for Security and Safety Services

Hiring, Training, and Education for Security Personnel

☐ Ensure security personnel complete training on gender inclusion before beginning work.

☐ Ask about candidates' experience with diverse communities and inclusive practices during the hiring process.

☐ Verify that outsourced security services follow inclusive training practices.

☐ Prioritize hiring diverse candidates, including openly transgender and nonbinary personnel, to build a more inclusive team.

Training on Inclusive Security Practices

☐ Provide comprehensive training on correct pronoun usage and respectful interactions with transgender and nonbinary individuals.

☐ Train security personnel to avoid assumptions based on gender expression or appearance.

☐ Include education on de-escalation tactics sensitive to gender identity in all training programs.

☐ Regularly update security personnel on changes in best practices for gender inclusion, including evolving terminology.

☐ Establish feedback mechanisms to continuously assess and improve security personnel's inclusivity training.

Respectful Interaction with Diverse Gender Identities

☐ Train security personnel to manage gender-related challenges with biometric technologies and body scanners sensitively.

☐ Ensure all security staff use gender-neutral language when interacting with individuals, particularly when gender identity is unknown.

☐ Encourage active listening and empathy in all security interactions, especially when addressing individuals from marginalized gender identities.

De-Escalation Through Inclusive Communication

☐ Implement de-escalation techniques grounded in empathy and respect for individuals' gender identities.

☐ Train security personnel to remain calm and clear during emergencies, using gender-neutral language and culturally competent communication.

☐ Encourage the use of context-specific communication strategies to prevent unnecessary conflict in high-pressure situations.

Inclusive Incident Management

☐ Ensure private, confidential spaces are available for individuals to report incidents without fear of being misgendered or outed.

☐ Handle sensitive gender identity information confidentially, with explicit consent from the individual involved.

☐ Develop comprehensive incident response protocols that address gender-based violence and discrimination with respect and confidentiality.

☐ Collaborate with HR and legal departments to ensure gender-related security incidents are handled in accordance with organizational policies and laws.

☐ Implement scenario-based training for security personnel, specifically addressing common issues such as misgendering or mismatched IDs.

CHAPTER 15

REAL-LIFE EXAMPLES OF INCLUSION AT WORK

A cross industries, from healthcare to aviation, energy to government, companies and municipalities are taking meaningful steps to create environments where everyone can belong. These case studies offer a glimpse into that journey, revealing how both private and public sectors can promote inclusion, regardless of their history or conventional norms.

Gender inclusion is a journey, sometimes seamless, sometimes messy, but always necessary. For some, the path has been one of trailblazing leadership, with groundbreaking policies and support systems leading the way. These organizations demonstrate how inclusion can be woven into the very fabric of their operations. For others, the road has been more complex; though strong policies exist, navigating the tensions between policy and practice remains a challenge. These real-life examples show that true inclusion is about more than what's written on paper; it's about how those policies are enforced and how organizations hold themselves accountable when missteps occur.

Resistance, whether rooted in outdated practices, systemic bias, or legislative opposition, is inevitable. But the work must continue. The struggles these organizations have faced serve as a reminder that creating inclusive environments requires constant reflection, adjustment, and, most importantly, persistence. The progress made is always worth the effort.

Inclusion is an ongoing commitment to change and growth. It's not a destination but a journey, one that demands engagement from all levels of an organization.

Sephora: Championing Transgender Inclusion

Sephora, a renowned beauty retailer, has garnered widespread acclaim from the LGBTQ+ community for its steadfast commitment to creating an inclusive and welcoming environment for all customers, regardless of their gender identity. The company has made significant strides in fostering diversity and promoting inclusivity within the beauty industry.

Inclusive Policies and Initiatives

Sephora's dedication to inclusion is evident in its policies and initiatives, designed to ensure that transgender and nonbinary individuals feel respected and valued when visiting Sephora stores:

- **Gender-Neutral Restrooms:** Sephora has taken the progressive step of providing gender-neutral restrooms in its stores. This initiative sends a powerful message of inclusivity, ensuring that customers of all gender identities can access these facilities comfortably.

- **Employee Training:** Sephora has invested in training programs for its employees, focusing on allyship and respectful interactions with transgender and nonbinary customers. This training helps ensure a welcoming and inclusive shopping experience for all.

- **Sephora Prism (LGBTQ+ ERG):** Sephora supports its LGBTQ+ employees through the Sephora Prism Employee Resource Group (ERG). This group offers professional development opportunities, a speaker series, and emotional support specifically designed for LGBTQ+ staff, creating a safe and empowering space for them to connect and thrive both personally and professionally.[238]

- **Community Partnerships and Volunteering:** Sephora offered their stores as designated safe spaces during Pride Month, promoting self-expression and offering support to the LGBTQ+ community. They encourage employees to volunteer with LGBTQ+ organizations, such as the Trevor Project, a suicide prevention and crisis intervention nonprofit for LGBTQ+ youth. Sephora employees have also volunteered their time and skills at events like the San Francisco Trans March, providing beauty services to participants.[239]

- **Inclusive Benefits:** Sephora provides extensive gender-affirming healthcare benefits for its employees, including transition support, hormone therapy, and gender-affirming surgery. Additionally, the company offers healthcare travel benefits to employees in states where gender-affirming care may be restricted.[240]

"We Belong to Something Beautiful" Campaign: Navigating Setbacks and Moving Forward

In 2019, Sephora launched the "We Belong to Something Beautiful" campaign, further strengthening its commitment to diversity and inclusion. However, the campaign's launch coincided with a controversy involving SZA, a Black R&B singer, who accused Sephora of racial profiling during a shopping trip at one of its stores. The incident occurred at a Sephora location in Calabasas,

California, where a store employee called security while SZA was shopping for Fenty Beauty products.[241]

In response to the incident, Sephora took immediate action by apologizing to SZA and announcing that all US stores would be shut down for an hour to conduct diversity training for over 16,000 employees. This move was part of a larger effort to address unconscious bias and ensure that its commitment to inclusion extended beyond marketing campaigns and into every aspect of the customer experience.[242]

Despite the setback, Sephora continued to push forward with its message of inclusion. In 2024, Sephora adopted "We Belong to Something Beautiful" as its global brand signature, expanding the campaign's message across all thirty-five of its markets worldwide.[243] This reaffirms the company's dedication to promoting a sense of belonging for all customers, regardless of gender identity or background. Sephora's perseverance through challenges demonstrates the importance of staying committed to inclusion even when faced with adversity.

"Identify as We"–A Celebration of Gender Diversity

In 2019, Sephora launched its "Identify as We" campaign during Pride Month, celebrating LGBTQ+ visibility in the beauty industry. Rather than just launching a typical Pride product line, Sephora wanted to do more. The brand aimed to highlight and celebrate the transgender and nonbinary community specifically, ensuring everyone felt included in the beauty space.

Directed by Matt Lambert, known for his work with the LGBTQ+ community, the campaign featured transgender and nonbinary models in front of the camera while LGBTQ+ (including transgender and gender-fluid) individuals worked behind the scenes.[244]

This campaign embraced the diverse spectrum of gender identities, making a bold statement about inclusion and representation. By focusing solely on gender-diverse individuals,

Sephora's "Identify as We" campaign became a milestone in the beauty industry, amplifying underrepresented voices and setting a new standard for inclusion.

As part of this initiative, Sephora also introduced the "Trans is Beautiful" group within its online Beauty Insider Community. This group provides a platform for trans and nonbinary individuals to ask questions, join challenges, share their looks, and connect with other Sephora customers virtually.[245]

Inclusive Makeup Classes and Tutorials

In 2016, Sephora initiated a groundbreaking program called "Classes for Confidence," offering complimentary in-store classes tailored to individuals undergoing significant life transitions. Initially, these classes focused on assisting individuals with workforce re-entry and those navigating beauty routines during battles with cancer.

In June 2018, Sephora expanded this program by launching a nationwide series of in-store classes specifically designed for the trans and nonbinary community. These sessions, developed and hosted by transgender Sephora employees, provide a safe and affirming space for customers to explore makeup and self-expression. Sephora also offers online classes, making these resources accessible to more individuals who may not be able to visit a store in person.[246]

Supporting LGBTQ+ Causes

Sephora's advocacy extends beyond advertising campaigns. The company introduced the "SEPHORAHeartPRIDE" collection, featuring ten branded offerings celebrating and supporting Pride. Sephora donates one dollar to LGBTQ+ organizations for every product sold, working in collaboration with the Tides Foundation to coordinate these donations.[247]

In a world where transgender, transitioning, and queer individuals often face discrimination and hostility, Sephora strives to be a safe haven where they can access beauty products without fear. The company's commitment to inclusion and advocacy helps create a greater sense of belonging for some of society's most vulnerable members.

Sephora's actions demonstrate that businesses can use their influence to make a positive impact and stand up for the rights and inclusion of marginalized communities. By championing diversity, Sephora sets a leading example of how the beauty industry can embrace change and promote inclusion.

The "We Belong to Something Beautiful" campaign, launched alongside the SZA incident, highlights the complexities of maintaining a commitment to diversity in the face of real-world issues. However, Sephora's continued dedication to inclusion, through diversity training, employee resource groups, and public campaigns, demonstrates how companies can learn from their missteps and keep moving forward. These efforts have helped Sephora earn a perfect one hundred score on the HRC Corporate Equality Index (CEI) for 2023–24, cementing its place as a leader in inclusivity within the beauty industry.

United Airlines: Fostering Inclusivity for Customers and Employees

United Airlines has consistently demonstrated its commitment to fostering a more inclusive and equitable workplace for employees of all gender identities. This commitment has earned United a perfect score on the HRC Corporate Equality Index (CEI) for over a decade, highlighting its leadership in creating an environment that supports diversity and inclusion.[248]

Fly How You Identify

United Airlines is at the forefront of gender inclusion in the aviation industry. In 2019, the airline became the first US airline to offer nonbinary gender options for passengers during the booking process, providing customers with the ability to select "U" (Undisclosed) or "X" (Unspecified) gender in addition to the traditional male and female options. United also introduced "Mx." to the list of title options, setting a precedent for inclusivity in the travel experience.[249]

At the time, United proudly announced this change with the message, "Fly how you identify. Our new non-binary gender options are now available."[250] In 2023, the airline expanded on this commitment to normalizing the use of pronouns by offering flight attendants and customer service representatives the option of including pronouns on their name badges.[251] This initiative not only allows employees to be recognized as their true selves but also signals a sense of safety and inclusion for transgender and nonbinary passengers, reinforcing United's dedication to making everyone feel respected and acknowledged.

Inclusive Policies for Employees

United Airlines has been proactive in creating policies that support all employees, regardless of gender identity. The company's transgender-inclusive healthcare benefits ensure that employees undergoing gender transitions are supported with access to necessary medical care. Additionally, in 2021, United relaxed its gender-based restrictions on tattoos, hair, nails, and makeup to promote self-expression and equity in the workplace. These updates allowed any employee to wear nail polish and makeup, and wear their hair down within professional guidelines, something previously restricted to only female staff.[252]

The airline has long been committed to employee education. United partnered with the HRC to deliver training programs, addressing topics such as pronoun usage, the persistence of gender norms, and how to be a better ally to both colleagues and customers.[253]

In its ongoing effort to promote gender inclusion, United Airlines invited employees to add their pronouns to email signatures. This is part of the company's broader push to foster an inclusive culture that respects all gender identities. Additionally, United Airlines has achieved "near-perfect pay equity for employees of all genders and races performing comparable work across US operations."[254]

Notice the words "all genders" in that last quote. Corporate conversations about the gender pay gap traditionally address equal pay for women; United acknowledges the need for equity across the gender spectrum. The airline demonstrates the use of inclusive language throughout its written communication across the organization.

Employee Resource Groups and Community Engagement

United Airlines provides ongoing support for employees through its Business Resource Group (BRG) called Equal. With over 5,800 members spanning 9 chapters, Equal offers networking, professional development, and educational opportunities to help LGBTQ+ grow within the company.[255] The group also focuses on community outreach, participating in numerous parades, festivals, and events such as Pride, Spirit Day, and other initiatives aimed at raising awareness and promoting inclusion.

In 2019, United Airlines became the first public company to be inducted into Pride Live's Stonewall Ambassador program, an honor that highlights its continued commitment to LGBTQ+ advocacy and community support. This milestone further solidifies United's position as a leader in promoting equality and inclusivity, both within the company and in the broader community.[256]

Mike Henning, Associate General Counsel and President of Equal, credits the success of these inclusion efforts to buy-in from senior leadership, which he believes "sets the tone and flows down throughout the company."[257]

United Airlines' dedication to inclusion exemplifies how a company can positively impact the experiences of both customers and employees. Its pioneering role in offering nonbinary gender options for travelers, normalizing the use of pronouns in name badges for employees, celebrating the LGBTQ+ community at large, and providing gender-inclusive policies that are both customer-facing and employee-facing make United Airlines a role model for the aviation industry.

Virtua Health: Leading the Way in Inclusive Patient Care

A few years ago, while traveling for work, I found myself needing medical care during an extended stay in Oregon. I was referred to Dr. Kyle Kurzet at Transition Health, a practice offering gender-affirming care. At the time, I didn't think much about the gender-affirming aspect; I was simply seeking medical attention for an unrelated issue, and Dr. Kurzet's credentials were impressive.

The experience was eye-opening. From the moment I walked in, I was treated with a level of respect and acknowledgment I hadn't realized was missing from my previous healthcare experiences. Every interaction was affirming, making me feel seen not just as a patient but as a person. When I returned home, I switched providers, not necessarily because of any particular negative experience, but because I came to understand how crucial it is to feel comfortable and respected in a healthcare setting, regardless of the reason for the visit.

Gender inclusion in the business of healthcare is an ethical imperative. When transgender and nonbinary patients receive poor or discriminatory treatment in any medical or behavioral health setting, they may avoid seeking healthcare altogether, worsening medical conditions and increasing the likelihood of preventable health crises. Some healthcare providers, including mental health care, view transgender and gender-questioning patients as individuals with problems that need their help to fix. When you are treated as if you are "not normal," you either begin to believe you are not normal, or you avoid the places that treat you this way. A study from the National Institutes of Health found that more than one in five transgender adults avoids healthcare altogether due to anticipated discrimination. Negative experiences contributing to this avoidance include slurs, microaggressions, sexual harassment, violence, and harassment regarding bathroom use.[258]

A Model for Inclusion

In response to these challenges, Virtua Health, one of the largest healthcare systems in New Jersey, recognized the need for a safe, inclusive space for the LGBTQ+ community and established the Virtua Pride Primary Care Practice in 2022. The practice serves as a critical resource for LGBTQ+ individuals and families, offering gender-affirming care alongside standard primary care services. Key services provided include hormone therapy, family planning, sexual health, behavioral health counseling, and medication-assisted treatment for opioid and alcohol abuse. In addition to inclusive patient care, all staff members are trained to assist LGBTQ+ patients, ensuring respectful interactions from the waiting room to the exam room.

Virtua Pride's commitment to inclusion is evident even in the small details. For instance, when patients request an initial appointment online, the form includes a pronoun field that goes beyond the basics. In addition to the standard options like "she"/ "her," "he"/ "him," and "they"/ "them," the form also offers "ze" (or "zie")/"hir" and an "other" option, which opens a field for the patient to specify their pronouns. This thoughtful approach allows patients to feel seen and respected, no matter their identity, even before they walk through the door.

Virtua Pride also refers patients to specialists who are sensitive to the LGBTQ+ community's unique needs, further reducing barriers to care. This focus on inclusion and affirming leads to better healthcare outcomes: patients are more forthcoming and engaged in their own care when they know they are being treated with dignity and respect.[259]

Gaps in Medical Education

One of the key issues Virtua Pride addresses is the lack of gender-affirming care education in medical schools. As Dr. Richard Levine of Virtua Pride notes, most primary care providers lack training in gender-affirming care, leaving gaps in care for transgender patients.[260] This systemic issue highlights the importance of LGBTQ+-focused clinics like Virtua Pride, where healthcare professionals receive specialized training in treating transgender and nonbinary patients with respect and competence.[261]

According to Virtua's leadership, this specialized training is crucial to building trust with patients, particularly those who have been marginalized by traditional healthcare settings.[262] By offering a dedicated practice that focuses on gender-affirming care, Virtua Health is actively filling these gaps and providing care that is often missing in other primary care practices.

Success and Results

The success of Virtua Pride has been notable. In its first year, the practice served nearly 600 patients across 1,600 visits, with 65% of these patients being new to the Virtua Medical Group network. This demonstrates the growing demand for inclusive, affirming healthcare. This growth has allowed Virtua Pride to expand its services. The practice is now adding specialists on a rotating basis, including a gastroenterologist and a social worker, further enhancing access to specialty care in an inclusive setting.[263]

City of Philadelphia, PA: Balancing Progress and Setbacks in Gender Inclusion

Philadelphia, widely recognized for its vibrant LGBTQ+ culture and historic advocacy, presents a nuanced case study in gender inclusion, showcasing both progressive accomplishments and systemic challenges. The city's ongoing efforts reflect the complexities of fostering inclusive environments for transgender and nonbinary individuals. From groundbreaking legislation to real-world challenges, Philadelphia stands as a leader in inclusivity, though its journey is far from complete.

Local Laws and Protections: Leading the Way

Philadelphia has long been a pioneer in LGBTQ+ rights. The city was one of the first in the US to include gender identity protections in employment, housing, and public accommodations, beginning with the Fair Practices Ordinance in 1963, expanding protections for sexual orientation in 1982, and for gender identity in 2002.[264] In recent years, Philadelphia has continued to build on this legacy.

- In 2022, the Philadelphia City Council passed a bill extending protections for transgender and gender-nonconforming youth, requiring institutions to respect pronouns and chosen names, provide access to appropriate facilities, and ensure confidentiality.[265]

- In 2023, Mayor Kenney signed Executive Order No. 4-23, protecting individuals seeking and providing gender-affirming healthcare from out-of-state investigations, further strengthening the city's protections.[266]

Philadelphia consistently earned a perfect score on the Human Rights Campaign's Municipal Equality Index, which evaluates non-discrimination laws, employment policies, municipal services, and law enforcement support for LGBTQ+ residents. [267]

The Philadelphia Police Department and Directive 4.15

In 2019, the Philadelphia Police Department (PPD) introduced Directive 4.15, a groundbreaking policy aimed at guiding respectful interactions with transgender and nonbinary individuals, whether they are suspects, arrestees, victims, or witnesses. This directive, developed in collaboration with the Office of LGBT Affairs and local advocates, includes key provisions such as:[268]

- **Recording chosen names:** Officers must record an individual's chosen name in addition to their legal name.
- **Respect for pronouns:** Officers are required to use an individual's chosen name and pronouns during interactions.
- **Healthcare access in custody:** Transgender individuals are guaranteed access to necessary healthcare, including hormone therapy.
- **Choice in officer gender for searches:** Transgender individuals may express a preference for the gender of the officer conducting searches.

The directive was designed to address historic police bias, and by 2020, the arrest rate for violence against transgender women had reached 100%, reflecting improvements in law enforcement response. However, as activist Deja Lynn Alvarez pointed out, policies alone cannot change personal biases, and ongoing education is critical.[269]

The Morrison-McLean Incident: Systemic Issues Remain

Despite the PPD's policy progress, the March 2024 arrest of Celena Morrison, a Black transgender woman and the executive director of the Office of LGBT Affairs, and her husband Darius

McLean, a Black man and the COO of the William Way LGBT Community Center, highlighted persistent systemic problems. The couple was subjected to a violent arrest by a state trooper, which involved racial profiling and gender discrimination. Video footage of the incident, where Morrison's phone was knocked away as she attempted to record, went viral, leading to widespread outrage. As Morrison and McLean called for accountability, community members described the incident as "another example in the long institutional history of over-policing and disproportional outcomes against Black, Brown, and LGBTQ+ people, particularly Black trans people."[270]

While the incident was being investigated, the trooper was removed from parole duty,[271] and within two months, he was removed from his position altogether.[272] This swift action showed that Philadelphia is willing to address serious missteps. However, the incident highlights the tension between progressive policies and their enforcement.

In the wake of this incident, Philadelphia's annual Trans Day of Visibility ceremony was canceled, though the transgender flag continued to fly at City Hall. The city cited "challenging times" without further explanation, which some saw as an opportunity to prioritize Morrison's self-care.[273] However, without an official reason and given that not everyone in the public may have known about the incident, the cancellation could be perceived differently by community members who may have hoped for the event to continue. For many, this decision underscores the complexities and challenges of upholding inclusion during difficult moments.

Community Engagement and Advocacy

Philadelphia's inclusivity extends beyond policies. The city actively participates in LGBTQ+ events like the Trans Wellness Conference and works closely with advocacy groups such as the William Way LGBT Community Center to support LGBTQ+ residents.[274]

In 2024, the Philadelphia Marathon introduced a nonbinary category, awarding equal prize money to nonbinary athletes, a further step toward broader gender inclusion in public life.[275]

The Office of LGBT Affairs continues to lead key programs, such as the "Supporting Transitioning Employees Guide" and the Michael S. Hinson, Jr. LGBTQ+ Leadership Pipeline, empowering and advocating for transgender and nonbinary residents. The office has also championed initiatives like the "More Color More Pride" flag, which adds black and brown stripes to the traditional Pride flag to represent LGBTQ+ people of color, highlighting the importance of intersectionality in the city's advocacy efforts.[276]

The Statewide Battle: Resistance and Ongoing Efforts

While Philadelphia pushes forward, it faces significant resistance at the state level. Pennsylvania currently has nine anti-trans bills pending for 2024. The proposed legislation includes measures limiting gender-affirming healthcare for minors and providing civil immunity for parents who refuse to use their children's correct pronouns or consent to gender-affirming services. Additionally, bills offer liability protections for educators who decline to use a student's pronouns and enforce the designation of school sports teams by biological sex.[277]

The city continues to advocate against these bills, with leadership from Mayor Cherelle Parker, who previously co-sponsored resolutions opposing legislation like House Bill 972, which would have prohibited transgender students from participating in sports aligning with their gender identity.[278] Parker's leadership reflects the city's ongoing commitment to ensuring equal rights and protections for its transgender residents.

Inclusion as a Work in Progress

Philadelphia serves as a powerful case study of real-life inclusion at work. The city's comprehensive approach, from protective legislation and community outreach to progressive police policies, demonstrates its deep commitment to inclusivity. However, incidents like the Morrison-McLean arrest remind us that achieving true inclusion is messy, requiring continuous work and accountability.

Philadelphia's progress underscores the importance of ongoing efforts to address resistance, systemic bias, and real-world challenges in creating safe and inclusive spaces. While policies like Directive 4.15 set the stage for change, the implementation of these policies, and the willingness to address violations, remains critical to advancing gender inclusion.

Chevron: Trailblazing Inclusivity in a Traditional Industry

Supporting transgender employees has been a long-standing commitment for Chevron since 1993, when it became the first major US oil and gas company to include gender identity and expression in its Equal Employment Opportunity policies.[279] This commitment to fostering inclusion revolves around education and engagement, earning the PRIDE Network the title of "Employee Resource Group of the Year" by Out & Equal. Their efforts include an educational pamphlet detailing employee transition guidelines, encompassing gender terminology, distinguishing sexual orientation, and a comprehensive workplace engagement strategy. Chevron's approach emphasizes peer-to-peer training, alleviating stress for transitioning employees by making social conduct everyone's responsibility, including management.[280]

Chevron's PRIDE Network and the "Transgender @ Chevron" Guidebook

Chevron's PRIDE Network (Promoting Respect, Inclusion & Dignity for Everyone), founded in 1991, has played a pivotal role in advancing LGBTQ+ inclusion within the company, long before employee networks were even sanctioned. The PRIDE Network spans over twenty countries, providing essential resources, programming, and training on topics such as trans allyship. In 2005, the PRIDE Network introduced the "Transgender @ Chevron" guidebook, which provides guidelines for transitioning employees and their allies, covering everything from gender terminology to workplace best practices. The guidebook was shared with the Human Rights Campaign Foundation as a model for other organizations, further solidifying Chevron's leadership in gender inclusion.[281]

In 2011, Chevron became the first company in its industry to offer fully inclusive transgender wellness benefits, setting a new standard for industry peers.[282] Additionally, Chevron's leadership in creating inclusive policies, such as the "Transgender @ Chevron" guidebook, has inspired organizations like the Transgender Law Center, which cited Chevron as a model for its own Model Transgender Employment Policy.[283] These efforts underscore Chevron's role as a trailblazer in promoting gender inclusion within the corporate world.

Supplier Diversity and Continued Inclusivity Efforts

Chevron's dedication to inclusivity extends to its business practices, especially its commitment to supplier diversity. In 2020, Chevron invested $40 million in women- and minority-owned businesses, reinforcing its belief that diversity drives innovation.[284] By 2023, the company was recognized on the National LGBT Chamber of Commerce's (NGLCC) "Best of the Best" list, underscoring Chevron's industry leadership in supporting LGBTQ+ businesses.[285]

Chevron's commitment to inclusion has been consistently recognized over the years. In both 2019[286] and again in 2024, Chevron was featured on Forbes' lists of "Best Employers for Diversity," "Best Employers for Women," and "Best Employers for New Grads."[287] Additionally, Chevron was recognized by *Newsweek* as one of America's Greatest Workplaces for LGBTQ+ in both 2023[288] and 2024,[289] further solidifying its reputation as a leader in fostering an inclusive environment.

Chevron's unwavering commitment to equality has earned the company a perfect score on the Human Rights Campaign's Corporate Equality Index (CEI) every year since 2005. In 2023, Chevron was further honored with the Equality 100 Award, recognizing its excellence in non-discrimination policies, equitable benefits, and corporate social responsibility.[290]

Chevron's approach to gender inclusion demonstrates that even in traditionally conservative industries like oil and gas, inclusion can thrive. The company's efforts, from its pioneering 1993 gender identity policies to the introduction of transgender wellness benefits in 2011, and its sustained commitment to supplier diversity, reflect how inclusion can drive business success. Chevron's PRIDE Network, which was established even before employee networks were formally recognized, continues to shape the company's inclusive culture across the globe.

As a company that leads by example, Chevron stands as a beacon of inclusive leadership, illustrating how corporate responsibility and a commitment to diversity can go hand in hand with innovation and business success.

INTEGRATED SUMMARY CHECKLIST

Summary Checklist for Leadership

Building Blocks of Inclusive Leadership

☐ Exhibit commitment to diversity and inclusion.
☐ Demonstrate awareness of personal and organizational biases.
☐ Show humility and seek input from others.
☐ Encourage diverse perspectives in decision-making.

Inclusive Leadership Behaviors

☐ Practice active listening and empathy.
☐ Encourage participation from all team members.
☐ Communicate transparently and advocate for diversity.
☐ Mitigate bias in team decisions and actions.

Empowering Voices for Inclusive Leadership

☐ Ensure all team members have a voice and create a safe space for innovation.
☐ Share successes and offer constructive feedback.
☐ Act on team input and delegate decision-making authority.

Creating Safe Spaces

- ☐ Establish non-judgmental listening sessions.
- ☐ Implement anonymous feedback mechanisms.
- ☐ Structure inclusive team meetings and provide diversity training.

Supporting Transitions

- ☐ Model trans-inclusive behaviors.
- ☐ Engage in trans-specific initiatives.
- ☐ Provide practical support and resources for transitioning employees.

Promoting Allyship and Inclusivity

- ☐ Offer workshops and training on allyship.
- ☐ Implement mentorship programs and share educational resources.
- ☐ Encourage pronoun usage and inclusive language.

Cultivating Continuous Learning

- ☐ Design and implement regular gender-inclusion training programs.
- ☐ Tailor content and ensure mandatory participation.
- ☐ Use interactive and engaging formats for training.
- ☐ Implement feedback channels and track progress.

Addressing Resistance

- ☐ Understand the root of resistance.
- ☐ Address concerns with awareness and education.
- ☐ Define and uphold inclusive practices.

Summary Checklist for Human Resources

HR as Champions of Inclusivity

- ☐ Model inclusive behavior: active listening, continuous education, and use of inclusive language.
- ☐ Foster open communication and create safe spaces for employees to provide feedback.
- ☐ Collaborate with leadership and departments to integrate inclusivity into the company culture.
- ☐ Develop training programs tailored to the unique needs of each department, addressing specific challenges and opportunities in their roles.
- ☐ Ensure training is accessible to all employees, from executives to entry-level positions, adapting formats to accommodate different needs (e.g., shift workers, remote employees, and private sessions for executives).
- ☐ Stay informed on legal developments by monitoring federal and state policies, consulting employment law experts, and ensuring company policies align with civil rights laws rather than shifting political agendas.

Workplace Policies and Practices

- ☐ Regularly review and update HR policies to ensure gender inclusion.
- ☐ Use gender-neutral language in the employee handbooks and all policy documents.
- ☐ Implement gender-neutral dress codes and job titles.

Addressing Resistance from Employees

- ☐ Address any instances of individual resistance with tailored approaches based on the specific type (psychological, moral/cultural, pragmatic, or group-based).

☐ Emphasize the shared benefits of inclusion to reinforce that inclusivity strengthens team cohesion and benefits all employees.

☐ Foster a collective identity that aligns with inclusive values and promotes a sense of belonging for everyone.

☐ Create an affirmation culture where individual contributions are valued, and inclusion is viewed as integral to a positive workplace.

☐ Model inclusive language and practices consistently in daily interactions, setting a standard for all employees.

Supporting Gender Transitions at Work

☐ Develop individualized transition plans respecting employee autonomy.

☐ Provide access to mental health resources and support networks.

☐ Update records to reflect affirmed gender identity and chosen names.

☐ Ensure access to gender-affirming healthcare and consistent coverage.

☐ Update security clearances and badges in alignment with the transition timeline.

☐ Respect restroom and facility preferences and educate staff on inclusivity.

Recruiting and Retaining Talent

☐ Use gender-neutral language in job descriptions, postings, and hiring materials.

☐ Implement blind resume reviews to mitigate unconscious bias.

☐ Ensure diverse hiring panels and inclusive interviewing techniques.

☐ Include equal opportunity employment information in job postings.

☐ Offer benefits that consider the needs of diverse genders.

☐ Conduct gender-sensitive exit interviews.

Training and Continuous Learning

☐ Implement comprehensive DEI training programs.

☐ Provide ongoing training on gender identity and inclusivity.

☐ Create spaces for private or anonymous questions.

☐ Stay informed about best practices and legal requirements through professional development.

Summary Checklist for Legal

Ensuring Legal Compliance and Handling Discrimination

- ☐ Stay informed on state, federal, and international laws, prioritizing established case law over shifting political directives.
- ☐ Monitor lawsuits challenging DEI rollbacks to anticipate potential legal changes.
- ☐ Prepare legal strategies to challenge unlawful mandates or defend against funding threats.
- ☐ Scrutinize all employment-related documents—handbooks, policies, NDAs—for legal compliance and gender inclusion.
- ☐ Ensure company policies remain inclusive and do not preemptively comply with unlawful mandates.
- ☐ Collaborate with HR and external consultants to uphold workplace protections and maintain an inclusive environment.
- ☐ Guide a thorough, unbiased, and confidential internal investigation for discrimination or harassment claims.
- ☐ Ensure compliance with legal reporting requirements, particularly in states with varying protections.
- ☐ Oversee disciplinary actions to align with company policy and legal obligations.

Crafting Gender-Neutral Documents

- ☐ Ensure generic and template legal forms and documents use gender-neutral language.
- ☐ Maintain gender accuracy when creating documents for known entities.
- ☐ Ensure precision and clarity when using "they" as a singular pronoun in court documents.
- ☐ Consider alternative gender-neutral methods for judicial documents.

Vendor and Third-Party Agreements

- ☐ Review terms and conditions of agreements for alignment with inclusion objectives.
- ☐ Negotiate to modify or remove problematic clauses.
- ☐ Include non-discrimination clauses and compliance requirements in agreements.
- ☐ Collaborate with procurement, HR, and leadership on vendor relationships.

Mergers and Acquisitions

- ☐ Review the target company's policies, employment practices, and history of discrimination.
- ☐ Assess the target company's reputation and public image for alignment with values on gender inclusion.
- ☐ Include inclusion clauses in M&A agreements.
- ☐ Recommend training programs and policy updates post-acquisition.

Continuing Legal Education

- ☐ Prioritize CLE courses focused on Diversity, Equity, and Inclusion (DEI).
- ☐ Incorporate gender-inclusive practices into everyday legal practice.
- ☐ Lead in sharing DEI insights with other departments.
- ☐ Collaborate with HR to facilitate in-house training sessions.

Summary Checklist for IT

Tech Language and Identity Representation

☐ Replace cybersecurity, networking, and project management terms to be gender neutral.

☐ Choose gender-neutral server naming conventions.

☐ Ensure employees' names, pronouns, and titles are accurately displayed across all digital platforms.

☐ Manage name changes across all systems to avoid deadnaming.

Inclusive Onboarding and Offboarding

☐ Include pronouns and chosen name in initial account setup.

☐ Configure training modules to address new hires by their pronouns and chosen name.

☐ Design digital badges to incorporate pronouns if disclosed and desired.

☐ Deactivate accounts using the departing employee's pronouns and chosen name.

☐ Ensure privacy in data retention and display pronouns and chosen name in historical posts and comments.

☐ Create an exit survey that is mindful of gender identity issues.

APIs and Third-Party Integrations

☐ Evaluate third-party services for non-inclusive language or settings.

☐ Ensure platforms allow for customizable options in form fields.

☐ Ensure all departments use updated information consistently to avoid deadnaming.

☐ Research and select biometric (or other) systems that allow for flexibility beyond binary gender recognition.

☐ Advise departments (e.g., HR, Security) on the limitations and inclusive practices of biometric (or other) systems.

☐ Test biometric (or other) systems for inclusivity across gender identities, focusing on misidentification risks for transgender and nonbinary users.

☐ Create custom fields or repurpose existing ones in identity and asset management systems for pronouns if fields do not exist.

☐ Develop feedback loops with transgender and nonbinary users to continually evaluate system inclusivity.

Creating Inclusive Virtual Spaces

☐ Ensure pronouns (optional) and chosen names are visible in virtual meetings.

☐ Provide nonbinary options for digital avatars.

☐ Establish guidelines for inclusivity in online meeting platforms and intranets.

Cybersecurity and Privacy for LGBTQ+ Staff

☐ Implement tools to detect and filter hate speech and cyberbullying (with human review).

☐ Store personal data securely with encryption and restricted access.

☐ Develop privacy policies outlining confidentiality levels for personal information.

☐ Establish anonymous reporting systems for digital harassment or privacy breaches.

☐ Create dedicated online spaces with controlled access for LGBTQ+ employees.

Auditing Language for Compliance

☐ Schedule regular audits of software, documentation, and code for inclusivity.

☐ Update non-inclusive language in error messages, system alerts, and API responses.

☐ Ensure inclusive language in all system documentation and interfaces.

Summary Checklist for Marketing and Branding

Gender-Neutral Marketing and Branding Strategies

- ☐ Conduct surveys and questionnaires to gather insights on gender identity and preferences.
- ☐ Utilize social media listening tools to monitor conversations about your brand and inclusivity.
- ☐ Include gender identity in audience segmentation, among other valuable criteria.
- ☐ Use gender-neutral language in all messaging and branding.
- ☐ Ensure advertisements and promotional materials portray a diverse range of gender identities.
- ☐ Choose color schemes that do not reinforce gender stereotypes.

Product and Service Development

- ☐ Offer gender-neutral product options.
- ☐ Ensure products cater to diverse identities.
- ☐ Reflect gender inclusion in product development.

Designing Inclusive Marketing Campaigns

- ☐ Ensure authentic representation of diverse gender identities in campaigns.
- ☐ Use inclusive language and pronouns.
- ☐ Include diverse visuals in marketing materials.
- ☐ Acknowledge intersections of gender identity with other aspects of identity.
- ☐ Avoid reinforcing gender stereotypes in product placement.
- ☐ Collaborate with individuals and influencers from diverse gender backgrounds.

Overcoming Challenges and Backlash

- ☐ Maintain consistency in messaging and avoid altering inclusion efforts.
- ☐ Address backlash selectively.
- ☐ Ensure inclusion is authentic and not limited to seasonal initiatives.
- ☐ Engage with a network of supporters, partners, and advocates who align with your values.

Gender Representation in Digital Content

- ☐ Use diverse imagery reflecting a wide spectrum of gender identities.
- ☐ Source inclusive visual content.
- ☐ Ensure website design and copy is gender inclusive.
- ☐ Provide options for gender beyond the binary in forms and surveys.
- ☐ Prioritize accessibility in website design.

Fostering Inclusive Online Interactions

- ☐ Use inclusive language in social media posts.
- ☐ Respect and use individuals' pronouns in online interactions.
- ☐ Challenge gender stereotypes in shared content.
- ☐ Amplify diverse voices within your community.
- ☐ Respond to comments and messages with inclusive language.
- ☐ Implement moderation guidelines to maintain a safe and inclusive online space.

Summary Checklist for Sales

Empowering Sales Teams Through Inclusion

☐ Secure C-suite advocacy for gender-inclusive sales approaches.

☐ Present the business case for inclusion to senior management, if necessary.

☐ Understand the shift from binary gender communication styles to a more nuanced approach.

☐ Recognize the ethical and strategic advantages of embracing diversity in sales.

☐ Provide ongoing education on diversity and inclusion for sales teams.

☐ Implement practical training programs focused on real-world applications of gender inclusion in sales.

Addressing Challenges to Improve Customer Relations

☐ Identify and understand resistance within the sales team.

☐ Provide comprehensive training to understand gender inclusion and pronoun usage.

☐ Encourage clear and open communication within sales teams.

☐ Solicit feedback from sales teams and clients to continuously improve practices.

☐ Track and measure the effectiveness of gender-inclusive strategies.

Building Inclusive Sales Pipelines

☐ Develop strategies to recognize and cater to diverse identities within the LGBTQ+ community.

☐ Integrate inclusion into lead generation and nurturing processes.

☐ Build a diverse sales team that reflects the clients you serve.

☐ Educate sales teams on gender identity and expression.

☐ Recognize and address intersectional identities and experiences.

Networking for Inclusive Sales

☐ Understand the strategic role of networking in fostering inclusivity.

☐ Join LGBTQ+-friendly networking organizations.

☐ Actively seek out and connect with individuals from diverse backgrounds.

☐ Use inclusive language and correct pronouns in networking settings.

☐ Engage with communities to promote diversity and inclusion.

☐ Amplify the voices and experiences of underrepresented groups within networks.

Summary Checklist for Customer Support and Service

Revamping Customer Service Training

☐ Update customer support scripts to enforce gender neutrality.

☐ Use gender-neutral greetings and remove courtesy titles such as "sir" and "ma'am."

☐ Identify and use customers' correct pronouns when provided.

☐ Avoid gender assumptions based on appearance or voice.

☐ Address misgendering with brief and sincere apologies.

☐ Implement roleplay scenarios related to gender identity in training sessions.

Intersectional Customer Support

☐ Train staff to understand the concept of intersectionality.

☐ Foster cultural competence through training on various cultures, traditions, and customs.

☐ Ensure accessibility in physical and digital spaces.

☐ Offer multilingual support and train staff to communicate effectively with non-native English speakers.

☐ Review marketing materials to ensure they represent diverse identities and backgrounds.

Leveraging Customer Feedback

☐ Encourage proactive engagement for feedback on gender inclusion practices.

☐ Utilize social media platforms for engaging with customers and responding to feedback.

☐ Send periodic customer satisfaction surveys that include questions about inclusion.

☐ Gather feedback on inclusive product and service options and share it with the marketing and branding department.

☐ Regularly review and analyze feedback to identify recurring themes or issues.

☐ Develop collaborative strategies with the marketing and HR teams to address specific issues.

☐ Communicate transparently about changes made in response to feedback.

☐ Use feedback to identify areas for creating safer and more welcoming environments.

Summary Checklist for Supply Chain and Procurement

Implementing Supplier Diversity

- ☐ Develop a Supplier Diversity Program, including leadership buy-in and measurable goals.
- ☐ Assess the current supplier landscape and identify opportunities for diverse suppliers.
- ☐ Engage with suppliers from underrepresented groups (minority-owned, women-owned, veteran-owned, LGBTQ+).
- ☐ Allocate procurement spend to diverse suppliers.
- ☐ Integrate supplier diversity efforts into finance, professional services, and technology sectors.
- ☐ Partner with minority- and women-owned businesses (MWBEs).
- ☐ Ensure alignment with corporate culture and inclusiveness.
- ☐ Commit to and invest in MWBE partnerships.
- ☐ Include diversity metrics in management's performance objectives.
- ☐ Address staffing and budget challenges for supplier diversity programs.

Practicing Inclusive Procurement

- ☐ Collaborate with diverse supplier advocacy groups.
- ☐ Engage with diverse suppliers.
- ☐ Ensure diversity in evaluation panels.
- ☐ Use inclusive language in RFPs.
- ☐ Implement gender-neutral procurement practices.
- ☐ Conduct gender-blind evaluations.
- ☐ Define objective evaluation criteria.
- ☐ Support supplier development programs.
- ☐ Monitor and report on gender neutrality in procurement processes.

Summary Checklist for Facilities Management

Introduction to Inclusive Facilities Management

☐ Recognize the importance of inclusive physical environments in promoting gender inclusion.

☐ Align all facilities management practices with company-wide inclusion principles.

Facilities Management Responsibilities and Scalable Strategies

☐ Adapt facilities management practices based on business size and resources.

- Small Businesses: Implement creative solutions for constrained or leased spaces.
- Mid-Sized Companies: Establish structured facilities management, including employee feedback.
- Large Corporations: Develop long-term infrastructure for inclusivity across multiple locations.

☐ Collaborate with HR and legal to develop clear, inclusive policies for facilities management.

☐ Regularly review and update facilities management strategies.

☐ Engage external experts for additional insights and resources.

Signage: More than Just Labels

☐ Use gender-inclusive signage to communicate values and inclusivity.

☐ Follow best practices for signage:

- Use universally recognized symbols.
- Use inclusive, nonbinary language.
- Ensure signage is visible and accessible.

☐ Implement gender-neutral language in all facility signage, including office signs and building directories.

☐ Regularly review and update signage to stay current with inclusive practices.

Ensuring Restroom Inclusivity and Privacy

☐ Provide inclusive restroom facilities:

- Convert single-stall restrooms to gender-neutral as permitted by law.

- Designate gender-neutral multi-occupant restrooms.

- Ensure multiple-stall restrooms have full-height partitions and full-length doors for privacy.

☐ Install privacy enhancements like full-length stall doors and occupancy indicator locks.

☐ Follow local laws on restroom signage and accessibility.

☐ Engage landlords about inclusive restroom options in leased spaces.

☐ Educate employees about restroom inclusivity policies.

Comprehensive Facility Considerations

☐ Ensure inclusivity in locker rooms and showers by providing private changing cubicles and shower stalls.

☐ Designate gender-neutral locker rooms and showers.

☐ Use clear, respectful signage for these facilities.

☐ Plan for inclusive emergency facilities:

- Designate safe spaces for emergencies.

- Ensure evacuation procedures consider gender identities and disabilities.

- Use gender-neutral language in emergency communications.

☐ Train staff on inclusivity in emergency procedures, restrooms, and locker room usage.

☐ Continuously gather feedback from employees on inclusivity in facilities.

Emergency Facilities and Considerations

☐ Designate and clearly mark safe spaces for emergencies, accessible to all employees, regardless of gender identity.

☐ Ensure that evacuation procedures avoid directing people to gender-segregated areas like locker rooms during emergencies.

☐ Provide training to designated emergency team leads on how to support vulnerable groups, including transgender and nonbinary individuals, during evacuations.

☐ Use gender-neutral language in all emergency communication to ensure clarity and inclusivity.

☐ Regularly review and update emergency plans to reflect the needs of diverse employees.

Summary Checklist for Security and Safety Services

Hiring, Training, and Education for Security Personnel
- ☐ Ensure security personnel complete training on gender inclusion before beginning work.
- ☐ Ask about candidates' experience with diverse communities and inclusive practices during the hiring process.
- ☐ Verify that outsourced security services follow inclusive training practices.
- ☐ Prioritize hiring diverse candidates, including openly transgender and nonbinary personnel, to build a more inclusive team.

Training on Inclusive Security Practices
- ☐ Provide comprehensive training on correct pronoun usage and respectful interactions with transgender and nonbinary individuals.
- ☐ Train security personnel to avoid assumptions based on gender expression or appearance.
- ☐ Include education on de-escalation tactics sensitive to gender identity in all training programs.
- ☐ Regularly update security personnel on changes in best practices for gender inclusion, including evolving terminology.
- ☐ Establish feedback mechanisms to continuously assess and improve security personnel's inclusivity training.

Respectful Interaction with Diverse Gender Identities
- ☐ Train security personnel to manage gender-related challenges with biometric technologies and body scanners sensitively.

- [ ] Ensure all security staff use gender-neutral language when interacting with individuals, particularly when gender identity is unknown.
- [ ] Encourage active listening and empathy in all security interactions, especially when addressing individuals from marginalized gender identities.

De-Escalation Through Inclusive Communication

- [ ] Implement de-escalation techniques grounded in empathy and respect for individuals' gender identities.
- [ ] Train security personnel to remain calm and clear during emergencies, using gender-neutral language and culturally competent communication.
- [ ] Encourage the use of context-specific communication strategies to prevent unnecessary conflict in high-pressure situations.

Inclusive Incident Management

- [ ] Ensure private, confidential spaces are available for individuals to report incidents without fear of being misgendered or outed.
- [ ] Handle sensitive gender identity information confidentially, with explicit consent from the individual involved.
- [ ] Develop comprehensive incident response protocols that address gender-based violence and discrimination with respect and confidentiality.
- [ ] Collaborate with HR and legal departments to ensure gender-related security incidents are handled in accordance with organizational policies and laws.
- [ ] Implement scenario-based training for security personnel, specifically addressing common issues such as misgendering or mismatched IDs.

EPILOGUE

My purpose for this book was to let you choose your own adventure based on your business size and needs. Now that we have reached the end, I hope your chosen adventure was both enlightening and motivating. As you advance in your career, through promotions or job changes, you might find it helpful to revisit chapters you may not have read yet. Different sections of this book can provide new insights and guidance.

I would be remiss if I did not take this final opportunity to reinforce a takeaway that I hope you will adopt in both your business and personal life: gender expression does not equal gender identity. You cannot know someone's gender just by looking at them. This is why we must stop using "sir" and "ma'am" with strangers. Until you know, you don't know.

Remember, gender inclusion at work cannot be accomplished with a workshop alone. Every department has work to do. Implementing change takes effort and dedication, but as I have hopefully shown you, the benefits to both your business and the individuals it serves are well worth it.

To further support you in your efforts, here are some valuable resources:

Support Organizations and Networks

- **Minus18** – An online network of LGBTQ+ youth in Australia that created an app to practice using different pronouns and neopronouns (minus18.org.au/pronouns-app).

- **PFLAG** – Offers support for LGBTQ+ individuals and their families (pflag.org).

- **Transgender Legal Defense & Education Fund** – Provides resources and pro bono legal services, including name change support (transgenderlegal.org).

- **Out & Equal** – Supports LGBTQ+ equity and workplace inclusion through programs and memberships (outandequal.org).

- **Trans Lifeline** – A peer support hotline run by trans people for trans people in the US and Canada. (translifeline.org).

- **Human Rights Campaign (HRC) Foundation** – "Transgender Inclusion in the Workplace: A Toolkit for Employers" for guidance on inclusive practices (hrc.org).

- **National LGBT Chamber of Commerce (NGLCC)** – LGBTQ+ business support and the exclusive certifying body for LGBTQ+-owned businesses (nglcc.org).

- **The Trevor Project** – Crisis intervention and mental health support for LGBTQ+ youth (thetrevorproject.org).

Certification, Training, and Education in Diversity, Equity, and Inclusion (DEI)

- **Universities Offering DEI Certificates** – Many colleges and universities, such as Cornell, Northwestern, and NYU, offer certificates in DEI.

- **Michigan State University's Gender and Sexuality Campus Center** – Offers an extensive, regularly updated glossary of terms covering gender, sexuality, legal issues, and racial identity (https://gscc.msu.edu).

Inclusivity Benchmarks and Ratings

- **Human Rights Campaign's Corporate Equality Index (CEI)** – Rates businesses on LGBTQ+ inclusion policies and practices (hrc.org).

- **Municipal Equality Index** – An HRC resource that evaluates municipal support for LGBTQ+ rights (hrc.org/mei).

- **Newsweek's America's Greatest Workplaces for LGBTQ+** – Annual ranking of US companies' inclusion based on employee reviews, spotlighting best practices in workplace LGBTQ+ inclusion (newsweek.com).

- **Campus Pride Index** – A directory rating LGBTQ+-friendly colleges and universities, highlighting best practices in inclusion for educational environments (campusprideindex.org).

Policy and Legal Resources

- **ACLU** – Provides legal advocacy, lawsuits, and resources for LGBTQ+ rights, including workplace protections and anti-discrimination cases (aclu.org).

- **Lambda Legal** – A national legal organization specializing in LGBTQ+ and HIV advocacy, offering legal support for workplace discrimination, healthcare access, and identity documentation issues (lambdalegal.org).

- **Transgender Law Center's Model Transgender Employment Policy** – Provides structured guidelines and best practices for supporting transgender employees in the workplace, including a model transgender employment policy (transgenderlawcenter.org).

- **Chevron's "Transgender @ Chevron" Guidebook** – An internal model supporting workplace transitions, long recognized as a resource in creating respectful, inclusive environments (chevron.com).

Legislative and Policy Tracking Tools

- **Anti-Trans Legislative Risk Map by Erin in the Morning** – A monthly interactive map showing legislative risks to transgender rights across US states, helping organizations monitor impacts on trans and nonbinary communities (erininthemorning.com).

- **LGBTQ+ Equality Maps by the Movement Advancement Project** – Provides a comprehensive overview of LGBTQ+ rights and policies across US states, covering healthcare, non-discrimination protections, and more (lgbtmap.org/equality-maps).

- **Litigation Tracker: Legal Challenges to Trump Administration Actions** – Tracks ongoing lawsuits against federal rollbacks, including challenges to anti-DEI executive orders and restrictions on transgender rights (justsecurity.org/107087/tracker-litigation-legal-challenges-trump-administration/).

- **Project 2025 Tracker** – Monitors efforts to implement *Project 2025*, a sweeping agenda that includes rolling back LGBTQ+ protections and dismantling DEI policies (project2025.observer).

Media and Communications Resources

- **GLAAD's Media Reference Guide** – Guidance on language and respectful representation of LGBTQ+ individuals in branding and content (glaad.org/reference).

Resources to Watch

- **Equal Employment Opportunity Commission (EEOC)** – Once a key enforcer of Title VII protections, the EEOC deprioritized gender identity discrimination cases in 2025 and even moved to drop active cases. While its archived guidance may still hold value, businesses should turn to civil rights organizations, state or local agencies, and legal experts for reliable enforcement guidance until federal priorities shift.

- **Society for Human Resource Management (SHRM)** – SHRM quietly removed "Equity" from DEI in 2024 and, by 2025, began advising HR professionals to comply early with restrictive executive orders. While its HR resource library remains extensive, its stance on inclusion is shifting, requiring careful scrutiny.

- **DOJ (US Department of Justice)** – The DOJ once provided legal guidance on transgender workplace protections, but in 2025, all related resources were removed. Some may still be available through archived sources, but at present, the DOJ is not a reliable resource for workplace inclusion guidance.

Books and Additional Reading

- *The Power of Employee Resource Groups: How People Create Authentic Change* by Farzana Nayani – Recommended for improving ERG success.

- *Advice from Your Trans Aunty* by Erica Vogel – Suggested for understanding the trans experience. A great book for HR to give transitioning employees.

- *What's Behind Your Brand: A Style Guide for Humanizing Your Content* by Jen O'Ryan, PhD – For any department that creates content, this book helps you design messages that bring people in without shutting others out.

- *How to Be an Inclusive Leader, Second Edition: Your Role in Creating Cultures of Belonging Where Everyone Can Thrive* by Jennifer Brown – An excellent resource for leadership.

Media and Films

- *Disclosure* – A 2020 documentary that examines transgender representation in film and television, exploring the impact of media on public perceptions of transgender people. Featuring interviews with prominent trans voices, *Disclosure* highlights both progress and challenges in inclusive representation. Available on Netflix.

- *Will & Harper* – A 2024 documentary following Will Ferrell and his friend Harper Steele, a transgender woman, on a heartfelt road trip across the US. The journey captures moments of humor, acceptance, and vulnerability, offering insights into friendship and gender identity. Available on Netflix.

KEEP THE CONVERSATION GOING

The work doesn't stop here. Scan the QR code to access additional resources, connect with like-minded professionals, and continue the conversation. Whether you're looking for practical tools, deeper insights, or a space to engage, you'll find ways to stay involved.

ABOUT AMELIA J. MICHAEL

Amelia is a consultant, speaker, and trainer with over 30 years of experience helping people navigate tough conversations and move through discomfort with confidence. They specialize in making complex ideas approachable and guiding organizations toward more inclusive workplaces.

A serial entrepreneur, Amelia has founded multiple businesses dedicated to inclusion and innovation. They owned an IT company before launching Aikotek, a consulting firm that bridges gender inclusion and workplace systems, primarily in the legal sector. They also founded Polycute.com, offering products that amplify LGBTQ+ identities and allyship. With experience spanning IT, legal, healthcare, mental health, and beyond, Amelia understands how different industries operate and how inclusion efforts fail when departments work in isolation. Their work breaks down these silos so real change can take root.

As a nonbinary person and a member of a gender-diverse family, Amelia brings both lived experience and strategic insight to their work. Their time as a crisis counselor shaped their belief that change happens when people feel safe enough to ask questions, challenge assumptions, and learn without fear of judgment. Whether training executives, advising HR teams, or equipping organizations with tools for lasting transformation, their work is rooted in curiosity, empathy, and practical solutions.

Amelia is also a parent, singer, meditator, yogi, and lifelong advocate for intersectional feminism. They live what they teach, continually stepping into discomfort and challenging themself to grow. Once terrified of singing and public speaking, they faced those fears and now front a band and speak nationwide—proof that facing discomfort moves us forward.

Bring Amelia to Your Organization or Classroom
Amelia delivers engaging keynotes and gender inclusion training for workplaces committed to equity and belonging. They also guest lecture at universities and teach in professional training programs for therapists, crisis counselors, and mental health professionals.

Learn more at ameliajmichael.com or connect on LinkedIn: @AmeliaJMichael

ENDNOTES

1   Jones, Jeffrey M., "LGBTQ+ Identification in U.S. Rises to 9.3%," Gallup, February 20, 2025, https://news.gallup.com/poll/656708/lgbtq-identification-rises.aspx

2   History.com editors. "The Stonewall Riots," History, A&E Television Networks, last updated June 28, 2023, https://www.history.com/topics/lgbtq/the-stonewall-riots

3   History.com editors, "Montgomery Bus Boycott," History, A&E Television Networks, last updated November 22, 2022, https://www.history.com/topics/black-history/montgomery-bus-boycott

4   Easterwood, Gabby, "1 in 4 teens identify as LGBTQ, according to CDC study," KDVR News, April 28, 2023, https://kdvr.com/news/1-in-4-teens-identify-as-lgbtq-cdc-study/

5   Hodshire, Soren, "Understanding the Transgender Portion of Our Population," Healthline, August 27, 2024, https://www.healthline.com/health/transgender/how-common-is-transgender

6   Brown, Anna, "About 5% of young adults in the U.S. say their gender is different from their sex assigned at birth," Pew Research Center, June 7, 2022, https://www.pewresearch.org/short-reads/2022/06/07/about-5-of-young-adults-in-the-u-s-say-their-gender-is-different-from-their-sex-assigned-at-birth/

7   Brown, Anna, "About 5% of young adults in the U.S. say their gender is different from their sex assigned at birth," Pew Research Center, June 7, 2022, https://www.pewresearch. org/short-reads/2022/06/07/about-5-of-young-adults-in-the-u-s-say-their-gender-is-different-from-their-sex-assigned-at-birth/

8   Parker, Mayor Annise, "Out for America 2022: A Census of Out LGBTQ Elected Officials Nationwide," LGBTQ Victory Institute, June, 2022, https://victoryinstitute.org/out-for-america-2022/gender-identity/

9   Taladrid, Stephania, "The First Gen Z Congressman Believes He Can Change Washington," The New Yorker, January 9, 2023, https://www.newyorker.com/news/dispatch/maxwell-frosts-vision-meets-washington

10 Swaminathan, Ravi, "Gen Zers are making their mark in the workplace – here are 4 things they expect," World Economic Forum, September 22, 2022, https://www.weforum.org/agenda/2022/09/the-4-expectations-gen-z-teams-have-workplace-future/

11 Fry, Richard and Parker, Kim, "Early Benchmarks Show 'Post-Millennials' on Track to Be Most Diverse, Best-Educated Generation Yet," Pew Research Center, November 15, 2018, https://www.pewresearch.org/social-trends/2018/11/15/early-benchmarks-show-post-millennials-on-track-to-be-most-diverse-best-educated-generation-yet/

12 Merriman, Marcie, "How can understanding the influence of Gen Z today empower your tomorrow? 2023 EY Gen Z Segmentation Study," Ernst & Young, 2023, https://www.ey.com/content/dam/ey-unified-site/ey-com/en-us/campaigns/consulting/documents/ey-2307-4309403-genz-segmentation-report-us-score-no-20902-231us-2-vf4.pdf

13 Phillips, Gregory L., II, Curtis, Michael G., Kelsey, Scar Winter, Floresca, Ysabel Beatrice et al., "Changes to Sexual Identity Response Options in the Youth Risk Behavior" Survey, JAMA Pediatrics, 2024;178(5):506–508.

14 Rohman, Melissa, "One in Four U.S. Adolescents Identify as Non-Heterosexual, Comparative Analysis Finds," Northwestern Medicine Feinberg School of Medicine News Center, April 12, 2024.

15 Parker, Kim and Igielnik, Ruth, "On the Cusp of Adulthood and Facing an Uncertain Future: What We Know About Gen Z So Far," Pew Research Center, May 14, 2020, https://www.pewresearch.org/social-trends/2020/05/14/on-the-cusp-of-adulthood-and-facing-an-uncertain-future-what-we-know-about-gen-z-so-far-2/

16 Brown, Anna, "About 5% of young adults in the U.S. say their gender is different from their sex assigned at birth," Pew Research Center, June 7, 2022, https://www.pewresearch.org/short-reads/2022/06/07/about-5-of-young-adults-in-the-u-s-say-their-gender-is-different-from-their-sex-assigned-at-birth/

17 EY. "Failure Drives Innovation, According to EY Survey on Gen Z." PR Newswire. September 18, 2018. https://www.prnewswire.com/news-releases/failure-drives-innovation-according-to-ey-survey-on-gen-z-300714436.html

18 Tallo, "The Survey is In: Gen Z Demands Diversity and Inclusion Strategy," October 21, 2020, https://tallo.com/blog/genz-demands-diversity-inclusion-strategy/

19 Merriman, Marcie, "How can understanding the influence of Gen Z today empower your tomorrow? 2023 EY Gen Z Segmentation Study," Ernst & Young, 2023, https://www.ey.com/content/dam/ey-unified-site/ey-com/en-us/

campaigns/consulting/documents/ey-2307-4309403-genz-segmentation-report-us-score-no-20902-231us-2-vf4.pdf

20 Martinez, L. R., Sawyer, K. B., Thoroughgood, C. N., Ruggs, E. N., and Smith, N. A., 2017, "The importance of being 'me': The relation between authentic identity expression and transgender employees' work-related attitudes and experiences," *Journal of Applied Psychology, 102*(2), 215–226, https://doi.org/10.1037/apl0000168

21 The White House, "Ending Illegal Discrimination and Restoring Merit-Based Opportunity," The White House, January 21, 2025, https://www.whitehouse.gov/presidential-actions/2025/01/ending-illegal-discrimination-and-restoring-merit-based-opportunity/

22 LinkedIn Corporate Communications, "LinkedIn and Microsoft Commit to Helping 250,000 Companies Hire for Skills," LinkedIn Pressroom, March 30, 2021, https://news.linkedin.com/2021/march/linkedin-and-microsoft-skills-commitment, Survey Methodology: Censuswide conducted research on behalf of LinkedIn, online between February 25 - March 2, 2021 among 1,009 Hiring Managers and 2,101 Job Seekers, ages 18-69, in the U.S.

23 Baumler, Rebecca J. and Percy, Cameron W., "Crystallized Trans Identity: How Authenticity and Identity Communication Affect Job and Life Satisfaction," Communication Research, March 10, 2024, https://doi.org/10.1177/00936502241234840

24 Martinez, L.R., Sawyer, K.B., Thoroughgood, C.N., Ruggs, E.N. et al., "The importance of being 'me': The relation between authentic identity expression and transgender employees' work-related attitudes and experiences," *Journal of Applied Psychology, 102*(2), 215–226, https://doi.org/10.1037/apl0000168

25 Martinez, L.R., Sawyer, K.B., Thoroughgood, C.N., Ruggs, E.N. et al., 2017), "The importance of being 'me': The relation between authentic identity expression and transgender employees' work-related attitudes and experiences," *Journal of Applied Psychology, 102*(2), 215–226, https://doi.org/10.1037/apl0000168

26 Scipioni, Jade, "A transgender CEO on coming out at age 49: 'The biggest transphobia' was 'my own'," CNBC Make It, January 30, 2022, https://www.cnbc.com/2022/01/30/ceo-caroline-farberger-on-leadership-coming-out-as-transgender.html

27 Alston, Fiona, "'I genuinely thought that the playing field was even when I lived as a man' – Caroline Farberger is now aware of the disparities in business," Tech.eu, May 4, 2023, https://tech.eu/2023/05/04/i-genuinely-thought-that-the-playing-field-was-even-when-i-lived-as-a-man-caroline-farberger-is-now-aware-of-the-disparities-in-business/

28 Scipioni, Jade, "A transgender CEO on coming out at age 49: 'The biggest transphobia' was 'my own'," CNBC Make It, January 30, 2022, https://www.cnbc.com/2022/01/30/ceo-caroline-farberger-on-leadership-coming-out-as-transgender.html

29 Alston, Fiona, "'I genuinely thought that the playing field was even when I lived as a man' – Caroline Farberger is now aware of the disparities in business," Tech.eu, May 4, 2023, https://tech.eu/2023/05/04/i-genuinely-thought-that-the-playing-field-was-even-when-i-lived-as-a-man-caroline-farberger-is-now-aware-of-the-disparities-in-business/

30 Scipioni., Jade, "A transgender CEO on coming out at age 49: 'The biggest transphobia' was 'my own'," CNBC Make It, January 30, 2022, https://www.cnbc.com/2022/01/30/

ceo-caroline-farberger-on-leadership-coming-out-as-transgender.html

31 Scipioni, Jade, "A transgender CEO on coming out at age 49: 'The biggest transphobia' was 'my own'," CNBC Make It, January 30, 2022, https://www.cnbc.com/2022/01/30/ceo-caroline-farberger-on-leadership-coming-out-as-transgender.html

32 Farley, Rachel, "Transitioning from a man to a woman as the CEO of an insurance company: Caroline Farberger shares her unique experience and remarkable insights on inclusive leadership," Heidrick & Struggles, October 14, 2024, https://www.heidrick.com/en/insights/podcasts/e175_caroline-farberger-shares-her-unique-experience-and-remarkable-insights-on-inclusive-leadership

33 Baboolall, David (they/them), Greenberg, Sarah (she/her), Obeid, Maurice (he/him), and Zucker, Jill (she/her), "Although corporate America has stepped up its public support of LGBTQ+ rights, it still has a long road ahead to foster a truly inclusive environment for transgender employees," McKinsey & Company, November 10, 2021, https://www.mckinsey.com/featured-insights/diversity-and-inclusion/being-transgender-at-work

34 Baboolall, David (they/them), Greenberg, Sarah (she/her), Obeid, Maurice (he/him), and Zucker, Jill (she/her), "Although corporate America has stepped up its public support of LGBTQ+ rights, it still has a long road ahead to foster a truly inclusive environment for transgender employees," McKinsey & Company, November 10, 2021, https://www.mckinsey.com/featured-insights/diversity-and-inclusion/being-transgender-at-work

35 Baboolall, David (they/them), Greenberg, Sarah (she/her), Obeid, Maurice (he/him), and Zucker, Jill (she/her), "Although corporate America has stepped up its public support of LGBTQ+ rights, it still has a long road ahead to foster a truly inclusive environment for transgender employees," McKinsey & Company, November 10, 2021, https://www.mckinsey.com/featured-insights/diversity-and-inclusion/being-transgender-at-work

36 Baboolall, David (they/them), Greenberg, Sarah (she/her), Obeid, Maurice (he/him), and Zucker, Jill (she/her), "Although corporate America has stepped up its public support of LGBTQ+ rights, it still has a long road ahead to foster a truly inclusive environment for transgender employees," McKinsey & Company, November 10, 2021, https://www.mckinsey.com/featured-insights/diversity-and-inclusion/being-transgender-at-work

37 Wolny, Nick, "What Is Pink Money? The LGBTQ+ Economy, Explained," Nick Wolny Blog, May 5, 2024, https://nickwolny.com/what-is-pink-money/

38 Winck, Ben, "Gen Z's surging economic power will permanently change the investing landscape over the next decade, Bank of America says," Business Insider, November 19, 2020, https://markets.businessinsider.com/news/stocks/gen-z-economic-impact-outlook-spending-permanently-change-investing-bofa-2020-11-1029822486

39 Merriman, Marcie, "How can understanding the influence of Gen Z today empower your tomorrow? 2023 EY Gen Z Segmentation Study," Ernst & Young, 2023, https://www.ey.com/content/dam/ey-unified-site/ey-com/en-us/campaigns/consulting/documents/ey-2307-4309403-genz-segmentation-report-us-score-no-20902-231us-2-vf4.pdf

40 DeMattia, Adam, "A Mature Approach to Diversity, Equity, and Inclusion Delivers Real Results," Enterprise Strategy Group, March, 2023, https://d1.awsstatic.com/executive-insights/en_US/esgamatureapproachtoDEI.pdf

41 Blumberg, Deborah Lynn, "How True Name helps transgender people make a name for themselves," Mastercard.com, June 23, 2022, https://www.mastercard.com/news/perspectives/2022/true-name-feature-for-transgender-community/

42 Liaukonyte, Jura, Tuchman, Anna and Zhu, Xinrong, "Lessons from the Bud Light Boycott, One Year Later," Harvard Business Review, March 20, 2024, https://hbr.org/2024/03/lessons-from-the-bud-light-boycott-one-year-later

43 Thompson, Sonia, "Dylan Mulvaney Isn't The Cause Of Anheuser-Busch InBev's Massive Q2 Decline," Forbes, August 3, 2023, https://www.forbes.com/sites/soniathompson/2023/08/03/bud-lights-second-quarter-sales-tanked-because-they-forgot-this-one-thing/

44 Meyersohn, Nathaniel, "Target Retreated on DEI. Then Came the Backlash," CNN, February 19, 2025, https://www.cnn.com/2025/02/19/business/target-dei-boycott/index.html

45 Meyersohn, Nathaniel, "Target Retreated on DEI. Then Came the Backlash," CNN, February 19, 2025, https://www.cnn.com/2025/02/19/business/target-dei-boycott/index.html

46 Lorenzo, Rocío, Voigt, Nicole, Tsusaka, Miki, Krentz, Matt et al., "How Diverse Leadership Teams Boost Innovation," Boston Consulting Group, January 23, 2018, https://www.bcg.com/publications/2018/how-diverse-leadership-teams-boost-innovation

47 Hunt, Dame Vivian, Yee, Lareina, Prince, Sara and Dixon-Fyle, Sundiatu, "Delivering through diversity," McKinsey

& Company, January 18, 2018, https://www.mckinsey. com/capabilities/people-and-organizational-performance/ our-insights/delivering-through-diversity

48 Han, Soyoung and Noland, Marcus, "Policy Brief 20-7: Women scaling the corporate ladder: Progress steady but slow globally," Peterson Institute for International Economics, May, 2020, https://www.piie.com/publications/ policy-briefs/women-scaling-corporate-ladder-progress-steady-slow-globally

49 Han, Soyoung and Noland, Marcus, "Policy Brief 20-7: Women scaling the corporate ladder: Progress steady but slow globally," Peterson Institute for International Economics, May, 2020, https://www.piie.com/publications/ policy-briefs/women-scaling-corporate-ladder-progress-steady-slow-globally

50 Han, Soyoung and Noland, Marcus, "Policy Brief 20-7: Women scaling the corporate ladder: Progress steady but slow globally," Peterson Institute for International Economics, May, 2020, https://www.piie.com/publications/ policy-briefs/women-scaling-corporate-ladder-progress-steady-slow-globally

51 Hewlett, Sylvia Ann, Marshall, Melinda and Sherbin, Laura, "How Diversity can Drive Innovation," Harvard Business Review, December, 2013, https://hbr.org/2013/12/ how-diversity-can-drive-innovation

52 Hewlett, Sylvia Ann, Marshall, Melinda and Sherbin, Laura, "How Diversity can Drive Innovation," Harvard Business Review, December, 2013, https://hbr.org/2013/12/ how-diversity-can-drive-innovation

53 Glassdoor, "Diversity & Inclusion Workplace Survey," September, 2020, https://www.glassdoor.com/blog/diversity-inclusion-workplace-survey/

54 NALP, "Report on Diversity in U.S. Law Firms," January, 2023, https://www.nalp.org/uploads/Research/2022NALPReportonDiversity_Final.pdf

55 Thoroughgood, Christian N., Sawyer, Katina and Webster, Jennica R, "Creating a Trans-Inclusive Workplace," Harvard Business Review, March–April 2020, https://hbr.org/2020/03/creating-a-trans-inclusive-workplace

56 James, Sandy E., Herman, Jody L., Rankin, Susan, Keisling, Mara et al., "The Report of the 2015 U.S. Transgender Survey," Washington, DC: National Center for Transgender Equality, December, 2015, NOTE: SAVED AS USTS-Full-Report-Dec17.pdf

57 Thoroughgood, Christian N., Sawyer, Katina B., and Webster, Jennica R., "Finding calm in the storm: A daily investigation of how trait mindfulness buffers against paranoid cognition and emotional exhaustion following perceived discrimination at work," Organizational Behavior and Human Decision Processes, Volume 159, July 2020, Pages 49-63, https://www.sciencedirect.com/science/article/abs/pii/S0749597818300037

58 Thoroughgood, Christian N., Sawyer, Katina and Webster Jennica R., "Creating a Trans-Inclusive Workplace," *Harvard Business Review*, March–April, 2020, https://hbr.org/2020/03/creating-a-trans-inclusive-workplace

59 Dupreelle, Pierre, Schachtner, Michael, Yousif, Nadjia, Zawadzki, Annika et al., "Companies Are Failing Trans Employees," Harvard Business Review, March 31, 2023, https://hbr.org/2023/03/companies-are-failing-trans-employees

60 Crail, Chauncey, "15 Effective Employee Retention Strategies In 2024," *Forbes*, April 30, 2024, https://www.forbes.com/advisor/business/employee-retention-strategies/

61 Navarra, Katie, "The Real Costs of Recruitment," SHRM, April 11, 2022, https://www.shrm.org/topics-tools/news/talent-acquisition/real-costs-recruitment

62 Novacek, Gabrielle, Yousif, Nadjia, Dartnell, Ashley, Farsky, Mario et al., "Inclusion Isn't Just Nice. It's Necessary," BCG Diversity, Equity, and Inclusion Report, February 22, 2023, https://www.bcg.com/publications/2023/how-to-improve-inclusion-in-the-workplace

63 Gibbons, Sammy, "Nearly 30 towns excluded LGBTQ people from marriage license applications, state says," NorthJersey.com, March 8, 2023, https://www.northjersey.com/story/news/state/2023/03/08/nj-towns-exclude-lgbtq-people-from-marriage-license-forms/69985660007/

64 De La Cruz, Jesselly, Argote-Freyre, Frank, and Baroni, Francesca, "Marriage Equality in NJ: A Latina/o/x Perspective." Latino Action Network Foundation, Hudson P.R.I.D.E., and Garden State Equality. June 27, 2022. https://www.lanfoundation.org/post/marriage-equality-in-nj-a-latina-o-x-perspective

65 Gibbons, Sammy, "Nearly 30 towns excluded LGBTQ people from marriage license applications, state says," NorthJersey.com, March 8, 2023, https://www.northjersey.com/story/news/state/2023/03/08/nj-towns-exclude-lgbtq-people-from-marriage-license-forms/69985660007/

66 City of Linden, New Jersey, "City Clerk Applications, Forms, Licenses, Permits & Information," https://linden-nj.gov/documents/city-clerk-applications-forms-licenses-permits-information/

67 Gibbons, Sammy, "Nearly 30 towns excluded LGBTQ people from marriage license applications, state says," NorthJersey.com, March 8, 2023, https://www.northjersey.com/story/news/state/2023/03/08/nj-towns-exclude-lgbtq-people-from-marriage-license-forms/69985660007/

68 US Equal Employment Opportunity Commission, "Removing Gender Ideology and Restoring the EEOC's Role of Protecting Women in the Workplace," January 28, 2025, https://www.eeoc.gov/newsroom/removing-gender-ideology-and-restoring-eeocs-role-protecting-women-workplace

69 EEOC v. R.G. & G.R. Harris Funeral Homes, Inc., (884, F.3d 560,6thCir.2018),https://www.aclu.org/cases/rg-gr-harris-funeral-homes-v-eeoc-aimee-stephens?document=eeoc-v-rg-gr-harris-funeral-homes-ruling

70 US Equal Employment Opportunity Commission, "Harris Funeral Homes to Pay $250,000 to Settle Sex Discrimination Lawsuit Involving Transgender Employee," EEOC Press Release, December 1, 2020, https://www.eeoc.gov/newsroom/harris-funeral-homes-pay-250000-settle-sex-discrimination-lawsuit-involving-transgender

71 US Equal Employment Opportunity Commission, "A&E Tire Agrees to Pay $60,000 to Settle Sex Discrimination Lawsuit," EEOC Press Release, April 8, 2019, https://www.eeoc.gov/newsroom/ae-tire-agrees-pay-60000-settle-sex-discrimination-lawsuit

72 EEOC v. Deluxe Financial Services, Inc., (0:15-cv-02646. D. Minn. Jan. 20, 2016), https://clearinghouse-umich-production.s3.amazonaws.com/media/doc/81176.pdf

73 US Equal Employment Opportunity Commission, "Deluxe Financial to Settle Sex Discrimination Suit on Behalf of Transgender Employee," Press Release, January 21, 2016,

https://www.eeoc.gov/newsroom/deluxe-financial-settle-sex-discrimination-suit-behalf-transgender-employee

74 Helmore, Edward, "US civil rights agency seeks to dismiss gender-identity discrimination cases," The Guardian, February 15, 2025, https://www.theguardian.com/us-news/2025/feb/15/transgender-equal-employment-opportunity-commission

75 Human Rights Campaign, "Corporate Equality Index FAQ," HRC Foundation, January 27, 2022, https://www.hrc.org/resources/corporate-equality-index-faq

76 Human Rights Campaign, "2023 Corporate Equality Index Criteria," HRC Foundation, November 30, 2023, https://www.hrc.org/resources/corporate-equality-index-criteria

77 Newsweek, "Newsweek and Plant-A Insights Group Announce Second Annual America's Greatest Workplaces for LGBTQ+ Ranking, Newsweek, May 29, 2024, https://www.globenewswire.com/news-release/2024/05/29/2890161/0/en/Newsweek-and-Plant-A-Insights-Group-Announce-Second-Annual-America-s-Greatest-Workplaces-for-LGBTQ-Ranking.html

78 Campus Pride, "Campus Pride Index," https://campusprideindex.org/

79 Reed, Erin, "Anti-Trans Legislative Risk Assessment Map: September 2024 Edition," Erin In The Morning, September 30, 2024, https://www.erininthemorning.com/p/anti-trans-legislative-risk-assessment-212

80 Alaska Airlines, "Alaska Airlines earned a score of 100 on HRC's 2023-2024 Corporate Equality Index," Alaska Airlines, November 30, 2023, https://news.alaskaair.com/company/alaska-airlines-earns-100-on-hrc-2023-corporate-equality-index/

81 Glassdoor, 40+ Stats For Companies to Keep In Mind for 2021," Glassdoor, https://www.glassdoor.com/employers/resources/hr-and-recruiting-stats/

82 Kratz, Juie, "Gen Z Is Unwavering About Inclusion. Cutting Back Will Cost You," *Forbes*, February 23, 2025, https://www.forbes.com/sites/juliekratz/2025/02/23/gen-z-demands-inclusion-cutting-dei-costs/

83 Jupp, Ethan, "Women are 47 percent more likely to be seriously injured in a crash," Motoring Research, March 10, 2020, https://www.motoringresearch.com/car-news/women-more-likely-injured-crash/#:~:text=Statistics%20show%20women%20have%20a,as%20severe%20as%2079%20percent

84 University of California – Berkeley, "Lack of females in drug dose trials leads to overmedicated women," ScienceDaily, August 12, 2020, www.sciencedaily.com/releases/2020/08/200812161318.htm

85 The Trevor Project, 2020, 2020 National Survey on LGBTQ Youth Mental Health, New York, New York: The Trevor Project, https://www.thetrevorproject.org/survey-2020/?section=Diversity-of-Gender-Identity-Sexual-Orientation

86 Michigan State University Gender and Sexuality Campus Center, "Glossary," https://gscc.msu.edu/education/glossary.html

87 Trans Student Educational Resources, 2015, "The Gender Unicorn," http://www.transstudent.org/gender

88 American Psychological Association, "Understanding transgender people, gender identity and gender expression," March 9, 2023, https://www.apa.org/topics/lgbtq/transgender-people-gender-identity-gender-expression

89 American Psychological Association, "Understanding transgender people, gender identity and gender expression," March 9, 2023, https://www.apa.org/topics/lgbtq/transgender-people-gender-identity-gender-expression

90 The White House, "Defending Women from Gender Ideology Extremism and Restoring Biological Truth to the Federal Government," The White House, January 20, 2025, https://www.whitehouse.gov/presidential-actions/2025/01/defending-women-from-gender-ideology-extremism-and-restoring-biological-truth-to-the-federal-government/

91 Schnebly, Risa Aria, "Sex Determination in Humans," Arizona State University Embryo Project Encyclopedia, July 16, 2021, https://embryo.asu.edu/pages/sex-determination-humans#:~:text=They%20named%20the%20region%20of%20the%20Y,causes%20the%20embryo%20to%20develop%20as%20male

92 Suhomlinova, Olga, O'Shea, Saoirse C. and Boncori, Ilaria, 2023, "Rethinking Gender Diversity: Transgender and Gender Nonconforming People and Gender as Constellation," Gender, Work & Organization: 1–20, https://doi.org/10.1111/gwao.13073

93 Defosse, Dana, "I Coined The Term 'Cisgender' 29 Years Ago. Here's What This Controversial Word Really Means," Huffington Post, February 18, 2023, https://www.huffpost.com/entry/what-cisgender-means-transgender_n_63e13ee0e4b01e9288730415

94 Defosse, Dana, "I Coined The Term 'Cisgender' 29 Years Ago. Here's What This Controversial Word Really Means," Huffington Post, February 18, 2023, https://www.huffpost.com/entry/what-cisgender-means-transgender_n_63e13ee0e4b01e9288730415

95 Lorshbough, Erika, "Black Trans Lives Matter – Here's How our Criminal System Fails Them," ACLU of New York, June 30, 2020, https://www.nyclu.org/en/news/black-trans-lives-matter-heres-how-our-criminal-system-fails-them

96 Lorshbough, Erika, "Black Trans Lives Matter – Here's How our Criminal System Fails Them," ACLU of New York, June 30, 2020, https://www.nyclu.org/en/news/black-trans-lives-matter-heres-how-our-criminal-system-fails-them

97 Carpenter, C.S., Eppink, S.T. and Gonzales, G., 2020, Transgender Status, Gender Identity, and Socioeconomic Outcomes in the United States, ILR Review, 73(3), 573-599, https://doi.org/10.1177/0019793920902776

98 Mulcahy, A., Streed, C.G., Jr., Wallisch, A.M., Batza, K. et al., Gender Identity, Disability, and Unmet Healthcare Needs among Disabled People Living in the Community in the United States, Int J Environ Res Public Health, 2022 Feb 23;19(5):2588, https://doi.org/10.3390%2Fijerph19052588

99 Mulcahy, A., Streed, C.G., Jr., Wallisch, A.M., Batza, K. et al., Gender Identity, Disability, and Unmet Healthcare Needs among Disabled People Living in the Community in the United States, Int J Environ Res Public Health, 2022 Feb 23;19(5):2588, https://doi.org/10.3390%2Fijerph19052588

100 Choi, Soon Kyu, and Meyer, Ilan H., "LGBT Aging: A review of research findings, needs, and policy implications," UCLA Williams Institute School of Law Report, August, 2016, https://williamsinstitute.law.ucla.edu/publications/lgbt-aging/

101 Thurston, Isabella, "The History of Two-Spirit Folks," The Indigenous Foundation, June 29, 2023, https://www.theindigenousfoundation.org/articles/the-history-of-two-spirit-folks

102 Harvard Divinity School, "The Third Gender and Hijras," 2018, https://rpl.hds.harvard.edu/religion-context/case-studies/gender/third-gender-and-hijras

103 George, Jude, "Celebrating Gender Diversity Around the World," Outright International, June 8, 2023, https://outrightinternational.org/gender-diversity

104 Barry, Kevin and Levi, Jennifer L., "Embracing the ADA: Transgender People and Disability Rights," Harvard Law Review, February 22, 2021, https://harvardlawreview.org/blog/2021/02/embracing-the-ada-transgender-people-and-disability-rights/

105 The Trevor Project, 2020, 2020 National Survey on LGBTQ Youth Mental Health. New York, New York: The Trevor Project, https://www.thetrevorproject.org/survey-2020

106 Merriam-Webster, "The History of 'Thon', the Forgotten Gender neutral Pronoun," https://www.merriam-webster.com/wordplay/third-person-gender neutral-pronoun-thon

107 Andrew, Scottie, "A guide to neopronouns, from ae to ze." CNN, August 12, 2023, https://www.cnn.com/us/neopronouns-explained-xe-xyr-wellness-cec/index.html

108 Washington, Ella F., "Recognizing and Responding to Microaggressions at Work," Harvard Business Review, May 10, 2022, https://hbr.org/2022/05/recognizing-and-responding-to-microaggressions-at-work

109 Emberton, Mihal, "Unconscious Bias Is a Human Condition," The Permanente Journal, Vol. 25, March 17, 2021, https://www.ncbi.nlm.nih.gov/pmc/articles/PMC8784036/

110 Kacala, Alexander, "Laverne Cox on Black transgender lives: 'We cannot leave anyone behind'," Today, June 25, 2020, https://www.today.com/popculture/laverne-cox-black-trans-lives-t185180

111 Cutler, Sylvia, "Sexist Job Titles and the Influence of Language on Gender Stereotypes," BYU College of Humanities, 2015, https://humanities.byu.edu/sexist-job-titles-and-the-influence-of-language-on-gender-stereotypes/

112 Prewitt-Freilino, Jennifer, Caswell, Andrew T. and Emmi Laakso, "The Gendering of Language: A Comparison of Gender Equality in Countries with Gendered, Natural Gender, and Genderless Languages," Sex Roles, 66 (3-4), February, 2011, https://www.researchgate.net/publication/257663669_The_Gendering_of_Language_A_Comparison_of_Gender_Equality_in_Countries_with_Gendered_Natural_Gender_and_Genderless_Languages

113 Braver, Rita, "Ms. After 50: Gloria Steinem and a feminist publishing revolution," CBS News Sunday Morning, September 17, 2023, https://www.cbsnews.com/news/ms-magazine-gloria-steinem/

114 Merriam-Webster, "Words We're Watching: 'Nibling'," https://www.merriam-webster.com/wordplay/words-were-watching-nibling

115 Caldera, Camille, "Fact check: US House members can use gendered language; rules change affected one document," USA Today, January 16, 2021, https://www.usatoday.com/story/news/factcheck/2021/01/16/fact-check-house-rules-only-changed-gendered-language-one-document/4175388001/

116 Swenson, Ali, "Removal of gender-specific terms from House rules does not amount to a ban," AP News, January 15, 2021, https://apnews.com/article/fact-checking-9901710773

117 Wirkus, A. and Zarnow, Z., "Gender-Inclusive Language in the Courts: How to Communicate with Fairness, Dignity, Impartiality, and Accuracy," National Center for State Courts, 2024, https://www.ncsc.org/__data/assets/pdf_file/0028/84916/Gender-Inclusivity-in-the-Courts.pdf

118 Wiggins, Christopher, "House Democrats Introduce Gender-Neutral Laws Bill," Advocate, January 25, 2023, https://www.advocate.com/politics/democrats-push-gender-neutral-laws

119 Sheehey, Maeve and Tourial, Greg, "House GOP Adds 'Family Centric' Wording in Shot at LGBTQ+ People," Bloomberg Government, January 3, 2025, https://news.bgov.com/bloomberg-government-news/house-gop-adds-family-centric-wording-in-shot-at-lgbtq-people

120 Stahl, Jeremy and Stern, Mark Joseph, "Pam Bondi Instructs Trump DOJ to Criminally Investigate Companies That Do DEI," MSN, February 5, 2025, https://www.msn.com/en-us/news/politics/pam-bondi-instructs-trump-doj-to-criminally-investigate-companies-that-do-dei/ar-AA1ywSr4

121 Zurcher, Anthony, "Combative Trump blames diversity policies after air tragedy," BBC, January 31, 2025, https://www.bbc.com/news/articles/cpvmdm1m7m9o

122 Doan, Laura and Clark, Alex, "Trump criticized DEI and the FAA's diversity policies after a deadly plane crash. Here's what we know," CBS News, January 31, 2025, https://www.cbsnews.com/news/trump-dei-diversity-policies-plane-crash/

123 Gartenberg v. The Cooper Union for the Advancement of Science and Art, No. 1:24-cv-02669 (S.D.N.Y. 2025), https://storage.courtlistener.com/recap/gov.uscourts. nysd.619155/gov.uscourts.nysd.619155.39.0.pdf

124 Novacek, Gabrielle, Yousif, Nadjia, Dartnell, Ashley, Farsky, Mario et al., ,"Inclusion Isn't Just Nice. It's Necessary," Boston Consulting Group's BLISS Index, February, 2023, https://web-assets.bcg.com/4c/ca/ dfd11bc1457a8668048a10606859/bcg-inclusion-isnt-just-nice.-It's-Necessary_Feb-2023.pdf

125 Novacek, Gabriella, Yousif, Nadjia, Dartnell, Ashley, Far-sky, Mario et al., "Inclusion Isn't Just Nice. It's Necessary," Boston Consulting Group's BLISS Index, February, 2023, https://web-assets.bcg.com/4c/ca/ dfd11bc1457a8668048a10606859/bcg-inclusion-isnt-just-nice.-It's-Necessary_Feb-2023.pdf

126 Dillon, Bernadette and Bourke, Juliet, "The six signature traits of inclusive leadership: Thriving in a diverse new world," Deloitte University Press, 2016, https://www2. deloitte.com/content/dam/insights/us/articles/six-sig-nature-traits-of-inclusive-leadership/DUP-3046_Inclu-sive-leader_vFINAL.pdf

127 Hewlett, Sylvia Ann, Marshall, Melinda and Sherbin, Laura, "How Diversity can Drive Innovation," Harvard Business Review, December, 2013, https://hbr.org/2013/12/ how-diversity-can-drive-innovation

128 Morris, Simone E., "How Inclusive Leaders Create Safe Spaces For Authenticity At Work," *Forbes*, December 23, 2023, https://www.forbes.com/sites/simonemor-ris/2023/12/23/how-inclusive-leaders-create-safe-spaces-for-authenticity-at-work/

129 LeaderFactor, "Google's Project Aristotle and Psychological Safety," LeaderFactor, January 27, 2025, https://www. leaderfactor.com/learn/google-and-psychological-safety

130 Darley, James, "Google Calendar Removes Black History Month & Pride Month," *Sustainability Magazine*, February 14, 2025, https://sustainabilitymag.com/articles/ google-calendar-removes-black-history-month-pride-month

131 Salesforce, "'Driving Systemic Change': Salesforce Chief Equality Officer on Priorities for the Year Ahead," Salesforce.com, February 28, 2023, https://www.salesforce. com/news/stories/chief-equality-officer/

132 Scheer, Ilhan, "Psychological safety: Crack the work behavior code," Accenture, December 6, 2022, https://www. accenture.com/us-en/blogs/business-functions-blog/ psychological-safety-corporate-culture

133 Reuters, "Accenture scraps diversity and inclusion goals, memo says," Reuters, February 7, 2025, https://www. reuters.com/technology/accenture-scraps-diversity-inclusion-goals-ft-reports-2025-02-07/

134 Thoroughgood, Christian N., Sawyer, Katina and Webster Jennica R., "Creating a Trans-Inclusive Workplace," Harvard Business Review, March–April, 2020, https://hbr. org/2020/03/creating-a-trans-inclusive-workplace

135 Thoroughgood, Christian N., Sawyer, Katina and Webster, Jennica R., "Creating a Trans-Inclusive Workplace," Harvard Business Review, March–April, 2020, https://hbr. org/2020/03/creating-a-trans-inclusive-workplace

136 Shalev, Nate, "How Managers can Support a Team Member Who's Transitioning," *Harvard Business Review*,

November, 17, 2022, https://hbr.org/2022/11/how-man-agers-can-support-a-team-member-whos-transitioning

137 Martinez, L.R., Sawyer, K.B., Thoroughgood, C.N., Ruggs, E.N. et al., 2017, "The importance of being 'me': The relation between authentic identity expression and transgender employees' work-related attitudes and experiences," *Journal of Applied Psychology, 102*(2), 215–226, https://doi.org/10.1037/apl0000168

138 Gelles, David, "The Moral Voice of Corporate America," *The New York Times*, August 19, 2017, https://www.nytimes.com/2017/08/19/business/moral-voice-ceos.html

139 Martinez, Lori Castillo, "Gender Inclusive Benefits for Salesforce Employees," Salesforce, November 15, 2021, https://www.salesforce.com/in/news/stories/announcing-new-gender-inclusive-benefits-for-salesforce-employees/

140 Tucker, Jill, "Marc Benioff's cheerleading for Trump has horrified liberals. In exclusive interview, he defends his stance," San Francisco Chronicle, December 9, 2024, https://www.sfchronicle.com/sf/article/salesforce-marc-benioff-trump-19953758.php

141 Gelles, David, "The Moral Voice of Corporate America," The New York Times, August 19, 2017, https://www.nytimes.com/2017/08/19/business/moral-voice-ceos.html

142 Shugerman, Emily, "Marc Benioff's embrace of Trump has Time staffers freaking out," The San Francisco Standard, January 6, 2025, https://sfstandard.com/2025/01/06/as-marc-benioff-warms-to-trump-time-staffers-cool-to-their-owner/

143 Trans Legislation Tracker, "2024 anti-trans bills tracker," Trans Legislation Tracker, Accessed October 25, 2024, https://translegislation.com/

144 GLAAD, "Trump's Anti-Trans Ad Fails Politically Among Likely Voters," GLAAD, October 24, 2024, https://glaad.org/trumps-anti-trans-ad-fails-politically-among-likely-voters/

145 Feminist, "Feminism is not gender specific: Activist & actor @janefonda in conversation with @blairimani of @feminist," Instagram video, May 15, 2023, https://www.instagram.com/feminist/reel/CsG9e3KMIvY/

146 Nate Shalev, "How Managers can Support a Team Member Who's Transitioning," Harvard Business Review, November, 17, 2022, https://hbr.org/2022/11/how-managers-can-support-a-team-member-whos-transitioning

147 Martinez, L.R., Sawyer, K.B., Thoroughgood, C.N., Ruggs, E.N. et al., 2017, "The importance of being 'me': The relation between authentic identity expression and transgender employees' work-related attitudes and experiences," *Journal of Applied Psychology, 102*(2), 215–226, https://doi.org/10.1037/apl0000168

148 Martinez, L.R., Sawyer, K.B., Thoroughgood, C.N., Ruggs, E.N. et al., 2017, "The importance of being 'me': The relation between authentic identity expression and transgender employees' work-related attitudes and experiences." *Journal of Applied Psychology, 102*(2), 215–226, https://doi.org/10.1037/apl0000168

149 Gonzales, Matt, "States are Banning Preferred Pronouns at Work, but Federal Guidelines Promote Inclusion. What Should HR Do?" SHRM, October 25, 2023, https://www.shrm.org/topics-tools/news/inclusion-diversity/states-are-banning-preferred-pronouns-at-work-but-federal-guidelines-promote-inclusion

150 The White House, "Executive Order: Defending Women from Gender Ideology Extremism and Restoring

Biological Truth to the Federal Government," The White House, January 20, 2025, https://www.whitehouse.gov/presidential-actions/2025/01/defending-women-from-gender-ideology-extremism-and-restoring-biological-truth-to-the-federal-government/

151   The White House, "Executive Order: Protecting Children from Chemical and Surgical Mutilation," The White House, January 28, 2025, https://www.whitehouse.gov/presidential-actions/2025/01/protecting-children-from-chemical-and-surgical-mutilation/

152   The White House, "Executive Order: Prioritizing Military Excellence and Readiness," The White House, January 27, 2025, https://www.whitehouse.gov/presidential-actions/2025/01/prioritizing-military-excellence-and-readiness/

153   The White House, "Executive Order: Keeping Men Out of Women's Sports," The White House, February 5, 2025, https://www.whitehouse.gov/presidential-actions/2025/02/keeping-men-out-of-womens-sports/

154   Alabama State Legislature, Alabama Senate Bill 79, Regular Session 2025, accessed February 20, 2025, https://alison.legislature.state.al.us/files/pdf/SearchableInstruments/2025RS/SB79-enr.pdf

155   Budd, Joe, "EEOC Releases Final Workplace Harassment Guidance," CBIA, May 3, 2024, https://www.cbia.com/news/hr-safety/eeoc-workplace-harassment-guidance/

156   Sneed, Tierney and Condon, Emily R., "Judge temporarily blocks Trump administration from carrying out certain anti-DEI directives," CNN, February 21, 2025, https://

www.cnn.com/2025/02/21/politics/judge-temporarily-blocks-trump-dei-directive/index.html

157 Helmore, Edward, "US civil rights agency seeks to dismiss gender-identity discrimination cases," The Guardian, February 15, 2025, https://www.theguardian.com/us-news/2025/feb/15/transgender-equal-employment-opportunity-commission

158 Smith, Allen, "How to Adjust your I&D Initiatives Under Trump's New Guidelines," SHRM, January 28, 2025, https://www.shrm.org/topics-tools/employment-law-compliance/how-to-adjust-dei-initiatives-under-trumps-new-guidelines

159 Button, Danni, "Virgin Atlantic Airways Makes a Bold Policy Change," TheStreet, November 3, 2022, https://www.thestreet.com/employment/virgin-airlines-changes-policies-sees-job-application-boom

160 Smith, Gordon, "Virgin Atlantic Reviews 'Gender Neutral' Policy for New Saudi Route," Skift Research, September 3, 2024, https://skift.com/2024/09/03/virgin-atlantic-reviews-gender-neutral-policy-for-new-saudi-route/

161 King, Chris, "Virgin Atlantic Has Announced a New Gender-Neutral Uniform Policy," Condé Nast Traveler, October 3, 2022, https://www.cntraveler.com/story/virgin-atlantic-has-announced-a-new-gender-neutral-uniform-policy

162 Hansford, Amelia," Alaska Airlines ordered to drop gendered uniforms after non-binary flight attendant's lawsuit," The Pink News, April 28, 2023, https://www.thepinknews.com/2023/04/28/alaska-airlines-gendered-uniforms/

163 Satran, Rory, "Flight Attendant Uniforms Ditch Gender. How Does That Fly in the Air?" The Wall Street

Journal, January 28, 2023, https://www.wsj.com/articles/ flight-attendant-uniforms-gender-neutral-11674860130

164 Tajfel, H. and Turner, J.C., "The Social Identity Theory of Intergroup Behavior," In J. T. Jost & J. Sidanius (Eds.), Political psychology: Key readings (pp. 276–293), Psychology Press, 2024, https://doi.org/10.4324/9780203505984-1

165 Jaspal, Rusi and Breakwell, Glynis M., "Identity Process Theory: Identity, Social Action and Social Change," Cambridge University Press, 2014, https://assets.cambridge.org/97811070/22706/frontmatter/9781107022706_frontmatter.pdf

166 Shuman, Eric, van Zomeren, Martijn, Saguy, Tamar, Knowles, Eric et al., "Defend, Deny, Distance, and Dismantle: A New Measure of Advantaged Identity Management," Personality and Social Psychology Bulletin, Published online January 29, 2024, https://doi.org/10.1177/01461672231216769

167 Thoroughgood, Christian N., Sawyer, Katina and Webster, Jennica R., "Creating a Trans-Inclusive Workplace," Harvard Business Review, March–April, 2020, https://hbr.org/2020/03/creating-a-trans-inclusive-workplace

168 Thoroughgood, Christian N., Sawyer, Katina and Webster, Jennica R., "Creating a Trans-Inclusive Workplace," Harvard Business Review, March–April, 2020, https://hbr.org/2020/03/creating-a-trans-inclusive-workplace

169 Frei, Darren, "'Johnson & Johnson helped me transition': Meet an employee who's now living his true self," Johnson & Johnson Personal Stories, May 31, 2018, https://www.jnj.com/personal-stories/how-johnson-johnson-helped-one-transgender-employee-with-his-transition

170 Frei, Darren, "'Johnson & Johnson helped me transition': Meet an employee who's now living his true self," Johnson & Johnson Personal Stories, May 31, 2018, https://www.jnj.com/personal-stories/how-johnson-johnson-helped-one-transgender-employee-with-his-transition

171 Al Idrus, Amirah, "For 2 biotech employees, coming out as trans means asking others to transition with them," Fierce Biotech, July 17, 2018, https://www.fiercebiotech.com/biotech/for-2-biotech-employees-coming-out-as-trans-means-asking-others-to-transition-you

172 Frei, Darren, "'Johnson & Johnson helped me transition': Meet an employee who's now living his true self," Johnson & Johnson Personal Stories, May 31, 2018, https://www.jnj.com/personal-stories/how-johnson-johnson-helped-one-transgender-employee-with-his-transition

173 Frei, Darren, "'Johnson & Johnson helped me transition': Meet an employee who's now living his true self," Johnson & Johnson Personal Stories, May 31, 2018, https://www.jnj.com/personal-stories/how-johnson-johnson-helped-one-transgender-employee-with-his-transition

174 Frei, Darren, "'Johnson & Johnson helped me transition': Meet an employee who's now living his true self," Johnson & Johnson Personal Stories, May 31, 2018, https://www.jnj.com/personal-stories/how-johnson-johnson-helped-one-transgender-employee-with-his-transition

175 Johnson & Johnson, "Johnson & Johnson Position on Providing a Safe and Harassment-Free Workplace," Johnson & Johnson, Accessed October 30, 2024, https://www.jnj.com/about-jnj/policies-and-positions/our-position-on-providing-a-safe-and-harassment-free-workplace

176 EY, "Failure Drives Innovation, According to EY Survey on Gen Z," PR Newswire, September 18, 2018, https://www.prnewswire.com/news-releases/failure-drives-innovation-according-to-ey-survey-on-gen-z-300714436.html

177 Klinghoffer, Dawn, Young, Candice and Haspas, Dave, "Every New Employee Needs an Onboarding 'Buddy'," Harvard Business Review, June 6, 2019, https://hbr.org/2019/06/every-new-employee-needs-an-onboarding-buddy

178 von Dadelszen, Mark, "Understanding Legalese – The Characteristics, Use and Issues to be considered," Legalwise, February 22, 2023, https://legalwiseseminars.co.nz/insights/understanding-legalese-the-characteristics-use-and-issues-to-be-considered

179 Rowe, Suzanne E., "Finessing Gender Pronouns: When 'He' or 'She' Just Won't Do," Oregon State Bar Bulletin, June, 2007, https://www.osbar.org/publications/bulletin/07jun/legalwriter.html

180 Lockwood, Ellen, "The Ethics of Pronouns in Legal Writing," Texas Paralegal Journal, Fall, 2021, https://txpd.org/ethics-articles/the-ethics-of-pronouns-in-legal-writing/

181 Strzelczyk, Kati Pajak, "How to Write Gender-Neutral Contracts," Mintz, January 27, 2020, https://www.mintz.com/insights-center/viewpoints/2911/2020-01-27-how-write-gender-neutral-contracts

182 Holiday Inn, "Holiday Inn 1997 Super Bowl Ad," YouTube video, 0:30, January 12, 2007, https://www.youtube.com/watch?v=MyE5mIXIu-M

183 Absolut, "Absolut Vodka - Darla #ABSOLUTNIGHTS," Vimeo video, 0:56, September 21, 2018, https://vimeo.com/291140598

184 Absolut, "Out & Open," Absolut, https://www.absolut. com/en-us/campaigns/out-and-open/

185 Franz, Annette, "7 Ways to Boost Customers' Emotional Connection and Loyalty with your Brand," MarTech, October 3, 2024, https://martech.org/7-ways-to-boost-customers-emotional-connection-and-loyalty-with-your-brand/

186 Door Modefabriek, "Gender neutral fashion: the new norm?" Modefabriek, September 1, 2020, https://www. modefabriek.nl/en/news/gender-neutral-fashion-the-new-norm?hide_register_modal=1

187 Luckerson, Victor, "Target to Stop Separating 'Girls' Toys From 'Boys' Toys in Stores," Time, August 8, 2015, https:// time.com/3989850/target-gender-signs/

188 Morris, Chris, "Mattel, Creator of Barbie, Bets Big on 'Gender Neutral' Dolls," Fortune, September 25, 2019, https:// fortune.com/2019/09/25/mattel-gender-neutral-doll-barbie-creative-world/.

189 Etcoff, Nancy, Orbach, Susie, Scott, Jennifer, D'Agostino, Heidi, "The Real State of Beauty: A Global Report," Commissioned by Dove, September, 2004, https://www. clubofamsterdam.com/contentarticles/52%20Beauty/ dove_white_paper_final.pdf

190 Boechat, Beta and Diedrichs, Phillippa, "The Real State of Beauty: A Global Report," Dove, April, 2024, file:/// Users/amichael/Downloads/125436646.pdf

191 Maas, Megan K., "How Toys Became Gendered – and why it'll take more than a gender neutral doll to change how boys perceive femininity," The Conversation, December 5, 2019, https://theconversation.com/

how-toys-became-gendered-and-why-itll-take-more-than-a-gender neutral-doll-to-change-how-boys-perceive-femininity-124386

192 Monteil, Abby, "Kids' YouTuber Ms. Rachel Said 'Happy Pride' and the Right-Wing Tantrums Commenced," Them, June 4, 2024, https://www.them.us/story/ms-rachel-youtube-pride-conservative-right-wing-backlash-outrage

193 Chen, Stefanos, "Macy's Parade Shuns Boycott Demands From Anti-L.G.B.T.Q. Group," The New York Times, November 17, 2023, https://www.nytimes.com/2023/11/17/nyregion/thanksgiving-parade-nonbinary-lgbt-protest.html

194 Tuyetnhi Tran, Emi, "British chain Costa Coffee faces boycott calls over transgender illustration," NBC News, August 2, 2023, https://www.nbcnews.com/nbc-out/out-news/costa-coffee-faces-boycott-calls-transgender-illustration-rcna97523

195 Business Wire, "Nike Debuts Unlimited Courage - The First of Three Upcoming Films That Celebrate Everyday Athletes as Part of Its Global Nike Unlimited Campaign," August 8, 2016, https://www.businesswire.com/news/home/20160808006267/en/Nike-Debuts-Unlimited-Courage---The-First-of-Three-Upcoming-Films-That-Celebrate-Everyday-Athletes-as-Part-of-Its-Global-Nike-Unlimited-Campaign

196 Cooper, Alex, "Nike Ad Features Argentina's First Trans Woman Soccer Player," Advocate, November 10, 2021, https://www.advocate.com/business/2021/11/10/nike-ad-features-argentinas-first-trans-woman-soccer-player

197 Barker, Tyler, "Nike responds to backlash over transgender partnership, instructs customers to 'Be kind, be inclusive'." Lootpress, April 7, 2023, https://www.newsbreak.

com/lootpress-1588259/2984596385977-nike-responds-to-backlash-over-transgender-partnership-instructs-customers-to-be-kind-be-inclusive

198   Nike, "No Pride, No Sport: Sport without the LGBTQIA+ Community is incomplete," June 29, 2023, https://www.nike.com/a/no-pride-no-sport

199   Morik, Ryan, "Apparel company calls out Nike for not supporting biological females amid trans inclusion in sports," Fox News, October 10, 2024, https://www.foxnews.com/sports/apparel-company-calls-out-nike-not-supporting-biological-females-amid-trans-inclusion-sports

200   Baldwin, Heather, "Gender Matters," Selling Power, February 2, 2010, https://www.sellingpower.com/2010/02/02/5153/gender-matters

201   Hyde, J.S., 2005, The gender similarities hypothesis, *American Psychologist*, 60(6), 581-592, https://psycnet.apa.org/doiLanding?doi=10.1037%2F0003-066X.60.6.581

202   Forrester Consulting, "Diversity Drives Sales Success: The Link Between Successful Sales Teams And Diversity, Equity, And Inclusion," November, 2021, https://business.linkedin.com/content/dam/me/business/en-us/amp/sales-solutions/pdf/forrester-diversity-report-2021.pdf

203   MedReps, "The Benefits of Workplace Diversity in Medical Sales," August 19, 2022, https://www.medreps.com/medical-sales-careers/the-benefits-of-workplace-diversity-in-medical-sales/

204   Forrester Consulting, "Diversity Drives Sales Success: The Link Between Successful Sales Teams And Diversity, Equity, And Inclusion," November, 2021, https://business.

linkedin.com/content/dam/me/business/en-us/amp/sales-solutions/pdf/forrester-diversity-report-2021.pdf

205 Prilepok, Milan, Stewart Shelley, III, Yearwood, Ken and Zegeye, Ammanuel, "Expand diversity among your suppliers—and add value to your organization," McKinsey & Company, May 17, 2022, https://www.mckinsey.com/capabilities/operations/our-insights/expand-diversity-among-your-suppliers-and-add-value-to-your-organization

206 Human Rights Campaign, "LGBTQ+ Supplier Diversity Programs," Human Rights Campaign, https://www.thehrcfoundation.org/professional-resources/lgbtq-supplier-diversity-programs

207 Ousterout, Jamie, "Supplier Diversity: What it is and Why it Matters for Your Business," The Diversity Movement, January 4, 2023, https://thediversitymovement.com/supplier-diversity-what-it-is-and-why-it-matters-for-your-business/

208 Marriott International, "EXCHANGES – A Diverse Supplier Program by Marriott," Marriott, https://www.marriott.com/diversity/supplier-diversity.mi

209 Ousterout, Jamie, "Supplier Diversity: What it is and Why it Matters for Your Business," The Diversity Movement, January 4, 2023, https://thediversitymovement.com/supplier-diversity-what-it-is-and-why-it-matters-for-your-business/

210 Brown, Pamela, Lucas, Charlotte, Zizaoui, Israe, Burns, Tiffany et al., "The rise of the inclusive consumer," McKinsey & Company, February 8, 2022, https://www.mckinsey.com/industries/retail/our-insights/the-rise-of-the-inclusive-consumer

211 Human Rights Campaign, "LGBTQ+ Supplier Diversity Programs," Human Rights Campaign, https://www.thehrcfoundation.org/professional-resources/lgbtq-supplier-diversity-programs

212 Basom, Aylin, "2022 State of Supplier Diversity Report: Progress, Process, Empowerment," Supplier.io, 2022, https://supplier.io/wp-content/uploads/2022/03/Supplier-io_StateofSupplierDiversityReport_v2.pdf

213 Ried, Leopold, Polyviou, Mikaella and Wiedmer, Robert, "The Case for Federal Programs That Help Small and Diverse Suppliers," Harvard Business Review, February 4, 2025, https://hbr.org/2025/02/the-case-for-federal-programs-that-help-small-and-diverse-suppliers

214 The White House, "Fact Sheet: President Donald J. Trump Protects Civil Rights and Merit-Based Opportunity by Ending Illegal DEI," The White House, January 22, 2025, https://www.whitehouse.gov/fact-sheets/2025/01/fact-sheet-president-donald-j-trump-protects-civil-rights-and-merit-based-opportunity-by-ending-illegal-dei/

215 Prilepok, Milan, Stewart, Shelley, III, Yearwood, Ken and Zegeye, Ammanuel, "Expand diversity among your suppliers—and add value to your organization," McKinsey & Company, May 17, 2022, https://www.mckinsey.com/capabilities/operations/our-insights/expand-diversity-among-your-suppliers-and-add-value-to-your-organization

216 Ousterout, Jamie, "Build Your Brand by Sharing Your Supplier Diversity Stories," The Diversity Movement, August 25, 2022, https://thediversitymovement.com/build-your-brand-by-sharing-your-supplier-diversity-stories/

217 Bayada, "Bayada Diversity, Equity, and Inclusion: 2023 Progress Report," Bayada, 2023, https://jobs.bayada.

com/media/1qqb3aay/dei_26657666_design_deiannual-report_021424_peach_v16-compressed.pdf

218 Bayada, "Bayada Diversity, Equity, and Inclusion: 2023 Progress Report," Bayada, 2023, https://jobs.bayada.com/media/1qqb3aay/dei_26657666_design_deiannual-report_021424_peach_v16-compressed.pdf

219 Bayada, "Bayada Diversity, Equity, and Inclusion: 2023 Progress Report," Bayada, 2023, https://jobs.bayada.com/media/1qqb3aay/dei_26657666_design_deiannual-report_021424_peach_v16-compressed.pdf

220 US Department of Labor Occupational Safety and Health Administration, "Best Practices: A Guide to Restroom Access for Transgender Workers," June 1, 2015, https://www.dol.gov/sites/dolgov/files/OASP/legacy/files/TransgenderBathroomAccessBestPractices.pdf. (Removed in 2025; archived at http://web.archive.org/web/20190801192404/https://www.dol.gov/sites/dol-gov/files/OASP/legacy/files/TransgenderBathroomAc-cessBestPractices.pdf)

221 Grant, Teddy, "West Hollywood requiring all new businesses to have multi-stall gender-neutral bathrooms," ABC News, December 7, 2022, https://abcnews.go.com/US/west-hollywood-requiring-new-businesses-multi-stall-gender/story?id=94711648

222 KLCC, "UO Incorporates Gender Inclusive Bathrooms," KLCC News, January, 22, 2016, https://www.klcc.org/news/2016-01-22/uo-incorporates-gender-inclusive-bathrooms

223 Sevits, Kurt, "Gender-neutral restrooms: Denver businesses have until April 30 to comply with code," The Denver Post, April 7, 2018.

224 NBC Staff and Wire Reports, "Gender-Neutral Restrooms Become the Law," NBC Philadelphia, May 10, 2013, https://www.nbcphiladelphia.com/news/local/lgbt-gender-neutral-restrooms/1955908/

225 Perry, Sophie, "Trans people dragged from Butlin's toilets by security in act of 'unprovoked aggression'," The Pink News, October 11, 2024, https://www.thepinknews.com/2024/10/11/bang-face-butlins-skegness-trans-security/

226 Sunkel, Cameron, "DJ and Author of Transgender Inclusion Policies Kicked Out of Melbourne Nightclub Bathroom," EDM, March 16, 2021, https://edm.com/news/transgender-dj-kicked-out-of-nightclub-bathroom

227 Soto, Jose, "Remembering Banko Brown, A 'Bold' And 'Funny' Trans Man Shot Outside a San Francisco Walgreens by an Armed Security Guard," Human Rights Campaign, May 10, 2023, https://www.hrc.org/news/remembering-banko-brown-a-bold-and-funny-trans-man-shot-outside-a-san-francisco-walgreens-by-an-armed-security-guard

228 US Department of Justice Community Relations Service, "Engaging and Building Relationships with Transgender Communities," August 14, 2023, https://www.justice.gov/crs/our-work/training/engaging-building-relationships-with-transgender-community (Removed February 2025; archived January 12, 2025 at http://web.archive.org/web/20250112145552/https://www.justice.gov/crs/our-work/training/engaging-building-relationships-with-transgender-community)

229 US Department of Justice, "Press Release: Justice Department Releases New Training Video for Law Enforcement on Interacting with Transgender Community," US Department of Justice, August 25, 2016, (archived February 5,

2025), https://www.justice.gov/archives/opa/pr/justice-department-releases-new-training-video-law-enforcement-interacting-transgender

230 International Association of Chiefs of Police, "Interactions with Transgender and Gender-Nonconforming Individuals," Law Enforcement Policy Center, August, 2018, https://www.theiacp.org/sites/default/files/2021-09/Transgender%20FULL%20-%202021%20format.pdf

231 AT4E, "Identity Documents & Privacy," Advocates for Trans Equality, 2024, https://transequality.org/issues/identity-documents-privacy

232 The White House, "FACT SHEET: Biden-Harris Administration Advances Equality and Visibility for Transgender Americans," The White House Briefing Room Statement, March 31, 2022, https://www.whitehouse.gov/briefing-room/statements-releases/2022/03/31/fact-sheet-biden-harris-administration-advances-equality-and-visibility-for-transgender-americans/ (Removed 2025; archived January 18, 2025, at http://web.archive.org/web/20250118023301/https://www.whitehouse.gov/briefing-room/statements-releases/2022/03/31/fact-sheet-biden-harris-administration-advances-equality-and-visibility-for-transgender-americans/#content)

233 Transportation Security Administration, "TSA Cares: Gender Diversity," TSA, 2024, https://www.tsa.gov/travel/tsa-cares/gender-diversity (Removed 2025; archived January 22, 2025 at https://web.archive.org/web/20250122224652/https://www.tsa.gov/travel/tsa-cares/gender-diversity)

234 Transportation Security Administration, "TSA Cares: Gender Diversity," TSA, 2024, https://www.tsa.gov/travel/tsa-cares/gender-diversity (Removed 2025;

archived January 22, 2025 at https://web.archive.org/web/20250122224652/https://www.tsa.gov/travel/tsa-cares/gender-diversity)

235 Fergus, Rachel, "Biased Technology: The Automated Discrimination of Facial Recognition," ACLU Minnesota, February 29, 2024, https://www.aclu-mn.org/en/news/biased-technology-automated-discrimination-facial-recognition

236 Transportation Security Administration, "Inclusion Action Committee Report," Transportation Security Administration, December, 2021,https://www.tsa.gov/sites/default/files/inclusion_action_committee_report.pdf (Removed 2025; archived January 20, 2025 at https://web.archive.org/web/20250120160504/https://www.tsa.gov/sites/default/files/inclusion_action_committee_report.pdf)

237 Harmon-Marshall, Caleb, "Are Transgender Screening Rights at Risk at TSA?" Yahoo! Creators, February 12, 2025, https://creators.yahoo.com/lifestyle/story/are-transgender-screening-rights-at-risk-at-tsa-181143897.html

238 Parisi, Kristen, "How Sephora achieved 14% LGBTQ+ representation," HR Brew, June 27, 2024, https://www.hr-brew.com/stories/2024/06/27/how-sephora-achieved-14-lgbtq-representation

239 Parisi, Kristen, "How Sephora achieved 14% LGBTQ+ representation," HR Brew, June 27, 2024, https://www.hr-brew.com/stories/2024/06/27/how-sephora-achieved-14-lgbtq-representation

240 Sephora, "DE&I Heart Journey Progress Report, Sephora, July, 2024, https://www.inside-sephora.com/en/usa/diversity-equity-inclusion

241 Bromwich, Jonah E., "Sephora Will Shut Down for an Hour of Diversity Training Tomorrow," The New York Times, June 4, 2019, https://www.nytimes.com/2019/06/04/style/sephora-will-shut-down-for-an-hour-of-diversity-training-tomorrow.html

242 Bromwich, Jonah E., "Sephora Will Shut Down for an Hour of Diversity Training Tomorrow," The New York Times, June 4, 2019, https://www.nytimes.com/2019/06/04/style/sephora-will-shut-down-for-an-hour-of-diversity-training-tomorrow.html

243 Sephora, "Sephora Adopts A Global Brand Signature "We Belong To Something Beautiful," PR Newswire, March 8, 2024, https://www.prnewswire.com/apac/news-releases/sephora-adopts-a-global-brand-signature--we-belong-to-something-beautiful--302080996.html

244 Prinzivalli, Leah, "Sephora's Pride 2019 Campaign Was Made By and For the LGBTQ+ Community," Allure, June 4, 2019, https://www.allure.com/story/sephora-pride-2019-identify-as-we-campaign

245 Dooley, Tatum, "Sephora Is Supporting Trans People with Its Latest Campaign And Collection," TeenVogue, June 6, 2019, https://www.teenvogue.com/story/sephora-campaign-supports-trans-people

246 Sicardi, Arabelle, "Sephora is Launching In-Store Beauty Classes for Trans People," Them, May 22, 2018, https://www.them.us/story/sephora-launches-beauty-classes-for-trans-community

247 Dooley, Tatum, "Sephora Is Supporting Trans People with Its Latest Campaign And Collection," TeenVogue, June 6, 2019, https://www.teenvogue.com/story/sephora-campaign-supports-trans-people

248 United, "Flying with Pride," United Airlines, Retrieved October, 2024, https://www.united.com/en/us/fly/company/responsibility/lgbtq.html

249 Lewis, Sophie, "United Airlines becomes first airline to add non-binary gender booking options," CBS News, March 22, 2019, https://www.cbsnews.com/news/united-airlines-becomes-first-airline-to-add-non-binary-gender-booking-options/

250 United Airlines (@united), "Fly how you identify. Our new non-binary gender options are now available," X, March 22, 2019, https://x.com/united/status/1109050841200250880

251 Klint, Matthew, "United Airlines Adds Pronoun Option To Employee Name Tags," Live and Let's Fly, May 19, 2023, https://liveandletsfly.com/united-airlines-name-tags/

252 Rawles, Timothy, "United Airlines relaxes rules on gender-specific uniforms," Out Voices, August 23, 2021, https://outvoices.us/travel/united-airlines-relaxes-rules-on-gender-specific-uniforms

253 United Airlines, "United Airlines Earns 100% Score on Human Rights Campaign Foundation's Annual Scorecard on LGBTQ+ Workplace Equality," United Airlines Media Room, Accessed October 19, 2024, https://united.mediaroom.com/2020-01-27-United-Airlines-Earns-100-Score-on-Human-Rights-Campaign-Foundations-Annual-Scorecard-on-LGBTQ-Workplace-Equality

254 United Airlines, "Diversity, Equity, and Inclusion in Action," United Airlines, Accessed October 19, 2024, https://www.united.com/en/us/fly/company/responsibility/dei-in-action.html

255 Niewiarowski, Erik, "How United Airlines supports the 'employees of tomorrow'," Pink News, January 25, 2024, https://www.thepinknews.com/2024/01/25/how-united-airlines-supports-the-employees-of-tomorrow/

256 United Airlines, "United Airlines Inducted as Stonewall Ambassador in Recognition of Ongoing Commitment to LGBTQ+ Community," PR Newswire, June 28, 2019, https://www.prnewswire.com/news-releases/united-airlines-inducted-as-stonewall-ambassador-in-recognition-of-ongoing-commitment-to-lgbtq-community-300877586.html

257 Niewiarowski, Erik, "How United Airlines supports the 'employees of tomorrow'," Pink News, January 25, 2024, https://www.thepinknews.com/2024/01/25/how-united-airlines-supports-the-employees-of-tomorrow/

258 Casey, Logan S., Reisner, Sari L., Findling, Mary G., Blendon, Robert J. et al., "Discrimination in the United States: Experiences of lesbian, gay, bisexual, transgender, and queer Americans," Health Services Research 54 Suppl 2(Suppl 2):1454-1466, December, 2019, https://doi.org/10.1111/1475-6773.13229

259 Mancini, Maggie, "Virtua Health's new primary care practice to focus on LGBTQ+ community in South Jersey," Philly Voice, June 23, 2022, https://www.phillyvoice.com/virtua-health-pride-lgbtq-primary-care-practice-marlton-south-jersey/

260 Slock, Sarah, "LGBTQ say they're ignored, abused by doctors. These Bucks, Montco providers are listening," Philly Burbs, August 18, 2022, https://www.phillyburbs.com/story/news/special-reports/2022/08/08/lgbtq-community-health-equity-transgender-discrimination/65388432007/

261 Slock, Sarah, "LGBTQ say they're ignored, abused by doctors. These Bucks, Montco providers are listening," Phillyburbs.com, August 18, 2022, https://www.phillyburbs.com/story/news/special-reports/2022/08/08/lgbtq-community-health-equity-transgender-discrimination/65388432007/

262 Virtua Health, "Pride Primary Care," Virtua Health, Accessed October 27, 2024, https://go.virtua.org/pride-primary-care

263 Virtua Health, "Virtua's Primary Care Practice for LGBTQ+ Community Celebrates First Anniversary During Pride Month," Virtua Health, June 6, 2023, https://www.virtua.org/news/virtuas-primary-care-practice-for-lgbtq-community-celebrates-first-anniversary-during-pride-month

264 Hikes, Amber, "Philadelphia's LGBTQ Protections," City of Philadelphia Action Guide, December 4, 2017, https://www.phila.gov/2017-12-04-philadelphias-lgbtq-protections/

265 City of Philadelphia, "City Expands Protections for Transgender and Gender Nonconforming Youth," City of Philadelphia, July 19, 2022, https://www.phila.gov/2022-07-19-city-expands-protections-for-transgender-and-gender-nonconforming-youth/

266 City of Philadelphia, "Mayor Kenney Signs Executive Order Protecting Individuals Seeking, Receiving and Providing Gender-Affirming Health Care," City of Philadelphia, October 17, 2023, https://www.phila.gov/2023-10-17-mayor-kenney-signs-executive-order-protecting-individuals-seeking-receiving-and-providing-gender-affirming-health-care/

267 Human Rights Campaign, "Philadelphia, Pennsylvania: 2024 Municipal Equality Index Scorecard," 2024, https://hrc-prod-requests.s3-us-west-2.amazonaws.com/files/documents/MEI-Scorecard-Assets/MEI-24-Scorecards/2024-MEI-Philadelphia-Pennsylvania.pdf; 2023, https://hrc-prod-requests.s3-us-west-2.amazonaws.com/MEI-2023-Assets/MEI-2023-Philadelphia-Pennsylvania.pdf; 2022, https://hrc-prod-requests.s3-us-west-2.amazonaws.com/MEI-2022-Philadelphia-Pennsylvania.pdf; 2021, https://hrc-prod-requests.s3-us-west-2.amazonaws.com/MEI-2021-Philadelphia-Pennsylvania.pdf; 2020, https://hrc-prod-requests.s3-us-west-2.amazonaws.com/MEI-2020-Philadelphia-Pennsylvania.pdf

268 Hikes, Amber, "Police Announce Policy Guiding Treatment of Trans and Non-Binary People," City of Philadelphia News and Events, June 25, 2019, https://www.phila.gov/2019-06-25-police-announce-policy-guiding-treatment-of-trans-and-non-binary-people/

269 Zipkin, Michele, "Philadelphia's Resident Survey shows LGBTQ dissatisfaction with police, healthcare," Philadelphia Gay News, January 24, 2020, https://epgn.com/2020/01/24/philadelphias-resident-survey-shows-lgbtq-dissatisfaction-with-police-healthcare/

270 Riedel, Samantha, "The 'Very Concerning' Arrest of a Black Trans Philadelphia Official Is Being Investigated," Them, March 7, 2024, https://www.them.us/story/cherelle-parker-very-concerning-arrest-black-trans-philadelphia-official-being-investigated

271 Alsharif, Mirna, Persaud, Yasmeen and Solis, George, "The arrest of a Philadelphia city official and her husband that was captured on video is under investigation," NBC News,

March 24, 2024, https://www.nbcnews.com/news/us-news/arrest-philadelphia-city-official-husband-was-captured-video-investiga-rcna141702

272 NBC10 Staff, "Trooper who arrested Philly LGBTQ officials on I-76 no longer with state police," NBC10 Philadelphia, May 10, 2024, https://www.nbcphiladelphia.com/news/local/trooper-who-arrested-philly-lgbtq-officials-on-i-76-no-longer-with-state-police/3796725/

273 Ring, Trudy, "Philadelphia cancels Trans Day of Visibility ceremony in 'challenging times'," Advocate, March 28, 2024, https://www.advocate.com/transgender/philadelphia-cancels-trans-day-ceremony

274 Walters, Zach, "2023 Year in Review," City of Philadelphia Office of LGBT Affairs, December 6, 2023, https://www.phila.gov/2023-12-06-office-of-lgbt-affairs-2023-year-in-review/

275 McCann, Steven, "Philadelphia Marathon Expands Non-binary Inclusion, But Activists Demand More," Philly Gay Calendar, September 5, 2024, https://phillygaycalendar.com/2024/09/05/philadelphia-marathon-expands-non-binary-inclusion-but-activists-demand-more/

276 Walters, Zach, "2023 Year in Review," City of Philadelphia Office of LGBT Affairs, December 6, 2023, https://www.phila.gov/2023-12-06-office-of-lgbt-affairs-2023-year-in-review/

277 Trans Legislation Tracker, "Pennsylvania 2024 Bills," Trans Legislation Tracker, Accessed October 20, 2024, https://translegislation.com/bills/2024/PA

278 Rodriguez, Jeremy, "LGBTQ+ advocate Cherelle Parker wins Democratic primary for mayor," Philadelphia Gay

News, May 17, 2023, https://epgn.com/2023/05/17/lgbtq-advocate-cherelle-parker-wins-democratic-primary-for-mayor/

279 Chevron, "Chevron earns top marks on corporate equality index for 18th consecutive year," Chevron Newsroom, December 14, 2023, https://www.chevron.com/newsroom/2023/q4/chevron-earns-top-marks-on-corporate-equality-index-for-18th-consecutive-year

280 Chevron, "Celebrating 30 years of championing rights for LGBTQ+ employees," Chevron Newsroom, June 15, 2023, https://www.chevron.com/newsroom/2023/q2/celebrating-30-years-of-championing-rights-for-lgbtqplus-employees

281 Chevron, "Celebrating 30 years of championing rights for LGBTQ+ employees," Chevron Newsroom, June 15, 2023, https://www.chevron.com/newsroom/2023/q2/celebrating-30-years-of-championing-rights-for-lgbtqplus-employees

282 Chevron, "Chevron earns top marks on corporate equality index for 18th consecutive year," Chevron Newsroom, December 14, 2023, https://www.chevron.com/newsroom/2023/q4/chevron-earns-top-marks-on-corporate-equality-index-for-18th-consecutive-year

283 Transgender Law Center, "Model Transgender Employment Policy: negotiating for inclusive workplaces," Transgender Law Center, December, 2013, https://transgenderlawcenter.org/wp-content/uploads/2013/12/model-workplace-employment-policy-Updated.pdf

284 Chevron, "Diversity & Inclusion," Chevron Careers, Accessed October 20, 2024, https://careers.chevron.com/diversity

285 NGLCC, "2023 'Best-of-the-Best' Corporations for Inclusion Named by NGLCC and Partners in the National Business Inclusion Consortium (NBIC)," National LGBT Chamber of Commerce, November 9, 2023, https://nglcc.org/news/6837/

286 Bassford, Jennifer, Corgatelli, Sara and Diaz-Villasenor, Sandra, "Chevron Corporation: Business 361-Group Project," University of Redlands School of Business, April 13, 2020, https://storymaps.arcgis.com/stories/80f32fff6887418caf7c8d15099d9e67

287 Peachman, Rachel Rabkin, "America's Best Employers For Diversity," Forbes, April 23, 2024, https://www.forbes.com/lists/best-employers-diversity/; Peachman, Rachel Rabkin, "America's Best Employers For Women," Forbes, July 23, 2024, https://www.forbes.com/lists/best-employers-women/; Peachman, Rachel Rabkin, "America's Best Employers For New Grads," Forbes, May 21, 2024, https://www.forbes.com/lists/best-employers-for-new-grads/

288 Newsweek, "America's Greatest Workplaces for LGBTQ+ 2023," Newsweek, 2023, https://www.newsweek.com/rankings/americas-greatest-workplaces-lgbtq-2023

289 Newsweek, "America's Greatest Workplaces for LGBTQ+ 2024," Newsweek, 2024, https://www.newsweek.com/rankings/americas-greatest-workplaces-lgbtq-2024

290 Chevron, "Chevron earns top marks on corporate equality index for 18th consecutive year," Chevron Newsroom, December 14, 2023, https://www.chevron.com/newsroom/2023/q4/chevron-earns-top-marks-on-corporate-equality-index-for-18th-consecutive-year

THE B CORP MOVEMENT

Dear reader,

Thank you for reading this book and joining the Publish Your Purpose community! You are joining a special group of people who aim to make the world a better place.

Certified

Ⓑ

Corporation

What's Publish Your Purpose About?

Our mission is to elevate the voices often excluded from traditional publishing. We intentionally seek out authors and storytellers with diverse backgrounds, life experiences, and unique perspectives to publish books that will make an impact in the world.

Beyond our books, we are focused on tangible, action-based change. As a woman- and LGBTQ+-owned company, we are committed to reducing inequality, lowering levels of poverty, creating a healthier environment, building stronger communities, and creating high-quality jobs with dignity and purpose.

As a Certified B Corporation, we use business as a force for good. We join a community of mission-driven companies building a more equitable, inclusive, and sustainable global economy. B Corporations must meet high standards of transparency, social and environmental performance, and accountability as determined by the nonprofit B Lab. The certification process is rigorous and ongoing (with a recertification requirement every three years).

How Do We Do This?

We intentionally partner with socially and economically disadvantaged businesses that meet our sustainability goals. We embrace and encourage our authors and employee's differences in race, age, color, disability, ethnicity, family or marital status, gender identity or expression, language, national origin, physical and mental ability, political affiliation, religion, sexual orientation, socio-economic status, veteran status, and other characteristics that make them unique.

Community is at the heart of everything we do—from our writing and publishing programs to contributing to social enterprise nonprofits like reSET (www.resetco. org) and our work in founding B Local Connecticut.

We are endlessly grateful to our authors, readers, and local community for being the driving force behind the equitable and sustainable world we are building together.

To connect with us online or publish with us, visit us at www.publishyourpurpose.com.

Elevating Your Voice,

Jenn T Grace

Jenn T. Grace
Founder, Publish Your Purpose